Opening the Black Box

Closed circuit television (CCTV) cameras are a prominent, if increasingly familiar, feature of urbanism. They symbolise the faith that spatial authorities place in technical interventions for the treatment of social problems. CCTV was principally introduced to sterilise municipalities, to govern conducts and to protect properties. Vast expenditure has been committed to these technologies without a clear sense of how they influence things. CCTV cameras might appear inanimate, but *Opening the Black Box* shows them to be vital mediums within relational circulations of supervision.

The book excavates the social relations entwining the everyday usage of CCTV. It takes the reader on a journey from living beneath the camera, to working behind the lens. Attention focuses on the labour exerted by camera operators as they source and profile distanced spectacles. These workers are paid to scan monitor screens in the search for disorderly vistas, visualising stimuli according to its perceived riskiness and/or allurement. However, the projection of this gaze can draw an unsettling reflection. It can mean enduring behavioural extremities as an impotent witness. It can also entail making spontaneous decisions that determine the course of justice.

Opening the Black Box, therefore, contemplates the seductive and traumatic dimensions of monitoring telemediated 'riskscapes' through the prism of camera circuitry. It probes the positioning of camera operators as 'vicarious' custodians of a precarious social order and engages their subjective experiences. It reveals the work of watching to be an ambiguous practice – as much about managing external disturbances on the street as managing internal disruptions in the self.

Gavin J.D. Smith is a Senior Lecturer in Sociology at the Australian National University. He is the author of many reviews, book chapters, journal articles and media reports on the social impacts and implications of surveillance diffusion. His current research explicates the dynamic interplay between systems and subjects of surveillance, particularly the interpretive meanings people attribute to their visibility and the labour they invest in managing their ascribed 'data-body'.

Routledge Advances in Sociology

1 **Virtual Globalization**
Virtual spaces/tourist spaces
Edited by David Holmes

2 **The Criminal Spectre in Law, Literature and Aesthetics**
Peter Hutchings

3 **Immigrants and National Identity in Europe**
Anna Triandafyllidou

4 **Constructing Risk and Safety in Technological Practice**
Edited by Jane Summerton and Boel Berner

5 **Europeanisation, National Identities and Migration**
Changes in boundary constructions between Western and Eastern Europe
Willfried Spohn and Anna Triandafyllidou

6 **Language, Identity and Conflict**
A comparative study of language in ethnic conflict in Europe and Eurasia
Diarmait Mac Giolla Chríost

7 **Immigrant Life in the US**
Multi-disciplinary perspectives
Edited by Donna R. Gabaccia and Colin Wayne Leach

8 **Rave Culture and Religion**
Edited by Graham St John

9 **Creation and Returns of Social Capital**
A new research program
Edited by Henk Flap and Beate Völker

10 **Self-Care**
Embodiment, personal autonomy and the shaping of health consciousness
Christopher Ziguras

11 **Mechanisms of Cooperation**
Werner Raub and Jeroen Weesie

12 **After the Bell**
Educational success, public policy and family background
Edited by Dalton Conley and Karen Albright

13 **Youth Crime and Youth Culture in the Inner City**
Bill Sanders

14 **Emotions and Social Movements**
   *Edited by Helena Flam and
   Debra King*

15 **Globalization, Uncertainty and
   Youth in Society**
   *Edited by Hans-Peter Blossfeld,
   Erik Klijzing, Melinda Mills
   and Karin Kurz*

16 **Love, Heterosexuality
   and Society**
   Paul Johnson

17 **Agricultural Governance**
   Globalization and the new
   politics of regulation
   *Edited by Vaughan Higgins and
   Geoffrey Lawrence*

18 **Challenging Hegemonic
   Masculinity**
   Richard Howson

19 **Social Isolation in
   Modern Society**
   *Roelof Hortulanus,
   Anja Machielse and
   Ludwien Meeuwesen*

20 **Weber and the Persistence
   of Religion**
   Social theory, capitalism and
   the sublime
   Joseph W.H. Lough

21 **Globalization, Uncertainty and
   Late Careers in Society**
   *Edited by Hans-Peter Blossfeld,
   Sandra Buchholz and
   Dirk Hofäcker*

22 **Bourdieu's Politics**
   Problems and possibilities
   Jeremy F. Lane

23 **Media Bias in Reporting
   Social Research?**
   The case of reviewing ethnic
   inequalities in education
   Martyn Hammersley

24 **A General Theory of Emotions
   and Social Life**
   Warren D. TenHouten

25 **Sociology, Religion and Grace**
   Arpad Szakolczai

26 **Youth Cultures**
   Scenes, subcultures and tribes
   *Edited by Paul Hodkinson and
   Wolfgang Deicke*

27 **The Obituary as
   Collective Memory**
   Bridget Fowler

28 **Tocqueville's Virus**
   Utopia and dystopia in Western
   social and political thought
   Mark Featherstone

29 **Jewish Eating and Identity
   Through the Ages**
   David Kraemer

30 **The Institutionalization of
   Social Welfare**
   A study of
   medicalizing management
   Mikael Holmqvist

31 **The Role of Religion in
   Modern Societies**
   *Edited by Detlef Pollack and
   Daniel V.A. Olson*

32 **Sex Research and Sex Therapy**
A sociological analysis of
Masters and Johnson
Ross Morrow

33 **A Crisis of Waste?**
Understanding the
rubbish society
Martin O'Brien

34 **Globalization and
Transformations of Local
Socioeconomic Practices**
Edited by Ulrike Schuerkens

35 **The Culture of
Welfare Markets**
The international recasting of
pension and care systems
Ingo Bode

36 **Cohabitation, Family
and Society**
Tiziana Nazio

37 **Latin America and
Contemporary Modernity**
A sociological interpretation
José Maurízio Domingues

38 **Exploring the Networked
Worlds of Popular Music**
Milieu cultures
Peter Webb

39 **The Cultural Significance of the
Child Star**
Jane O'Connor

40 **European Integration as an
Elite Process**
The failure of a dream?
Max Haller

41 **Queer Political Performance
and Protest**
Benjamin Shepard

42 **Cosmopolitan Spaces**
Europe, globalization, theory
Chris Rumford

43 **Contexts of Social Capital**
Social networks in
communities, markets
and organizations
*Edited by Ray-May Hsung,
Nan Lin and Ronald Breiger*

44 **Feminism, Domesticity and
Popular Culture**
*Edited by Stacy Gillis and
Joanne Hollows*

45 **Changing Relationships**
*Edited by Malcolm Brynin and
John Ermisch*

46 **Formal and Informal Work**
The hidden work regime
in Europe
*Edited by Birgit Pfau-Effinger,
Lluis Flaquer and Per H. Jensen*

47 **Interpreting Human Rights**
Social science perspectives
*Edited by Rhiannon Morgan
and Bryan S. Turner*

48 **Club Cultures**
Boundaries, identities
and otherness
Silvia Rief

49 **Eastern European
Immigrant Families**
Mihaela Robila

50 **People and Societies**
Rom Harré and designing the social sciences
Luk van Langenhove

51 **Legislating Creativity**
The intersections of art and politics
Dustin Kidd

52 **Youth in Contemporary Europe**
Edited by Jeremy Leaman and Martha Wörsching

53 **Globalization and Transformations of Social Inequality**
Edited by Ulrike Schuerkens

54 **Twentieth Century Music and the Question of Modernity**
Eduardo de la Fuente

55 **The American Surfer**
Radical culture and capitalism
Kristin Lawler

56 **Religion and Social Problems**
Edited by Titus Hjelm

57 **Play, Creativity, and Social Movements**
If I can't dance, it's not my revolution
Benjamin Shepard

58 **Undocumented Workers' Transitions**
Legal status, migration, and work in Europe
Sonia McKay, Eugenia Markova and Anna Paraskevopoulou

59 **The Marketing of War in the Age of Neo-Militarism**
Edited by Kostas Gouliamos and Christos Kassimeris

60 **Neoliberalism and the Global Restructuring of Knowledge and Education**
Steven C. Ward

61 **Social Theory in Contemporary Asia**
Ann Brooks

62 **Foundations of Critical Media and Information Studies**
Christian Fuchs

63 **A Companion to Life Course Studies**
The social and historical context of the British birth cohort studies
Michael Wadsworth and John Bynner

64 **Understanding Russianness**
Risto Alapuro, Arto Mustajoki and Pekka Pesonen

65 **Understanding Religious Ritual**
Theoretical approaches and innovations
John Hoffmann

66 **Online Gaming in Context**
The social and cultural significance of online games
Garry Crawford, Victoria K. Gosling and Ben Light

67 **Contested Citizenship in East Asia**
Developmental politics, national unity, and globalization
Kyung-Sup Chang and Bryan S. Turner

68 **Agency without Actors?**
New approaches to collective action
Edited by Jan-Hendrik Passoth, Birgit Peuker and Michael Schillmeier

69 **The Neighborhood in the Internet**
Design research projects in community informatics
John M. Carroll

70 **Managing Overflow in Affluent Societies**
Edited by Barbara Czarniawska and Orvar Löfgren

71 **Refugee Women**
Beyond gender versus culture
Leah Bassel

72 **Socioeconomic Outcomes of the Global Financial Crisis**
Theoretical discussion and empirical case studies
Edited by Ulrike Schuerkens

73 **Migration in the 21st Century**
Political economy and ethnography
Edited by Pauline Gardiner Barber and Winnie Lem

74 **Ulrich Beck**
An introduction to the theory of second modernity and the risk society
Mads P. Sørensen and Allan Christiansen

75 **The International Recording Industries**
Edited by Lee Marshall

76 **Ethnographic Research in the Construction Industry**
Edited by Sarah Pink, Dylan Tutt and Andrew Dainty

77 **Routledge Companion to Contemporary Japanese Social Theory**
From individualization to globalization in Japan today
Edited by Anthony Elliott, Masataka Katagiri and Atsushi Sawai

78 **Immigrant Adaptation in Multi-Ethnic Societies**
Canada, Taiwan, and the United States
Edited by Eric Fong, Lan-Hung Nora Chiang and Nancy Denton

79 **Cultural Capital, Identity, and Social Mobility**
The life course of working-class university graduates
Mick Matthys

80 **Speaking for Animals**
Animal autobiographical writing
Edited by Margo DeMello

81 **Healthy Aging in Sociocultural Context**
Edited by Andrew E. Scharlach and Kazumi Hoshino

82 **Touring Poverty**
Bianca Freire-Medeiros

83 **Life Course Perspectives on Military Service**
Edited by Janet M. Wilmoth and Andrew S. London

84 **Innovation in Socio-Cultural Context**
Edited by Frane Adam and Hans Westlund

85 **Youth, Arts and Education**
Reassembling subjectivity through affect
Anna Hickey-Moody

86 **The Capitalist Personality**
Face-to-face sociality and economic change in the post-communist world
Christopher S. Swader

87 **The Culture of Enterprise in Neoliberalism**
Specters of entrepreneurship
Tomas Marttila

88 **Islamophobia in the West**
Measuring and explaining individual attitudes
Marc Helbling

89 **The Challenges of Being a Rural Gay Man**
Coping with stigma
Deborah Bray Preston and Anthony R. d'Augelli

90 **Global Justice Activism and Policy Reform in Europe**
Understanding when change happens
Edited by Peter Utting, Mario Pianta and Anne Ellersiek

91 **Sociology of the Visual Sphere**
Edited by Regev Nathansohn and Dennis Zuev

92 **Solidarity in Individualized Societies**
Recognition, justice and good judgement
Søren Juul

93 **Heritage in the Digital Era**
Cinematic tourism and the activist cause
Rodanthi Tzanelli

94 **Generation, Discourse, and Social Change**
Karen R. Foster

95 **Sustainable Practices**
Social theory and climate change
Elizabeth Shove and Nicola Spurling

96 **The Transformative Capacity of New Technologies**
A theory of sociotechnical change
Ulrich Dolata

97 **Consuming Families**
Buying, making, producing family life in the 21st century
Jo Lindsay and JaneMaree Maher

98 **Migrant Marginality**
A transnational perspective
Edited by Philip Kretsedemas, Jorge Capetillo-Ponce and Glenn Jacobs

99 **Changing Gay Male Identities**
Andrew Cooper

100 **Perspectives on Genetic Discrimination**
Thomas Lemke

101 **Social Sustainability**
A multilevel approach to social inclusion
Edited by Veronica Dujon, Jesse Dillard and Eileen M. Brennan

102 **Capitalism**
A companion to Marx's economy critique
Johan Fornäs

103 **Understanding European Movements**
New social movements, global justice struggles, anti-austerity protest
Edited by Cristina Flesher Fominaya and Laurence Cox

104 **Applying Ibn Khaldūn**
The recovery of a lost tradition in sociology
Syed Farid Alatas

105 **Children in Crisis**
Ethnographic studies in international contexts
Edited by Manata Hashemi and Martín Sánchez-Jankowski

106 **The Digital Divide**
The internet and social inequality in international perspective
Edited by Massimo Ragnedda and Glenn W. Muschert

107 **Emotion and Social Structures**
The affective foundations of social order
Christian von Scheve

108 **Social Capital and its Institutional Contingency**
A study of the United States, China and Taiwan
Edited by Nan Lin, Yang-chih Fu and Chih-jou Jay Chen

109 **The Longings and Limits of Global Citizenship Education**
The moral pedagogy of schooling in a cosmopolitan age
Jeffrey S. Dill

110 **Irish Insanity 1800–2000**
Damien Brennan

111 **Cities of Culture**
A global perspective
Deborah Stevenson

112 **Racism, Governance, and Public Policy**
Beyond human rights
Katy Sian, Ian Law and S. Sayyid

113 **Understanding Aging and Diversity**
Theories and concepts
Patricia Kolb

114 **Hybrid Media Culture**
Sensing place in a world
of flows
Edited by Simon Lindgren

115 **Centers and Peripheries in
Knowledge Production**
Leandro Rodriguez Medina

116 **Revisiting Institutionalism
in Sociology**
Putting the 'institution' back in
institutional analysis
Seth Abrutyn

117 **National Policy-making**
Domestication of global trends
*Pertti Alasuutari and
Ali Qadir*

118 **The Meanings of Europe**
Changes and exchanges of a
contested concept
*Edited by Claudia Wiesner and
Meike Schmidt-Gleim*

119 **Between Islam and the
American Dream**
An immigrant Muslim
community in
post-9/11 America
Yuting Wang

120 **Call Centers and the Global
Division of Labor**
A political economy of
post-industrial employment
and union organizing
Andrew J.R. Stevens

121 **Academic Capitalism**
Universities in the global
struggle for excellence
Richard Münch

122 **Deconstructing Flexicurity
and Developing
Alternative Approaches**
Towards new concepts and
approaches for employment
and social policy
*Edited by Maarten Keune and
Amparo Serrano*

123 **From Corporate to
Social Media**
Critical perspectives on
corporate social responsibility
in media and communication
industries
Marisol Sandoval

124 **Vision and Society**
Towards a sociology and
anthropology from art
John Clammer

125 **The Rise of Critical
Animal Studies**
From the margins to the centre
Nik Taylor and Richard Twine

126 **Social Networks and
Music Worlds**
*Edited by Nick Crossley,
Siobhan McAndrew and
Paul Widdop*

127 **Opening the Black Box**
The work of watching
Gavin J.D. Smith

Opening the Black Box
The work of watching

Gavin J.D. Smith

LONDON AND NEW YORK

First published 2015 by Routledge

2 Park Square, Milton Park, Abingdon, Oxon OX14 4RN
711 Third Avenue, New York, NY 10017, USA

Routledge is an imprint of the Taylor & Francis Group, an informa business

First issued in paperback 2016

Copyright © 2015 Gavin J.D. Smith

The right of Gavin J.D. Smith to be identified as author of this work has been asserted by him in accordance with sections 77 and 78 of the Copyright, Designs and Patents Act 1988.

All rights reserved. No part of this book may be reprinted or reproduced or utilised in any form or by any electronic, mechanical, or other means, now known or hereafter invented, including photocopying and recording, or in any information storage or retrieval system, without permission in writing from the publishers.

Notice:
Product or corporate names may be trademarks or registered trademarks, and are used only for identification and explanation without intent to infringe.

British Library Cataloguing-in-Publication Data
A catalogue record for this book is available from the British Library

Library of Congress Cataloging-in-Publication Data
Smith, Gavin J. D.
  Opening the black box : the work of watching / by Gavin Smith.
    pages cm. – (Routledge advances in sociology)
  1. Crime prevention–Social aspects. 2. Video surveillance–Social aspects. 3. Supervision. 4. Public safety–Social aspects. 5. Privacy, Right of–Social aspects. I. Title.
  HV7431.S6145 2014
  363.2'32–dc23
                    2014008549

ISBN 978-0-415-58729-7 (hbk)
ISBN 978-1-138-20004-3 (pbk)

Typeset in Times New Roman
by Taylor & Francis Books

This book is dedicated to John Souter and to Chris Wright for their outstanding contribution and amity.

Contents

Acknowledgements   xvii

PART I
Problematising and contextualising watching practices   1

1   Towards supervisory circulations: circuitry coordinates   3

    Sensing disruption: the work of watching 3
    Interpreting dedicated watching: the surveillance fix 5
    Flattening surveillance: envisioning supervisory circulations 12
    A fusion of horizons: visibility-visuality alternations 15
    Opening closed circuitries: purpose and focus 23
    Chapter structure and content 23

2   Engaging circuitries: researching supervisory circulations   27

    Setting the scene 27
    The (un)visibility of CCTV: protecting the privileged, problematising the poor 37
    Under the lens: research on CCTV 45
    Contacting supervisory lifeworlds: issues and techniques 49

PART II
Engaging the means of watching   61

3   Instigating circuitries: inception and reception   63

    Sedimenting inflexibility: instigating circuitries 64
    The socio-material sedimentation of expedience: structural and operational solidity 77
    The socio-material sedimentation of improvidence: structural and operational fragility 83
    Chapter 3 synopsis 102

4 Construing circuitries: supervisory projection — 105

CCTV struggles: strategies and tactics 106
Contact points: supervisory circuitries as para-social mediums 108
Spectacle enchantment: the seduction of watching 113
Chapter 4 synopsis 124

5 Enduring circuitries: supervisory subjection — 126

Affective labour: managing emotionality and caring for the self 127
Spectacle disenchantment: the work of watching 130
Techniques of neutralisation: managing external and internal disturbances 137
Chapter 5 synopsis 149

6 Sustaining circuitries: supervisory fluctuation — 151

Empowered watchers: on capacities for influence 152
Disempowered workers: on experiences of impotence 155
Supervisory boxes of enlightenment 159

References 164
Index 175

Acknowledgements

Writing and journeying share comparable properties. Each involves motion and indeterminacy of one form or another, commencing at a start place and terminating at an end point: a process of movement from one destination to the next, a transition of being into a state of becoming. Each activity evokes vistas of terrestrial topographies and encourages speculative projections on observed dimensions. The hope, for most writers and travellers, is that the undertaking will be rewarding and the carriage safe. Of course this is not an aspiration that can ever be guaranteed. There are too many influence-wielding intermediaries and interdependencies. Velocity, for instance, has a habit of interfering, as do the forces of nature. There are always hidden turbulences, fuel blockages and unexpected delays: a multitude of obstacles that were not anticipated, or a section in the plan that just does not make intuitive sense. For those trying to escape persecution or flee from environmental extremities, journeying seems a non-negotiable pursuit. It is a means of *survival*. For those privileged critters determining their own migratory itineraries, journeying can provide introspective openings and invite kudos. It is, in contrast, a means of *enriching*. Exactly how an arrival is made and in what mode of conveyance, influences the nature of the transit endured and the reception experienced, especially in human contexts. Ponder, for example, the contrasting ways in which undocumented refugees and documented industrialists get treated at international borders, notwithstanding their equivalent genetic constitutions and fleshy boundaries. Yet the wonder of journeying for all creatures of the world is essentially the same. It provides an experiential medium for storytelling and an opportunity to pit life and limb against the elements. The enchantment of voyaging, as writer or as wanderer, resides less in reasons for peregrination than in gradual realisation that a story you embark on is not necessarily the one you finish with.

Reaching the terminus of this journey would not have been possible without the obliging support of many carriers. Innumerable people have tendered encouragement, insight and succour, all in an effort to propel me along the path. There are, however, a number of conveyors to whom I owe special gratitude. I wish to thank the Economic and Social Research Council (ESRC) for awarding me a graduate studentship to research CCTV. I also wish to thank colleagues, staff and students at the University of Aberdeen, City University London, the University of Sydney and the Australian National University, for listening to my ideas and augmenting my thinking while in residence. In particular, each of the following scholars has played a part in this escapade: the late Mike Hepworth, Richard Giulianotti, Norman Stockman, Andrew Blaikie, Karen O'Reilly, David Inglis, Mary Holmes, John Brewer, Archie Simpson, Alenka Jelen, Eugene McLaughlin, Chris Greer, Carrie-Anne Myers, David Lyon, Kevin D. Haggerty, David Murakami Wood, Kirstie Ball, Clive Norris, Sami Coll, Aaron K. Martin, Pat O'Malley, Amanda Elliot, Peter Rogers, Martijn Konings, Marios Elles, Simon Tormey, Peter Marks, Janet Chan, Lucia Zedner, Ian Loader, Mark Andrejevic, researchers at the Centre for Criminology at the University of Oxford, and members of the Surveillance and Everyday Life Research Group at the University of Sydney.

Chris Wright deserves special acknowledgement for his selfless provision of time, effort and acuity. The durable features of this book reflect his contribution, while the weaker aspects evince the author's deficiencies. Similarly, Martin French was a stalwart comrade when the going got tough, and a first-rate collaborator. Thanks for everything, both.

Enormous credit must go to my mother, Norma Smith, for her phenomenally proficient proofreading and for rendering unfaltering belief. My father, Euan Smith, has been a staunch benefactor and sponsor. I am indebted to my Aunt Linnie for her sage advice and ongoing companionship. My late grandmother deserves recognition for ensuring that my student years were more auspicious than they should have been. My confidants in each 'corner' of the globe have had, on many occasions, to tolerate an absent friend. Special thanks to Reidy, Johnboy and the Smith brothers for their patience, perseverance and all-round fabulousness. I also wish to thank my partner, Rebecca, for texturing each day with supportive blessedness and for being a more than adept ideas sounding board.

I wish to thank my publishers in the Taylor and Francis Group. In particular, special thanks to Gerhard Boomgaarden, Emily Briggs, Alyson Claffey and Dominic Corti for their efforts, for their encouragement and, more than anything, for their patience. Segments of this book have appeared, partially and/or in earlier drafts, in the journal *Surveillance & Society* (Chapter 4), and in the following edited volumes: *Technologies of InSecurity: The Surveillance of Everyday Life*, ed. Katja Franko Aas, Helene Oppen Gundhus and Heidi Mork Lomell (Routledge-Cavendish) (Chapter 6); *Eyes Everywhere: The Global Growth of Camera Surveillance*, ed. Aaron Doyle, Randy Lippert and David Lyon (Routledge) (Chapter 3); *Routledge Handbook of Surveillance Studies*, ed. Kirstie Ball, Kevin D. Haggerty and David Lyon (Routledge) (Chapter 5).

Last, but by no means least, significant thanks is owed to each of the camera operators and managers who participated in the research and who gracefully tolerated my inquisitive intrusiveness in their working milieux. I hope that the account presented here sufficiently reflects their experiences and, perhaps, incorporates several appreciative nuances.

Gavin John Douglas Smith
February 2014

Part I
Problematising and contextualising watching practices

1 Towards supervisory circulations
Circuitry coordinates

Sensing disruption: the work of watching

It seems prudent to commence a book on supervision with an overview of two pivotal processes that have come to distinguish the contemporary supervisory landscape. For 'visibility' and 'visuality' characterise in important ways two crucial components of supervision: one, the capacity of an observer to expose things teleoptically (the *visibility* part); and two, the phenomenological experience of confronting and being able either directly or indirectly to manipulate the representational form of an exposed phenomenon (the *visuality* part). Such scene setting is critically important, for our purpose here is to examine sociologically a specific para-social relation and set of concomitant sensations induced as a consequence of life becoming increasingly *visible* (exposed) and *visual* (textualised). We are concerned with addressing exactly how a group of closed circuit television (CCTV hereafter) camera operators – or 'reality inspectors' – respond to their working environments and to their role as social order supervisors; and how in the course of their organisational duties they, as absent onlookers, source and process a concatenation of telemediated sequences. It is the gaze these workers repetitively project through a machinic interface that is the impetus for producing a visibility relation (i.e. rendering visible an external object) and for encountering a reflected visuality text (i.e. a visualised scene relating to an observed item). Precisely what a given image expresses – often disruptive bodies, risky behaviours and disturbing manifestations in the case of CCTV produced vistas – and how it is deciphered and managed by the spectator as part of an industrial contract and affective experience, are to be our principal focal points.

While sight is a paramount, albeit taken-for-granted, sense for many, vision for those positioned behind a camera lens and television screen has additional significance: it becomes a sensorial resource for marketisation. Camera operators are in the peculiar business of exploiting their sensory faculties to detect incongruous incidents and to receive financial and moral recompense. They are, in other words, an assembly of professionalised watchers who, from

4 Problematising and contextualising watching practices

a remote position or vantage point, exploit teleoptic[1] means in an attempt to manufacture orderly ends. However, the projection of this gaze can draw an unsettling reflection. It can mean enduring behavioural extremities as an impotent witness. It can also entail making spontaneous decisions that determine the course of justice. The camera operators' attention, therefore, is formally directed to the detection of disorderly rhythms: to sensing impending social disruption. Powers of sight are utilised to identify risky scenarios or calamitous actualities, to diagnose behaviour that is either threatening or transgressing appropriate codes. Tacit knowledge is expended in the screening and profiling of sequences, in surmising antecedent derivations and predicting probable eventualities from telemediated stimuli. These workers render 'motion profiling' as a sellable skill: a distinctive service that can be actioned for accomplishing organisationally stipulated goals. Systematised watching becomes an occupational activity. It becomes a career. It starts influencing perceptions of self-identity.

Individual camera operators, of course, possess more than just a workattributed personality. Their subjectivities are also inscribed with an array of alternative social identities and cultural values, as women, as young people, as parents, as citizens, as incapacitants, as believers, as consumers, etc. Considering exactly how these contrasting biographical filters influence what is caught on camera, and get contorted by what is viewed on screen, is what motivates this particular inquiry. That is to say, we are interested in how telemediated images operate as *technologies of domination* (how they ferment particular perceptions), and how they are absorbed by the *territories of the self* (how they intersect with internalised wills for stability, solidity and amusement) (Foucault 1988, 18). It is the dynamic and relational nature of this exposure, and the conflation processes it stimulates at the level of subjective experience, that is the object of analytical attention. This involes our asking how CCTV operators influence what is seen, and are affected by this contact.

This book is ultimately about the distanced, but intimate, involvement of camera operators in parlous occurrences – the opportunities and challenges contingent on such perspicacity. It contemplates the seductive and traumatic dimensions of monitoring telemediated 'riskscapes' through the prism of camera circuitries. It seeks to discern how supervisory practices *re*flect and *in*flect selfhood. By engaging the subjective experiences of camera operators as they cogitate their role, *Opening the Black Box*, therefore, probes the distinctive positioning of these spectators as vicarious custodians of a precarious social order. It reveals the work of watching – that is to say, disruption 'sensing' and 'processing' – to be an ambiguous pursuit: as much about managing external disturbances on the street as managing internal discomposure within the self. By excavating the social relations entwining the everyday use of CCTV, the reader is taken on a journey from living beneath the camera, to labouring behind the lens. Although CCTV cameras might appear inanimate and inertial, this interpretation overlooks their implementation as relational and motional mediums: as communicative propagators and as societal gauges. Cameras, in fact, serve as conduits for circulations of supervision. An empirical excavation and problematisation of their circulatory capacities is what forms the substantive focus of this book.

Interpreting dedicated watching: the surveillance fix

> While surveillance is now ubiquitous, it is also diverse, multi-faceted, and employed in such a panoply of projects that *it is almost impossible to speak coherently about 'surveillance' more generally.*
> (Haggerty and Ericson 2006, 22, emphasis added)

CCTV camera operators partake in supervision. They are telesupervisors of the moral and social order. But why conceptualise their actions in supervisory terms? Why not conceive their activities as being tantamount to surveillance? The latter term, for instance, is well established, and has a distinguished history, cultural resonance, intellectual orbit and political leverage. Indeed, surveillance is typically regarded as the means through which supervisory flows are transmitted and executed (Lyon 1994, 2001, 2007). What's more, the author has professional interests in the idiom: I convene an undergraduate course in Australia entitled 'Surveillance and Society' and I am an editor of the international journal *Surveillance & Society*. Further, I am a member of a nascent and dedicated scholarly community ('The Surveillance Studies Network' – SSN) who research the social impacts of surveillance interventions. Beyond the cautionary remarks issued in the citation above, the principal justifications for not exploiting a surveillance-centric vocabulary here reside in: (a) the descriptor's etymology; (b) the form of activity it typically depicts; and (c) the precipitous way that it is applied popularly as a cliché to describe a set of diverse watching procedures. There are supplementary reasons for selecting supervisory terminology. It provides superior semantic resources for probing relational *processes*. We shall return to this matter later.

Defined ordinarily as either 'close observation, especially of a suspected spy or criminal' (*Oxford English Dictionary*) or as 'watching *over*' someone or something, surveillance has obvious 'overseer' and 'oversight' connotations. It has a proximate affinity to the unidirectional espionage executed by undercover security personnel, specifically military servicemen and servicewomen, intelligence agents, law enforcement officers and state officials, in their attempt to reveal conspiracies, identify suspicious targets and anticipate risky events. It may refer to the furtive monitoring of spouses by private investigators. As the dictionary denotation makes evident, the intended object of the inspection is a proclaimed miscreant or suspected wrongdoer of one sort or another. That is to say, surveillance tends to be evoked when we typify an act of dedicated watching by an authority figure for the purposes of knowledge acquisition or dominion. The National Security Agency's (NSA) highly controversial PRISM programme, a scheme permitting the personal communications of citizens and dignitaries to be intercepted and profiled by analysts without appropriate consultation or consent, has been couched in such language by the world's media.

However, watching rituals like those forming the focal point of this study comprise activities (i.e. meanings and repercussions) in excess of those specified in standard surveillance definitions. In fact, a watching repertoire is contrastive to a surveillant repertoire. The former, for instance, is unbounded (not necessarily affixed to a purpose) while the latter tends to be bounded (resolutely attached to formal outcomes). The term 'surveillance' rationalises the act of watching as a systematised mode of inquiry, and renders it a means to an end, rather than an end in itself (or simply a means). While knowledge accretion and power wielding can be derived from the act of spectating, they need not be exclusive motivations or objectives. Visceral nuances like spontaneity, curiosity, desire and evasiveness might feature as subliminal influences on the projection of a gaze. Watching, in other words, is not always consciously structured or instrumentally programmable, nor is it necessarily fettered to compulsions of governance. It has relational properties, and these dictate in profound ways its directional bearing and the effects it spawns. Indeed, although divergent and benevolent instances of surveillance usage do exist, for example in health care (e.g. conducting pre-emptive breast screening to identify malignant cells), or in child development contexts (e.g. measuring the assimilation of socialisation and educational programs), the locution is typically evoked when we evaluate the *utility* of an observational intervention to modulate, or to classify, phenomena. Alternatively, surveillance surfaces when we contemplate the ethical proportionality (or otherwise) of voyeuristic/intrusive scrutiny. The media's growing disenchantment with CCTV camera schemes – and its critique of their assumed effectiveness and value for money – is a good illustration of the former concern (see Smith 2012a), while George Orwell's (1949) literary dystopia, *Nineteen Eighty-Four*, is an apt exemplification of the latter deliberation.

Surveillance struggles and ambiguities

There is a figurative dimension to the term 'surveillance' which is the source of much rhetorical dissension: a consequence of who historically has tended to use it (the powerful), and for what objectives (tyranny, jurisdictional control, social ordering, coordination, procedural efficiency and commercial enterprise). Advocates in industry and state sectors, and concerned activists and libertarians, perpetually represent and contest distinct surveillance narratives in an array of media (Haggerty and Ericson 2006, 8). The former group accentuate the efficaciousness of new technologies in their formalised depictions, while the latter group either project a despotic spectre of 'Big Brother' or direct public attention toward impending privacy annihilation. Each party lobbies hard to get its opinion heard. The news media is the premier battlefield, its function to host conflicting accounts and to moderate content as a seemingly 'impartial' intermediary (Jewkes 2004a). Social meanings attendant on surveillance processes are commandeered to: (a) arouse collective sentiment (often hysteria); (b) illuminate the security-enhancing or liberty-reducing features of particular interventions; and (c) highlight either the positive instances or discriminatory actualities resulting from social profiling techniques. Both units share one thing in common: they acknowledge the ubiquity of social monitoring, albeit from opposed value orientations. Surveillance has, as a consequence, come to be a politically charged trope exploited by partisan communities in order to promote specific doctrines – or in some cases, high-tech hardware solutions and commercial services (Jewkes 2004b; Haggerty and Ericson 2006, 13–14; Ball and Snider 2013a; Samatas 2013; Clavell 2013). Its texts and textualism – that is, the images and data produced as a result of accelerating social visibility – are manipulated strategically by each alliance to convince a broader audience of their contrasting proclamations (see Smith *et al.* 2013). Thus, struggles by social groups over surveillance connotations and practices add supplementary ambiguity to the label and obscure further its utility in registering and expounding watching rituals.

Surveillance is, owing to its popular application and ideological variances, a thoroughly equivocal notion (Haggerty and Ericson 2006, 21–22; Lyon 2007, 14). How we conceive surveillance will be either directly or indirectly influenced by our embodied acquaintances with it, by our financial circumstances, by our political convictions, and by the issue's public prominence or newsworthiness – its semantic and semiotic representation at a specified moment (Jewkes 2004a). In fact, it has come in recent times to be an absorbent cliché with imperial attributes. It is all too readily elicited in daily life when we – or a discrete interest group – wish to describe external monitoring practices or the broadcasting performed by those wishing to reveal subjective states or court the attention of an audience. Yet simply 'surveillifying'[2] myriad observational processes does little: (a) to distinguish monitoring systems comparatively in terms of their genealogical histories, machinic parts, underlying purposes, operating realities and social effects; and (b) to differentiate contextually divergent exposing techniques and exposure experiences. On the contrary, unrestrained applications of surveillance, in governmental articulations, in commercial advertising and in cultural discourse, debases any empirical precision or explanatory merits that the descriptor might otherwise offer to a social inquirer, especially one interested in registering relational mutations and phenomenological facets. It weakens, in important ways, the trope's epistemological practicality and ergo its conceptual purchase. As Hier and Greenberg (2009, 74) note, 'In the absence of a clear set of criteria to define surveillance *qua* surveillance, conceptual confusion will continue to detract from the analytical value and political significance of surveillance studies'. In other words, our volition to surveillify overzealously any structure or system embodying a watching component constrains significantly our ability to engage imaginatively with the variation of social relations springing from visibility-visuality interplays. It leads to our simplifying and making

8 *Problematising and contextualising watching practices*

pedestrian a multiplicity of elaborate social processes: socio-technical convergence, rule negotiation, representational semiotics, instinctive hermeneutics, labour exertion and affectivity, to name only a few.

Surveillance studies: foci and characterisations

Firmer ground in terms of research rigour and conceptual sophistication (though not necessarily political objectivity) has been populated by a province of inquiry orientated to the critical analysis of surveillance-subject interrelations. Comprising a globally distributed and transdisciplinary scholarly collective and abundant thematic concerns, the surveillance studies field has expanded its purview, profile and portfolio exponentially in the last two decades.[3] Its constellations organise yearly transcontinental conferences, events composed of diverse audiences and featuring a profusion of topic threads. An extraordinary array of books and papers are now appearing, and a brief survey of the field's premium journal, *Surveillance & Society*, exhibits the empirical and theoretical heterogeneity that is moulding and extending the parameters of this research domain. Yet even within this progressive and valuable scholastic realm, surveillance – the central object of inquiry – tends either to be deficiently described or to be viewed rather superficially as a vehicle for securing social asymmetries and for managing social problems. A comprehensive conceptual definition of surveillance that adequately accounts for its many operational nuances and relational specificities – that is, its contrasting meanings and expressions – has still to materialise. Perhaps this expectation is unrealistic and misplaced, especially given the term's historical significance, its politicised quintessence and its generalised enculturation (Haggerty and Ericson 2006). One of the more noteworthy attempts to provide notional precision has been tendered by the Canadian sociologist David Lyon, who offers two overlapping elucidations:

> Where we find purposeful, routine, systematic and focused attention paid to personal details, for the sake of control, entitlement, management, influence or protection, we are looking at surveillance. To break that down, the attention is first purposeful; the watching has a point that can be justified, in terms of control, entitlement, or some other publicly agreed goal. Then it is routine; it happens as we all go about our daily business, it is in the weave of life. But surveillance is also systematic; it is planned and carried out according to a schedule that is rational, not merely random. Lastly, it is focused; surveillance gets down to details.
> (Lyon 2008, 2)

> Surveillance directs its attention in the end to individuals. It is focused. By systematic, *I mean that this attention to personal details is not random, occasional or spontaneous*; it is deliberate and depends on certain protocols and techniques … it is crucial to remember that surveillance is

always hinged to some specific purposes ... On the one hand, then, surveillance is a set of practices, while, on the other, it connects with purposes. *It usually involves relations of power in which watchers are privileged.*

(Lyon 2007, 14–15, emphases added)

Although instructive in elucidating (a) the generalised rationalities and processes lurking behind the valorisation of personal information capture, circulation and analysis, and (b) the everydayness of observational encounters, these characterisations present surveillance in terms that are either too broad or, conversely, too narrow.[4] They take as points of inquiry a relatively coherent and fixed 'system' and a rationalised set of rules that define the operating agenda and, by extension, the operational lifeworld (see also Lyon 2007, 1). Agency, in terms of the effort that goes into activating systems and dispensing oversight, is typically depicted as a mechanised propulsion that unites in a fairly unproblematic manner with systemic ordinances, even if these are ambivalent and disagreeable in nature or serve to inflict social harms. That is to say, agency is predominantly expended in operationalising procedural means and in realising formalised ends – goals in sync with state and corporate agendas. Where watchers, or 'sorters'/'miners', are considered discretely as calculating units, they are epitomised as power conduits engaged in the reification of specific hegemonic values and interests (see Gandy 1993; Norris and Armstrong 1998, 1999; Monahan 2011; Fisher and Monahan 2011; Monahan and Regan 2012). They are depicted as conditioned puppets whose imperious strings are tugged by commercial incentives and class-based intolerances (Coleman 2004b).

Asymmetrical (il)legibility

The hierarchical or 'top-down' rendition of surveillance operativity as an asymmetrical practice has become a seductive approach for dissecting, demystifying and unsettling contrasting power distributions, specifically those incorporating an observational element (Rosenberg 1969; Conrad 1992; Cartwright 1995; Davies 1996; Gandy 1996, 2006; Parker 2000; Lyon 2003b; Ferreday 2011; Browne 2012). It prompts us to regard surveillance as an architectural expedient, a tool with which ruling groups penetrate social recesses, extract specialist knowledge, sculpt expert discourses, accumulate capital and govern errant bodies. Visualisation of social phenomena is, from this perspective, connected principally to disciplinary projects, biopolitical interests, contingency coordination and intervention rationalisation (Dillon and Lobo-Guerrero 2009). It serves volitions to wisdom, wills to modulate and desires to construct, vivisect and correct 'problematic' expressions of 'Otherness'. Visibility, the condition yielded from such scopic incursions, is thereby presented as a pathological 'trap' – or adversary – for the persons it enfolds (Foucault 1977, 200). The exposure of subjects to a meticulous gaze supports three interlaced outcomes. First, it anatomises and problematises subjectivity (objectivation). Second, it inscribes upon subjectivity assigned values and attitudes (subjectivation). Third, it gives gaze initiators a set of 'truth categories' and expertise that can be wielded for definitional leverage and for professional distinction (reification) (Foucault 1988, 49). In sum, intensifying visibility conditions provide for some groups greater diagnostic and prognostic privileges, and for other groups greater scrutinisation, heightened vulnerability and further disqualification from systems of influence (Gandy 2009). They are systematically manufactured and exploited as contrivances for categorising, stratifying and ordering realities, and as resources for sharpening decision-making protocols (Foucault 1991).

The hierarchic paradigm, therefore, has limited room in its purview for power obscurities and discretionary appropriations. Surveillance is instead regarded as a hyper-rationalised structure that produces perpendicular cascades of power – unidirectional percolations constituting the exterior surfaces and interior recesses of embodied subjects, and helping preserve prevailing jurisdictional arrangements. It is utilised for its capacity to supply expertise and claims to truth. Surveillance mediums:

> provide a virtualised surface for etching personal narrations and bodily actions, whether volitionally (informally/aesthetically) or mandatorily (formally/procedurally), and for contrasting these against predefined taxonomies of normality for indicators of risk, deviance, exceptionalism, grandeur or profitability … surveillance systems are [thereby] text-making assembly lines, reproducing selected details procured from social intra-relationalities, encoding them for circulation before mediating them as compressed signals to a remote audience for diagnosis, calibration and calculation.
>
> (Smith *et al.* 2013, 215)

Thus, the primary object of dissection for surveillance studies analysts is the system *qua* its supporting narratives, mechanical structures, underlying logics and social impacts: specifically its harmful effects on groups already experiencing cumulative disadvantage (Gandy 2009). The virtuous aspirations of many surveillance scholars are to excavate knowledge/power dispensations, to debunk rhetorical assertions, and to challenge visualisation hegemony and visibility susceptibility. The hierarchic hermeneutic is a critically orientated approach that is not necessarily predisposed to apprehend (a) directional complexities spawned by supervisory processes, and (b) phenomenological variances in exposure types and experiences (see, for instance, McGrath 2004; Koskela 2006). That is to say, operational incentives and technical specificities figure heavily in these characterisations, while the varying roles performed by intersecting and marginal players, notably the relational interplay between personal information probes (*capturing sensors*), informatic flows (*circulation swells*) and data processing units (*arranging metrics*), are consequently understated – underestimated even. An upshot is that formal and informal labour processes, and emerging micro configurations (specifically 'unintended consequences' (Haggerty and Ericson 2006, 6–7)), are often overlooked by meso and macro analyses that inadvertently concern themselves with systemic rationalities, efficacies, convergences and repercussions, and with unveiling existent and imminent dangers (see, for instance Bogard 1996; Haggerty and Ericson 2000; Grey 2003; Hier 2003; Graham 2006; Los 2006; Murakami Wood 2012; Mathiesen 2013).

This is not to propose that such formulations are dispensable or are erroneous. Far from it. They provide an ideological scaffold on which to appraise governmental ambitions and sovereign tendencies, and they extend a framework for anticipating future innovations. They reveal how power is dispatched and how it acts on things. They assist in reprimanding and rebuking influential agencies when data-processing violations transpire. They hatch astute theoretical contrivances, ways of thinking that enthuse audiences and mobilise their sensitisation and participation. However, each of these contributions proceeds from a position of relative disengagement in terms of lifeworld heuristics. Purviews are set at a specific diagnostic scale. The 'system', as a consistent and purposeful schematic, tends to be the master focal point and source of interest. Its power producing properties tend to be the objects of conceptual attention, and not its social dimensions and operational practicalities. A circumscribed normativity, that visibility is an apparently coherent, totalising and inevitable stratagem or political economic design, seems to preclude a focus on direct engagement and the sourcing of evidential details. Personal accounts and circumstances are often indirectly assumed rather than empirically solicited. Black boxed, or deliberately trivialised, in these representations is a sense of the contextualised social meanings that those actually involved in exposure practices ascribe to their embodied repertoires and inhabited milieu.

Yet by fixating on power conveyances to the exclusion of other factors, these expositions often fail to index just how intrinsically messy, anomalous and precarious occupational cultures are prone to be. They overlook inconsistencies in the temporal transition of supervisory systems from envisaged diagrams to materialised animations; that is, lived social arrangements contingent on multiplex fields of praxis. They disregard important fissures and gaps in the surveillant architecture – the many interrelationalities that 'not only provide provision and fecundity for the expansion of visibility, but that also act in restrictive and frictional ways: at times unravelling what might initially appear to the uninformed observer as highly mechanised and sophisticated socio-technical enterprises' (Smith *et al.* 2013, 217). Whole layers of social reality are consequently neglected: genealogies of emergence, idiosyncrasies in operational practices and affective contours of subjective experience.

Flattening surveillance: envisioning supervisory circulations

From perpendicular cascades to relational vortexes

If we are to make sense of what it means to view telescreens for a living, to participate vicariously in street rhythms, then it is evident that we need to employ terminologies – and styles of thought – that move us beyond the observational rationalism approaches previously depicted. A vocabulary is needed that affords more scope for processes of volition and experiences of ambivalence, and that accounts for relational interdependencies in gaze determination. It is here that the supervisory analytic makes a conceptually rich contribution. It forges an epistemological avenue for the 'operativity problem' identified above – and provides intellectual tools for problematising prevailing reifications of vigilance as a mere technique of power. This is principally because *supervision* broadens out what it means to engage in dedicated watching rituals and to be exposed as an object of attention – it illuminates the mutual entanglement of watchers and watched, and conceives each as exercising an influence over the other. It allows for relational oscillations and visceral propulsions to be better registered. It accentuates the multiplex proportions of the gaze – its projective and reflective dynamics. It brings a degree of spontaneity and affectivity to the action of looking, and it demystifies ideals of procedural objectivity and automation (and paranoia around machinic control). It permits us to regard the work of watching as a practice entirely: (a) influenced by contextualised factors; (b) reliant on technical components; and (c) contingent on complex sensory exchanges with points of perception – persons, topographies, statistics, pathogens, and so on. It flattens out what have been traditionally depicted as perpendicular and hierarchical cascades of power.

Supervision is an action that can be deliberate or impetuous. It is a process shaped by multiple appetites and objectives: behavioural compliance; authority wielding; knowledge accretion; tacit learning; scopic entertainment; curiosity; and interpersonal contact. It signifies the contingent nature of oversight, that those responsible for the overseeing might not be able to control directly the affairs they remotely witness. This is a thematic to which we will later return when we expound the narratives and practices of CCTV operators as they seek to preserve a precarious and transient social order; a mandate exceeding their legislative and applied influence, and their spatialised positioning. Supervision better encapsulates the multi-directional and relativistic character of viewing – as not merely a targeted and privileged pursuit (or one-way thrust of power) but a grounded and lateralised undertaking that is determined in large part by the object that demands visualisation. This is another issue that will be subsequently addressed when we consider the projected gaze as a conveyance directed as much by the values of an observer, as by the 'risky' or 'enticing' properties of an observed item. Supervision also accentuates the fact that directed attention is often prompted by desires to instruct, to analyse and to rectify. It informs us of the prescribed normative ecology operating in a particular context. However, directed attention also necessitates personal investment and commitment on the part of the supervisor – attentiveness to a thing for some duration and purpose. This can be motivated by relations of care, control and curiosity, and can generate a set of complex relational arrangements. Supervision, therefore, encompasses the co-produced and processual dimensions of monitoring and it signals the intricate nature of the vigil.

Engaging supervisory coordinates

Let's examine what supervision implies a little more concretely. Taken literally, supervision connotes a technical capacity for superior (teleoptic) or enhanced vision. A microscope, for instance, permits cells to be magnified. At a more semantic level, supervision refers to 'the action of supervising someone or something' (*Oxford English Dictionary*). A professional golf instructor supervises a novice so that she or he can learn approved techniques and play the game more competently. A work manager supervises staff to increase their productivity and proficiencies, to ensure that formal rules and targets are actualised and to improve employee welfare. Supervision, therefore, is primarily about order making, socialisation and service provision. To supervise someone or something is to wield visibility-enhancing instruments and/or assume – based on attributed knowledge and status – an authoritative responsibility for the integrity of a process, person or entity. That is to say, supervision tends to necessitate on the part of the supervisor some kind of exertion, engagement and commitment. It implies a supervisor entering into a dialectically relational – that is, co-constructive, co-dependent and collaborative – exchange with a mediated point of perception: a cell, a child, a celebrity, a commodity, etc. Supervisory practices thereby presuppose a multiplicity of contingent human actors and non-human actants, often dislocated in time-space. In the context of CCTV monitoring, supervision of the streets is facilitated by teleoptic technologies that sharpen vision, by data capturing transmitters that relay signals and by screens that display the visualised content. It hinges on a 'visibility-visuality' alternation, where visibility exertions (a projected gaze) interweave with visuality spectacles (a reflected outlook). The distinguishing components of this oscillating circulation are exposure of stimuli, data circulation, interactivity loops, technological mediation and translational inference.

Supervision necessarily involves processes of sociality and sociability. To analyse supervisory circulations, therefore, is to concentrate on the para-social contact points where supervisors and supervisees of human and/or non-human distinction interface (Horton and Wohl 1956).[5] Employing supervisory terminology permits us to expand on *system*-centric and *power*-centric (i.e. vertical) construals, endoxas that take as a given the potency, inevitability, coherence and obduracy of observational structures. It means that we can problematise templates presupposing the ascendancy contingent on *exposing* and the vulnerability attendant on being *exposed* (Yar 2003; Ball 2009). It allows us to foreground pulsating exposing-exposure gyrations and accompanying social torsions. It focuses our attention on the work of watching, an activity that is much more than the sum of its technical parts and formalised structure. Indeed, a supervisory approach fosters a critical recalibration of the gaze as a socially embedded practice typified by desire projection *and* by spectacle reflection, and influenced by the chain of events that it helps eventuate. It demands that we confront methodologically the experiential effects of visibility on both viewer *and* viewed, and contemplate relational vibrations concomitant on telemediated connectivity. It is, accordingly, a recipe for conceptualising the role and function of camera operators as teleopticians of the social order.

If we are to probe supervisory coordinates in sufficient detail then we must engage an intellectual framework that transcends conventional presumptions concerning wilful power asymmetries. We have to adopt a methodology that can assimilate the depths of subjective experience. This implies electing an epistemology with four interconnected propositions. First, that we discern supervisory acts of exposing and experiences of exposure as being intrinsically processual, transitional and orbital. Second, that we understand these supervisory circulations as being contingent on *exchange*, as having 'lived', 'mutual' and 'transposed' dimensions. Third, that we wield a newfangled supervisory ontology, a system of thought prioritising – and problematising – the various affects that are contingent on 'visibility-visuality' alternations. Fourth, that we exploit an ethnographic and phenomenological approach so that social meanings and affective states culminating from visibility-visuality interplays can be adequately comprehended. None of these premises overlook the structures and spheres of influence that fix supervisory regimes to specific targets. Rather, they seek to situate supervisory processes within broader relational frameworks, and to exploit an alternative parlance for formulating their sociological (and practical) significance.

Realising that supervision is as much a social process as it is a systemic procedure gives us scope to unveil what might be thought of as the latent dynamics. It catalyses our moving beyond the 'means-end' or instrumental rationality trope that has historically preoccupied surveillance scholarship.[6] It provides opportunities to extend our notional horizons and apply terms like friction, struggle, negligence, trauma, alienation, pleasure, intimacy, affinity and malfunction. It opens up possibilities for reconfiguring supervision in accordance with contrasting types of social action (Weber 1978). How, for instance, might value-orientated (cultural) action, traditional (habitual) action or affectual (emotive) action sculpt contours on the supervisory topography – in terms of what is seen and unseen by camera operators? How might these rationalities conflict and coalesce, and with what social resonances (Kalberg 1980, 1147)? Supervision may well have certified objectives, but supervisory acts can just as easily be dictated by random or spontaneous events. That is to say, revealing and viewing are not always purposeful or systematised in formally rational ways. In fact, supervisory schemes at times commence their operations from an illogical or spurious substratum and customise interventions (or 'lines of sight') accordingly (Holm 2009; Smith 2012). They are certainly not predictable in terms of their cause and effect. Revealing a social intimacy of some sort – and viewing it as a visualised simulacra – may, for example, materialise out of curiosity, out of boredom or out of habit. It might spring from a speculative suspicion or from biographical recollection. What's more, the act of onlooking, far from being merely discretionary, is primarily determined by the entrancing properties (i.e. dangerousness or seductiveness) of an observed signifier. Moreover, neither revealing nor spectating need be conducted in a routine manner, and they do not necessarily provoke a standard response from an exposer or exposee. On the contrary, each action can be subject to a set of arbitrary influences, demand fervent effort, induce spasmodic results or prompt ritualistic reactions (Gilliom 2001; Dupont 2008; Martin *et al.* 2009). Hence why characterising supervisory impulses through a variance of social action rationalities and visibility-visuality interplays seems contextually judicious; it helps us to register the spatial and temporal dimensions of exposing/ exposure and it improves our prospects of comprehending the embodied and experiential undertones attendant on relational entanglements. It enables the inquirer to approach visibility-visuality transactions from a more politically impartial and empirically informed perspective, as it demands that we study at close quarters – and in fine-grained detail – multi-sited and multi-period interactivity (Walby 2005b).

Although visibility and visuality are by no means novel tropes in this research area,[7] they subsist in a state of infancy in terms of their being applied to explicate empirical phenomena – specifically to describe tele-mediation work and outcomes associated with visibility-visuality interfacing. Starting to remedy this paucity is a primary objective for *Opening the Black Box*. CCTV camera operation is thereby conceived not as an act of 'surveillance' per se. It is interpreted instead as a supervisory practice, an activity defined by relational vortexes of visibility-visuality and by viewer conjecture and narration (the application of what Norris and Armstrong (1999, 117) call 'working rules'). Regarding it in this light helps restoratively *socialise* what in the popular (and scholarly) imaginary are often envisaged as de-socialised systemic processes: procedures characterised by mechanisation, impersonalisation and ineluctability. It is the author's wish to demonstrate in this research monograph just how disconnected from lived reality these abstract suppositions are prone to be.

A fusion of horizons: visibility-visuality alternations

As indicated previously, supervisory structures and rhythms materialise from, and in fact hinge on, two indispensable essences, 'visibility' and 'visuality'. Although each embodies distinctive qualities and purposes, it is germane in an analytical sense to treat them as co-relational, iterative and conjoined entities (hence the hyphen usage and the 'alternation' postscript). That both are necessarily elicited and operationalised as a CCTV camera operator, or any 'supervisory teleworker' for that matter (Smith 2012), performs her or his daily tasks makes it pertinent to regard visibility-visuality alternations as the foremost attribute of today's supervisory assemblages. Indeed, this confluence of *projection* and *reflection*, as we shall see, is the substratum upon which supervisory overseers formulate insights, refine calculi and determine lines of sight.

Vision manufacturing and visibility: gaze projection

According to the *Oxford English Dictionary*, the noun 'visibility' depicts a *state of being able to see or be seen*. Both intensions of the term coincide with our thematic concerns. The first intension, that is, our *being able to see*, is commonly used when we recount: (a) the clarity or otherwise of an object; (b) the luminosity or otherwise of a particular light manifestation; or (c) the (il)legibility invoked by a specific biospheric condition. It connotes, also, an active process where optic instruments are applied by observers to enhance their vision and to reveal in finer detail previously concealed phenomena; the use of eyesight and telescopic technologies for this purpose would be an apposite example. The second, and rather more abstract, intension, that is, our *being able to be seen*, is used when we reflect on: (a) the exposure external observational systems inflict upon us; (b) how we appear to others as representational signifiers (or as 'categorical identities', as Goold (2007, 55) terms them); (c) the desirability or undesirability of visibility; (d) the resources available or in fact unavailable to a thing or social being to control its level of visibility/invisibility. It connotes, moreover, the actual act of exposure itself, specifically its experiential, sensorial and ethical dimensions for both the observer and for the observed object/subject. Visibility, therefore, is multifaceted and processual in character: it is simultaneously a concept, a condition, an action and a lived state. It denotes: (a) a quality of vision; (b) the techniques and energies employed in making things visible; and (c) a relational experience. In essence, visibility is a thoroughly social entity in that it involves (and invokes) a spectating audience and a revealed spectacle – and often a complex set of intercessionary machineries, data circulations and translational rules; calculative frameworks that provide context and meaning for the displayed simulacra.

Vista rendering and visuality: spectacle reflection

According to the *Oxford English Dictionary*, the noun 'visuality' describes 'a picture, piece of film, or display used to illustrate or accompany something'. Predominantly belonging to the fields of visual culture and biomedicine, 'visuality' is an affinity term to that of visibility (Cartwright 1995). It refers to the textual and material – or informationalised – form a particular visibility (revealed phenomenon) takes as it is representationally mediated, and acted upon, by some viewer, that is, as it passes from a contextual point of origin to a screening station for profiling; or, more likely, to an Ethernet registry for computational measurement and/or interpretation (Waldby 2000, 2001). A visuality, therefore, is system-generated material, albeit depicting referential content relating to or signifying (though not necessarily depicting in any accurate way) a particular action or episode. It is, in other words, a duplicate copy or simulated portrayal of some occurrence or phenomenon. It eventuates as a result of a person or a thing being subjected to some optical intrusion, usually of the electromagnetic variety; a gaze that effectively compresses a captured event, activity or intimacy into a proxy incarnation that can be exteriorised and circulated as a textualised currency across a circuitry of some type (Waldby 2001). A 'molecular vision of life' has been the outcome of bodily and social informationalism and this vista, according to Nikolas Rose (2013, 5), increasingly renders 'living processes into digital elements that can be freed from organic origins and manipulated and circulated as mere data'. A sequence of CCTV footage is a good exemplar of such liquefaction. Video camera technologies are availed in the recording and relaying of decontextualised social events: as visual broadcasts on a monitor screen and as data files on a computer hard drive. Although the images they capture correlate to material things, data-providers are dispossessed of their informatic secretions as they get beamed across restricted conduits and sequestered as supervisory property.

Teleoptics and telemediation

Visibility and visuality have become inescapable attributes in the progressive encasing of social life within a virtualised reticulation, a physically unlocatable, but symbolically potent, nodal network of information flows, and processing metrics. They have become integral epistemological resources that establish knowledge principles, inform customary frameworks, foster expertise and mould identities (Castells 2010a, 2010b; Abi-Rached and Rose 2010). Desires to memorialise personalities and events, to probe unknown prodigies, to validate biographies, to mitigate ecological uncertainties, to sharpen decision-making protocols, and to exploit, explore and exhibit personal intimacies, alongside a concomitant proliferation of monitoring technologies[8] to serve in the realisation of these aspirations, have been particularly influential factors escalating conditions of visibility (i.e. the mass exposure of socio-material phenomena) and visuality circuitries (i.e. the mass circulation of representational signifiers), dramatically reconfiguring their scale, reach, nature and purpose. Visibility manufacturing (the energies exerted and techniques utilised in making social life visible) and visuality generation (the informatic simulacra arising as a consequence) are now social processes and textual verisimilitudes that fundamentally structure, and distinguish, both the institutional arrangement and cultural terrain of advantaged global regions. Visibility-visuality sequences are the edifying bedrock upon which most organisational resolutions and cultural mentalities eventuate. It underpins how we as a species come to perceive ourselves and the wider social world we inhabit. A gradual, albeit dramatic, consequence of these developments has been to valorise interfacing machineries as resources, and intermediation procedures as techniques, for experiencing our embodiment and for engaging the embodied lives of others (Latour 1994).

Telemediated renditions of social life are expanding, and involvement in social action increasingly occurs, particularly for younger generations, from behind – or indeed through – a video display monitor. As ever more transmitters connect our informatic transmissions to centralised servers, we find ourselves perpetually subject to data-capturing exposures and de-contextualised replications of our embodied actions appearing as compressed digits on the screens of data-profilers. Institutions are now in the business of curating (and capitalising on) our personalised etchings and calculating (determining) our probable lifecourse trajectories based on aggregated historical fragments and assumed socio-demographic details. Although data-profilers don't know us personally, their capacity to access various data-sets permits them to build a sense of virtual intimacy – a familiarity with our personal tastes, habits and disposition based on the analysis of emitted data traces. The reader might contemplate for a moment the degree of time per day she or he spends 'plugged in' to the cyber realm, the amount of personal data leakage duly experienced and her or his level of legibility – as goods are purchased on individuated credit cards, as journeys are made via global positioning technologies, as appointments are booked electronically with health care providers, as web browsers are visited, and as smart phone technologies are utilised, etc.

Social relations, as a repercussion of these transformations in technological capability, bureaucratic organisation and cultural attitudes, have now a compressed texture, telemediated character and 'leaky' complexion; they seep as data-flows very easily from context to context. They are increasingly occurring, and being intercepted and governed, from a distance (Giddens 1990; Miller and Rose 1990). This has had two principal reverberations. The first is that interactional exchanges between subjects progressively transpire remotely/indirectly and manifest in a 'flat' or one-dimensional guise. Mediation and delay have become prominent features of our communicational interchanges. Text messaging from a mobile phone, or initiating online courtship, would be apposite examples of such correspondence. The second is that the impersonalised and often anonymous nature of these mutual connections – the fact that they materialise either from behind a teleoptic lens or from behind a telescreen and do not necessarily involve co-presence – is generating novel behavioural norms, and corresponding requirements for superfluous identification protocols (Lyon 2009). Persons are being compelled and incentivised to self-reveal – to substantiate their reliability, to validate their biography, to court audience attention, and to parry their isolation (Smith 2014a), and this scenario endows multiple, often unknown, audiences with means to reach further into informants' interior recesses and to penetrate from afar bodily confidences (Andrejevic 2012, 2013). Although our relationships with other beings may have become shallower, transient and more aloof (see Bauman 2000), our longitudinal knowledge of their private lives is deepening markedly. Personal memoirs, as a consequence, are no longer the exclusive property of the embodied protagonist and her or his conscious memory; they are now etched in the cache sections of the databank – in a format that (a) transcends a requirement for proximity, (b) is instantly accessible, and (c) is eternally retrievable. The Web 2.0 platform Facebook provides a quintessential illustration. Despite disembodied and decontextualised data streams becoming the objects of capture and foci for a growing army of corporate, state and communal overseers, those being involuntarily exposed – and those engaged in voluntary data-sharing – are increasingly dispossessed from both the extraction and valuation process, and from the surplus capital that an emitted simulacra might come to accumulate as it passes through manifold calculation centres (processing points) (Smith 2014a).

It is important, as the French philosopher Jean Baudrillard (1994) so vividly expressed, to appreciate the heightened social significance and commercial value of telemediated visualities in the information-saturated cultural economies of the modern age. Tethered to specific discourses and objectives, visualities are ascribed meaning and act primarily as certainty indicators or as actuality fragments (Smith *et al.* 2013). They are seen to embody the evidential facts (or geometrics) – albeit in a compressed form – on which persons and organisations increasingly formulate impressions about external stimuli and base their calculative prognoses and interventions. As such, visualities, in a time of rapid change, uncertainty and scopophilia, have become tremendously valuable commodities, and when imbued with meaning they function both to inform and thrill the audiences whom they contact. They truly are mediums of subjectivation: masterful currencies, denotations determining organisational praxis and cultural arrangements, and dictating in profound ways how the social world is 'objectively' perceived and subjectively conceived. The more one directs technologies of visualisation (the techniques of visibility) and attendant visuality flows (the simulacra produced), the more diagnostic privileges and, data capital, one is likely to accrue and wield.[9] The converse, of course, is also true.

Social construal in gaze projection and reception

Although acts of objectivation and practices of subjectivation are intrinsically unified, and are core components of the supervisory ontology, this by no means implies that they necessarily yield coherent, or comprehensible, outcomes. Subjective inclinations and intuitive biases determine gaze projection as much as they distort how a reflected image is received (Norris and Armstrong 1999; Norris 2003; Norris and McCahill 2006; Walby 2006). Indeed, as Fiske (1998, 85) notes, 'technology can determine only what is seen, it is society and its politics that determines what is known'. Speculation, supposition and discretion really do dictate – and unfold – the course of history (Konings 2014). In a time of infoglut, it is processes of *conjecture* and *correlation* that predominantly characterise the organisational decision-making agenda (Andrejevic 2013). However, deciphering as 'evidence' information that is decontextualised and deficient in content can, of course, prompt the determination of false positives and the misconstruing of obliquely witnessed events (Haggerty and Ericson 2006, 16–18; Edmond and San Roque 2013). Results can be egregiously devastating when foci are construed through the prism of a particular dogmatic ideology or are interpreted hastily due to regulatory and/or impulsive pressures; the unlawful killing of Jean Charles de Menezes by the London Metropolitan Police after he was misidentified as a terrorist suspect is a chilling, albeit extreme, illustration of the embodied violence that can be endured as a corollary of informatic misrepresentation (McCulloch and Sentas 2006; Pugliese 2006; O'Driscoll 2008). Fallaciousness and mistakenness, alongside self-fulfilling intelligence prophecies, are inevitable companions on national security agency journeys to make predictive claims about, and pre-emptive interventions into, what are, of course, entirely unknowable futures (Amoore 2007, 2009; Amoore and de Goede 2008). This is especially so when operations that are contrived publically as methodologically objective and proportionally necessary, actually embody a set of unacknowledged stereotypical undercurrents and non-disclosed political economic interests: pivotal aspects influencing the framing of problems and the identification of threats. That is to say, what an authority searches for can differ markedly from what comes to be seen, and what gets indirectly regarded may differ substantially from what is actually being exposed (Amoore 2009). As we shall later discern when the social practices of camera operators are perused empirically, processes of hermeneutic construal (meaning making), linked to the viewer's social positioning, occupational enculturation, personal history and affective state, intervene notably in the relativity of supervisory structures and in the socially constructed process of 'spectacle rendering'.

Much like the process of artisan coffee making, which depends on an individual barista's tacit knowledge of the myriad set of interlinked variables that impact on product texture and flavour, order making, as performed by camera operators, requires mastery in biomechanics and deportment prognosis, and it necessitates forbearance, intuitiveness, diligence and composure. It demands an expertise in the art of cinematography, in the prophetic identification of risky mobilities and in the inferred recognition of suspicious behaviours. It also necessitates communicative fluency with respect to the relaying of critical information, geo-spatial awareness and definitional accuracy in terms of the social meaning or categorical value that is ascribed to the visualised topography. It is, by its very nature and by the unrealistic standards its proponents set, a highly complicated and convoluted socio-technical undertaking; one destined to produce at least a degree of systemic tension, debacle and failure. Hence why 'alternation' is utilised as the posterior descriptor for what, in supervisory contexts, are intricate visibility-visuality relations and dynamics: interactivity that inevitably spawns a mix of intended and unintended consequences. Critically considering such elaborate effects, and their various causalities, in the CCTV operations context will provide us with crucial expository clues as to the perplexing and arduous dimensions of visibility-visuality engagement, of confronting the social world through a teleoptic medium, either as a mechanical or anthropomorphic interlocutor.

Supervisory structures and rhythms: visibility making and visuality processing

In essence, then, supervisory systems are generative of visibility-visuality intersections. Entwined in para-social interactivity configurations are system constructed 'diagrams of curiosity' (the logics and rationalities dictating gaze projection and the problematisation of social constellations), and personally located 'points of perception' (the telemediated territories of attention which magnetise regimes of scrutiny). Thereby, supervisory actions incontrovertibly involve co-productive processes of 'visibility making' (revealing things) and 'visuality processing' (construing things). Visibility making refers to the bundle of energies, be they emotional or electric, expended by either a human operator or technological sensor (or a combination of both) in the production of a gaze and in the rendering of a representational spectacle (a simulacra), specifically one reflecting decontextualised motions in magnified detail. Visuality processing concerns precisely how the textualised 'testimonies' or mediated objects of focus created are then subjectively construed and experienced by a distant viewer, and how they are systematically exploited to inform decision making, to direct interventions, to evidence accusations, to coordinate resources, and to stimulate viscera (Edmond and San Roque 2013; Kruger 2013).

It is through a combination of the two processes that social analysts, instructors and authorities have come to define, and influence, reality's micro physics and macro patterns: its chief protagonists, infrastructural components, tonal composition and rhythmical dynamics. Such actions help establish taxonomies of (ab)normality for assessing and orchestrating conduct. CCTV camera systems, in fact, provide us with an apt exemplification. As observational mediums, they are employed to expose in excessively detailed, but unobtrusive, ways spatially located phenomena and to capture in perpetuity copies of that which is remotely screened (specifically unsuitable or exceptional actions). The textual footage these technologies harvest can then be availed as a means to: (a) identify potential or actual disorder; (b) manage more efficiently finite policing units; (c) generate evidence for criminal prosecution; (d) inform the crime science community; and (e) thrill, shock and entertain spectators in a combination of professional (security) and commercial (broadcasting) contexts.

Despite their social significance as industrialised processes and experiential practices, both visibility making and visuality processing are relatively poorly understood empirically. This is partially for organisational reasons: operational lifeworlds are often protected by legal clauses prohibiting any external interference (see Chapter 2). However, it is also an outcome of widely held assumptions: presumptions depicting them as elementary or secretive procedures, or as mechanised actions unworthy of concentrated attention. In reality, they are neither unremarkable, nor are they straightforward, and they certainly are far from automated. In contrast, each is a core activity determining in strategic ways how social life is anatomically comprehended and directorially disposed. By focusing on CCTV operation as an archetypal mode of visibility making and visuality profiling, we can start to unveil the intricacies and dimensions of what are increasingly important social ordering practices – that is to say, ways of problematising and governing social spaces from afar. We will see that CCTV camera operators, in the course of their searches for riskscapes, expend considerable ocular and interpretive energy, but they do so in exchange for income, insight and interest: factors influencing what is made visible, the purpose of the objectivation, and how exposed objects get effectively profiled. Yet in the process of such interfacing, camera operators contrive anomalous bonds with the telemediated spectacles they indirectly oversee. These familiarities have a determinative impact on self-identity conceptions and the deliverance of urban governance. Such analysis, therefore, helps us understand visibility making and visuality processing as *labour* duties: as entailing sensorial effort, specifically as this relates to managing territories of the street and territories of the self. This issue – or reality – is all too often overlooked when we think in more abstract ways about the occupational operativity of complex machineries (Gad and Hansen 2013).

Opening the Black Box thereby reveals the negotiated, contested, messy and affective character of supervisory labour. It substantively illuminates both the daily struggles faced, and the artistry employed, by those with a responsibility for orchestrating the means of vision and corresponding fields of visibility. Ethnographic renditions uncover how visibility-visuality circuitries conspire and eventuate as technologies of power and as technologies of the self (Foucault 1988), leveraging and enlightening subjective depths in a fashion that is both purposeful and inadvertent. The actions of those doing the supervision, and those being supervised, comprise the distinctive spirit – or *lifeblood* – of the supervisory lifeworld, and it is this entity that ultimately governs the formal and informal ends to which visibility-visuality alternations incline. Understanding supervision as a dynamic circulation, as an inspirited process of relational exchange, permits us to apprehend more sharply the ambivalent role of supervisory overseers, as prosumers (i.e. producers and consumers) of the spectacle. It allows us to perceive them as *teleoptic workers* and as *street technicians*, projectors of a suspicious gaze, and managers of a steady stream of (dis)orderly vistas. These order custodians experience in the course of their duties empowerment and disempowerment, enchantment and disenchantment.

Opening closed circuitries: purpose and focus

Although most people tend to experience supervisory processes in relatively ritualistic and obsequious ways, for example, when their image is systematically 'captured' by a CCTV camera or when they receive a formal request from the tax office to review tax return details, this conceals the panoply of actors, actants, sensors and sense-making procedures responsible for their previous or imminent exposure. Located behind each and every data-capturing sensor is a complex and extensive entanglement of socio-material components. The lifeworld of CCTV circuitries are constituted as a consequence of recurrent collisions and collusions between the following things: historical formations, technical paraphernalia, social deeds, political rhetoric, financial conditions, organisational rules, cultural norms, atmospheric tonalities and affective embodied states. Focusing in on, and trying to extricate, this interactivity helps the analyst transcend state and industry fetishisations that are prone to simplify matters, to valorise technologies and to manipulate publics into believing that CCTV camera hardware, devoid of its social embeddedness, is some panacea measure. It enables the inquirer instead to consider holistically the wider social system in which CCTV cameras are operationally implanted, and to appreciate the complexion of relational exchanges that conjoin in curious ways embodied subjects and disembodied simulacra. The result is an improved understanding of the social relations underpinning everyday supervisory applications and better comprehension of how temporal and spatial contexts both influence, and are influenced by, systems of supervision.

Chapter structure and content

From the perspective of those engaged in 'watching rituals', this book considers in heuristic detail the social relationships and forces that define – and matrix – a specific supervisory circulation. It is concerned to excavate and delineate the lived essence of supervisory work, the energies invested in socially constructing supervisory infrastructures and the exertions expended in the 'work of watching' – that is, the multi-dimensional labour performed by supervisors. I wish to present an empirically informed depiction of supervision, as a relational structure with a negotiated and emergent character, and as an intricate process steeped in torque and tension. *Opening the Black Box*, therefore, probes the 'supervisory gaze' at close quarters, specifically the meanings and values composing its projection and the resonances attendant on what it intimately exposes and reflects. Discerning exactly how camera operators use intuitive frames of reference for engaging sensory stimuli, and how they behave in situ and verbalise experiences, reveals much about the conditions of the lifeworld that they occupy, the self-identities they come to cultivate and the abstruseness of the social order into which they are cast as vicarious custodians.

Each of the following chapters investigates a particular relational thematic, and contemplates the impact of temporally and spatially external occurrences on internal constructions of the self. As an entirety, they reveal the interpersonal negotiations and social struggles influencing the bearing of a discrete supervisory circulation. They demonstrate that implanted within this formalised entity are informalised frictions, obduracies that surfaced as a consequence of historical factors and which continue to induce operational malleability.

Chapter 2, 'Engaging circuitries: researching supervisory circulations', commences proceedings by providing a substantive contextualisation, overviewing the so-called 'CCTV revolution' in the UK (the location for the research), and summarising the key factors and agendas rousing the technology's mass diffusion. It accentuates the proclamations that have influenced how we popularly envisage CCTV systems, as a socio-technical intervention for governing 'problem subjects' and for reconstructing public (securitising) space. It also introduces the reader to the study's methodological specificities and peculiarities.

Chapter 3, 'Instigating circuitries: inception and reception', considers the composition, interests and activities of a public-private sector committee responsibilised to materialise the observed camera network. Content analysis of official documents reveals the various rationalities, discourses and actions that helped cement CCTV provision in an urban district. It then examines empirically the camera operators' impressions of the socio-technical structure they eventually came to inherit and inhabit, and analyses several contradictory problems emanating from what is identified as a 'fusion of agency' – that is to say, aspirations from the past mingled with desiderata in the present.

Chapter 4, 'Construing circuitries: supervisory projection', focuses on the operators' interfacing with simulacra visualised through the camera system. It illuminates the complex nature of telemediation, and foregrounds the social meanings camera operators ascribe to the social bodies, spaces and events they distantly encounter. It contemplates relational asymmetries arising between watchers and watched as a consequence of a circumscribed interaction order.

Chapter 5, 'Enduring circuitries: supervisory subjection', then proceeds to problematise the operators' interrelationalities with the imagery they confront, focusing particular attention on how being vicariously involved in witnessing apparitions of brutality, disorder and suffering affects their territories of self, and how it accordingly realigns their subjective value systems and perceptions of trust.

Chapter 6, 'Sustaining circuitries: supervisory fluctuation', concentrates on the camera operators' multidimensional relationships with power as a currency that has contrasting proportionalities when set against their professionally assigned, and personally ingrained, roles and responsibilities.

Overture to Chapter 2

Having introduced the reader to the themes and foci of this particular text, and established a theoretical framework from which we can conceptualise supervisory systems and processes, I now wish to review in brief some of the hegemonic rhetoric and key events that have framed in ideological ways our perceptions of – and perspectives on – CCTV as a disciplinary intervention. This necessitates regard of the political economic structures and socio-cultural conditions that elucidate CCTV's historical popularity in the UK, the locality in which the ethnographic research for this book was conducted. It also entails situating this text relative to other correlative contributions, identifying points of similitude as well as items of divergence. Each procedure contributes in contextual ways to the reader's awareness of the fields of power and relational arrangements that have influenced CCTV's augmentation, and provides an opportunity to identify the distinctive genre of research question that we are to substantively engage. The latter measure demands that an account is presented specifying the methodological approach adopted to operationalise the study's *a posteriori* components. Each terrain will be traversed in the subsequent chapter as we concentrate on 'Engaging circuitries: researching supervisory circulations'.

Notes

1 A teleoptic detector, such as a CCTV camera or biometric reader, enables an overseer to magnify objects from afar.
2 'Surveillification' is the process of applying a narrow or imprecise conception of 'surveillance' to describe or to label relations encompassing an observational feature. It constitutes excessive usage of the term without detailing particular specifications or idiosyncrasies, specifically as these relate to either the labour that goes into making things visible and encountering object representations, or the experiential effects of being (in)voluntarily exposed.
3 See for instance: Lyon (2003a, 2006, 2007); Surveillance Studies Network (2006); Haggerty and Ericson (2006); Neyland (2006); Hier and Greenberg (2007); Aas *et al.* (2009); Goold and Neyland (2009); Monahan (2010); Coleman and McCahill (2011); Ball *et al.* (2012); Ball and Snider (2013b); Gilliom and Monahan (2013); Mathiesen (2013); Taylor (2013).
4 Lyon (2007, 14–15) recognises the absurdity (and futility) in trying to present a definitive account of surveillance that encapsulates every monitoring variation. Despite acknowledging its multifarious anatomy, he still proceeds to address surveillance perpendicularly (i.e. approaching it from a 'top-down and bottom-up' perspective), an approach with attendant limitations for conveying a relational and contingent (i.e. lateral and horizontal) exposition.
5 Para-social interaction was a term first used by Donald Horton and Richard Wohl (1956) in an early treatise on the social resonances of mass mediatisation and celebrity. The concept refers to the technological mediation that creates intimacy from a distance.

6 Specifically the questions: according to what principles and criteria does a system operate, and whose interests are principally served and whose voices are predominantly silenced by the actions of specific machineries?
7 As previously mentioned, the forefather of surveillance studies, Michel Foucault (1977), utilised 'visibility' allegorically in his analysis of panopticism. He wanted to show how visibility was connected to the effectuation of disciplinary power, specifically the privileging of vision (the gaze) and subject exposure/visualisation (objectivation). It was this relation that produced self-monitoring and self-governing individuals, subjects who had assimilated authority in a process of subjectivation.
8 A visualisation technology is a probe that operates to capture personal data and circulate it to various screening points.
9 This statement holds more weight when one considers, for example, the definitional privileges biomedicine has accrued as a result of directing the means of visibility and diagnosing the ends of visuality.

2 Engaging circuitries
Researching supervisory circulations

Setting the scene

> CCTV looks set to follow a similar pattern of development over the next 20 years, to become a kind of 'fifth utility'. Coverage seems set to extend towards ubiquity ... The more CCTV coverage becomes the norm, the more excluded areas will fight to gain coverage.
>
> (Graham 2001, 239)

Ubiquitous sensors/sensing

Today's social mobilities transpire within reticulations of legibility. They occur in contexts of unremitting signal emission (data provision) and mass sensing (data capture). This situation reflects the ideological penchant of governing authorities to avail visibility for the management of circulations, be they disease contagions or cargo logistics. In practical terms, it entails (and has meant) affixing sensors to the structural membranes and relational seams enclosing daily life in a bid to generate 'big data' – data-sets that can reveal the master patterns structuring social activity. Each motion-sensitive unit is programmed to capture and circulate electromagnetic radiation emanating from material substances and social flows. A toll road monitor, for instance, records (and then bills) drivers, whereas a microchip reader stores swipe card transactions. An upshot is that mobilitants (mobile bodies), as they contact detection points and as they traverse transparency-inducing grids, are interminably scanned and incessantly exude data fragments. Secreted details are then accreted by systems of supervision for their capacity to expose object parameters and inform decision making. Specifications of visibility include locational attestation (where a person is positioned, e.g. a café), activity indication (what a person is doing, e.g. meeting a friend), and mood intimation (how a person is feeling, e.g. exultant or depressed). Little, if any, sensorial output is relinquished for granular specks reveal expressions of temperament and thereby act as indicators of prospective bearing, and they catalyse assembly of future-orientated microcosmic simulators. The hypersecuritised and hypercommercialised airport concourse provides an appropriate, albeit extreme, empirical illustration of this process in operation (Adey 2009).

28 *Problematising and contextualising watching practices*

Consider the swarm of data-sharing interfaces passengers need engage before being permitted – or refused – travel prerogatives. Each detector, from pre-travel authorisation systems, airline check-in clerks and border security staff, to radiographic scanners, biometric readers and sniffer dogs, registers and probes transfer status. They are collectively wielded to identify, deter and striate risky flows and to present a visual, and symbolic, reminder of state sovereignty – and its monopoly over the means of both mobility and violence.

Everyday motions, far beyond the risk-averse confines of the transportation terminal, are getting textually redrawn as focal points (and currencies) for a range of legislative and commercial organisations. Personal information is sensed as we occupy recreational spaces and engage leisure pursuits, and as we inhabit work places and perform occupational duties. It is even sensed as we sleep (in terms of measuring durations of cell phone or online (in)activity and then drawing inferences from dormancy cycles). Mundane occurrences, like daily coffee intake, favourite food products, travel patterns, leisure habits and friendship networks, have, for external profilers, been recalibrated as character-revealing 'clues'. When longitudinally aggregated with metadata arising in discrete work, health and consumption milieux, the dispositions and motivations of *indivisuals* (i.e. visibilised persons) can be retrospectively uncovered – and then, of course, prospectively modulated (Smith 2014a). That is the implicit logic and ultimate purpose.

It seems apposite to heed an emerging 'sensor society', where social things, regardless of their notoriety or triviality, are subjected to pervasive sensing (Andrejevic and Burdon 2014) Sensed significations are susceptive to sense-making analytics, calculative codes that classify signs in accordance with statistically derived probability formulae. A sensor society is thereby defined by mass motion (mobility), mass motion sensing (detection) and mass motion computation (determination). In this distinctive social arrangement, ubiquitous detection, be that of consumption habits, productivity rates, financial markets, food circulations or interior states, becomes a normalised and naturalised procedure; a stipulated, yet banal, dimension of motionality itself. Maximised sensing permits spectators to mine, manipulate and consume 'biovalue' derived from bodily expressions and contortions (Waldby 2002). Biopolitical compulsions influence and incite sensing practices: wills to impose order; to exercise dominion; to unify entropy; to dissect component parts; to individuate populations; to programme selves; to predict lifecourse trajectories; to securitise risks; to manage pathologies; to unleash elite performance; to express (and explore) subjective states; to excavate surplus value; to eliminate uncertainty, etc. (Yurick 1985, 21).

Sensing unvisibility

Our susceptibility to sensorisation starts to become palpable when encounters with CCTV are tallied. A city dweller, for instance, is prone to having her or his image seized up to several hundred times a day as commutes are made to and from work (Norris and McCahill 2006). It matters not the type of place in which we appear, or the mode of public or private conveyance in which we travel, it is likely that a visualisation of our doings will appear on a telescreen somewhere. In fact, evading camera sensors as we navigate spatial enclosures in the modern metropolis has become an onerous, if nigh impossible, venture. The far-reaching permeation of CCTV into spatial circuitries of the municipality, however, belies its temporal immaturity as a civic confidant. CCTV is but a recent weapon in the prodigious history – and arsenal – of supervisory things (Norris and Armstrong 1999). Yet in a comparatively short duration of time it has made a notable imprint on scapes of metro and mind: expanding in prevalence whilst anomalously disappearing from view.

CCTV has, for many, come to incarnate an 'unvisible' status (Marks 2013). By the term unvisible, literary analyst Peter Marks refers to situations where certain oddities and inequities are deliberately forgotten or not seen by either a dominant or subservient population. This 'unseeing' can function in hegemonic and corruptive ways, tending to reproduce – rather than reorder – the status quo. Unseeing enables certain groups to conserve existing privileges, preserve authority, and manage any associated contrition or despondency. If one learns not to see then one fails to register the undue harm an action might effect. Conversely, if one is perpetually trained to *unsee* power differentials – treating circumstances as being purely self-determined (the outcome of personal choices) – then one, qua C. Wright Mills (1959), can very easily overlook the oppressive political structures responsible for personal troubles. The fact that influential political agendas and commercial interests lie behind – and are augmented by – the rolling out of CCTV networks, and that those whose voices count in these matters are not the predominant targets of the gaze, helps explain CCTV's material *visibility* and immaterial *unvisibility*. Its prominent presence in public space and corresponding absence in public consciousness, and its limited problematisation by those possessing the communicative means to alter the course of its history. The privacy-deprecating and authority-conformist mantra, 'If you've got nothing to hide, then you've got nothing to fear', has played an important role in the unseeing – and in the cultural legitimisation – of CCTV (Home Office 1994). This all too familiar campaign slogan, famously cited by Prime Minister John Major (and subsequently repeated by legislators on the left and right of politics[1]), dovetails nicely with neoliberal tenors, that responsible, law-abiding and self-determining members of the public, aside from sincerity, conceal nothing and reveal everything. That visibility, under the right conditions, is an important self-protector and way of accreting knowledge such that selves can be identified, securitised and ameliorated. To contest its logic is, of course, to condemn the self as harbouring malign or recalcitrant intent.[2] It is to infer that profundities in subjectivity should remain the property of the subjects to whom they directly correspond. In a post-privacy and sensor-driven world, this attitude has become the mindset of pariahs, and the stuff of outlaws.

Ingrained in public consciousness are impressions of CCTV as an allied urban occupant, a reassuring, benign and comforting 'eye in the sky' (Belina and Helms 2010), a spatially normalised and socially naturalised appliance for governing problem 'Others'. Indeed, it is so entirely orientated to *'them'* and to *'their* troublesome dependencies' that, with perhaps the exception of civil libertarians and career felons, precious few register, let alone critically engage with, CCTV, as they cross its field of vision (Goold *et al.* 2013) – this despite luminous signage warning mobilitants of their imminent (and incontestable/irreversible) visibility. So how might we comprehend this curious conundrum? What underlying political economic values and social concerns account for CCTV's extraordinary proliferation (as a novelty good) and its spectacular ordinariness (as a familiar appendage)? Why did a generation of British citizens elect to 'become with' – that is, predominantly tolerate and evolve alongside – CCTV? If we are successfully to unravel each of these interconnected puzzles, and understand the affinity we share with CCTV, then we need execute a genealogical review of the historical conditions and antecedent events that proved conducive (a) to CCTV's prolific dispersal, and (b) to its legitimacy as a 'quality of life' intervention. This occasions that we explicate its representational transition from that of revolutionary security measure, to that of platitudinous public service: CCTV's becoming, as Graham notes in the opening epigraph, a taken-for-granted 'fifth utility' in the architecture of the new urbanism. It implies contemplation of how precisely a former military appliance that once featured prominently in theatres of warfare and practices of espionage suddenly – and then progressively – became a mundane civil application (Norris and Armstrong 1999, 32). It necessitates, also, that we attend briefly to the propagandistic marketing techniques, the claims making and fear mongering, expended in manufacturing public consent: in sedimenting the virtues of CCTV in the popular imaginary and ensuring that voters (and investors) were agreeable to its introduction.

Focusing on CCTV's abrupt rise to prominence principally involves excavating the neoliberal ethos – and design diagrams – underlying the structural restoration of municipal spaces and civic conduct (Coleman 2004b). CCTV cameras serve an important accomplice role within such transformations in that they are deployed strategically to *manage in* desirable assets and to *manage out* undesirable nuisances (Norris and Armstrong 1999, 119). Although the CCTV story is evidently long and complex, culturally relative, and is a narrative exhaustively rehearsed in the extant scholastic literature,[3] I wish to focus here on what I regard as the pivotal factors and appetites responsible for CCTV's initial inauguration, and subsequent explosion, as a teleoptic overture in circulations of spatial supervision.[4] This contextualisation will transport us nicely to the empirical case study that follows, in terms of how CCTV circuitries are construed and used by their overseers. However, before explicitly attending to such matters, I will, by way of supplementary introduction, touch on CCTV's implicit symbolic and technical specificities, as these further explicate its prevalent cultural appeal – and salient embeddedness in social life.

CCTV's symbolic (im)materialism

The CCTV camera is a supremely iconic front end supervisory contrivance. Coming in a diverse assortment of shapes, colours and sizes, and tasked with protecting from external threats property of both the bodily and materialist kind, it is the preeminent image appearing in the psyches of most undergraduate students when they are asked to describe the technology best epitomising surveillance. Indeed, the CCTV camera is more than a mere entity affixed to manifold premises or a companion shadow in the rhythms of thoroughfares. It bears influential symbolic properties. It appears, for instance, as a tendentious political motif for encroaching surveillance creep in the epigrammatic murals of illustrious street artist Banksy, and even as a textual point of parody in an episode of the quintessential satirical American cartoon series *The Simpsons*. Cinematic movies like *Red Road* and *FACELESS* avail as major protagonists CCTV camera operators and camera-captured narratives. CCTV is a commonly discussed topic in print, broadcasting and online media, and CCTV images are ceaselessly displayed for their granular newsworthiness: their capacity to concretise the sacred and the profane.

CCTV cameras, though, have even greater totemic qualities in terms of what it is they precisely signify, and what scenarios they help eventuate. For example, they depict all manner of 'metroscapes' – metropolitan vistas – from a bird's-eye perspective. They produce an asymmetrical and anonymised field of vision. They affix to stanchions aloft the physical reach of those whose comportment they indirectly monitor. They have audio facilities for the deliverance of Big Brotheresque utterances. They integrate and converge with all manner of additional technologies and computerised software programs.[5] They procure trustworthy evidence that can influence the course of justice. They epitomise the collaborative energies of multi-agency crime management partnerships. They denote a city's prosperity and progressiveness (Graham 1998). They reify dominant ideals with respect to appropriate conduct (Coleman 2004b). They become the instruments through which discrediting labels are prejudicially ascribed to unruly or unbelonging groups (Smith 2004). They signal distrust of the body politic by governing municipalities (Goold 2004). They represent a 'capable guardian' figure for rationally thinking criminals to circumnavigate. They exemplify the faith spatial authorities place in technical interventions for the treatment of intricate social problems (Skinns 1998).

As monitoring technologies, CCTV camera systems evince and exhibit the rationalities of neoliberalism. The mass televisualisation of spatial topographies and remote ordering of comportment reflects an aspiration of the sovereign state to govern at, or from, a distance (Miller and Rose 1990). This involves use of teleoptic measures for riskscaping[6] and subcontracting responsibilities for policing to a range of public, private and community agencies (Garland 2001; Smith 2013). It entails cost reduction for state actors who can shift contractual accountability for crime incidence to other sources. CCTV camera systems are also implicated in the deliverance of socialisation protocols and in expressions of 'significant otherness'.[7] Camera conduits, for instance, do not merely capture and circulate spatialised interrelationalities in an uncontorted or neutral manner. Nor do they exist without influencing in some way the lived order of things. They are instead a relational medium in the urban ecosystem, *co-producing* intricate networks of sociality in the places they physically and vicariously overlook. They symbiotically formulate, and are formulated by, social identities and relations. They shape the substance of personal biographies. They impact on dispensations of justice. They reflect the dogmatic concerns of authority. They expose spectators to social grammars, and they subject the spectated to prevailing social rules. They modify insurance surcharges in provinces where they are (and are not) installed. They compress spatialities and temporalities while yielding virtualised archives of 'space-time'. They precipitate in those whom they scrutinise a set of affective states and attitudinal beliefs. They implicitly induce social vibrations of compliance, colloquy and controversy, and sway how persons perceive and behave in social space. They embody a variance of symbolic – or immaterial – dimensions, that is to say, expectations and significations, social meanings that effectively determine their appearance or disappearance in specific contexts, their reception by differing communities, and their durability and sustainability (Smith 2012a, 47–49).

Moreover, the footage these image-bearing machineries produce is wielded to convict and incarcerate individuals (Edmond and San Roque 2013). It is also utilised to absolve persons initially suspected of wrongdoing or to fashion as articles of titillation their behavioural eccentricities as they navigate the city. An example of the latter would be the unlawful release (and subsequent viralism) of security camera video footage depicting a mall shopper accidentally plunging into a water feature while texting on her mobile phone.[8] As 'harbingers of truth' and as 'vectors of subjectivation', CCTV films are implicated in verity claims and in the stimulation of scopophilic cravings (Finn 2012, 76). Displaying the socially egregious, the socially exalting and the socially frivolous, they regularly appear as storytelling mediums – as moral referents – in popular entertainment shows and on websites (Calvert 2000). They inform our appreciation of how fellow creatures actually live and, often, how fellow creatures ought not to live.

Owing to their expression of verisimilitude, producers and consumers alike tend to extol and esteem verified excerpts. For Levin (2002), the temporal indexicality of the motional (and real time) CCTV sequence is rapidly displacing the spatial indexicality of the motionless (and timeless) photographic image. Embellished CCTV montages (those featuring a recording date and time, and camera motion) are deemed to denote reality in authentic definition and to authoritatively manifest its vapid, inane, compelling and brutal proportions, a factor further enhancing their thrill appeal and their capacity to shock (Finn 2012, 75). What you see is what *really* happened. Viewers are presented with opportunities to converge time-space discontinuances and to access graphic stimuli in fine detail: to engage the intimate lives of others through vicarious means, to simultaneously be there and *not* be there. The ontological barrier of the screen, and transmission delay, tenders safety, anonymity and closure. Indeed, CCTV clips have become popular cultural currencies that typify vagaries in social experience: a way of telecasting the excesses and extremities associated with modern lifestyles, and a point of arousal for an audience undergoing disillusionment from undue exposure to staged performativities and/or propagandistic artificialities (Baudrillard 1994). They provide for many an object of escape and an object of comparison: an opportunity to indulge in fantasy and reflexivity. The cultural acceptance of CCTV is, in large part, a result of its productive qualities: its ability to manufacture textual realism, items of insight that are *influential* in, and *shareable* across, multiple contexts. It provides additional lenses – and bionic resources – through which spectators can revel in distanced events. But the acceptability of CCTV is also the product of a media 'love affair' with the technology. As Norris and Armstrong (1999, 67) aptly put it:

> Television is a visual medium. CCTV is a visual medium. They were made for each other. Add one other ingredient, crime, and you have the perfect marriage. A marriage that can blur the distinction between entertainment and news; between documentary and spectacle and between voyeurism and current affairs.

With this kind of similitude and affinity, the fact that CCTV footage in large part does the descriptive work for news producers in that it graphically represents a 'story', it is no surprise that CCTV has become so widely acclaimed and tolerated. Certainly when one inputs the honourable role it reportedly plays in crime reduction (the paramount promise on which CCTV was marketed to the public), the visually saturated culture for which it makes contributory materials, and the societal fascination with transgressive conduct, it becomes evident that CCTV has materialised as a cultural institution in its own right.

Coverage and comportment: CCTV's physical and cultural depth

It is no happenstance that the figure of the CCTV camera has infused cerebral territories of consciousness and has seeped into semiotic domains of popular culture. This absorption is both indicative and reflective of the technology's expeditious rise to prominence, its spawning a succession of high-profile visual 'texts',[9] and its pervasive propagation as an iconic teleoptic monitor of civic spatialities; that is to say, CCTV's becoming a salient conduit and symbol in the neoliberal restructuring of British municipalities. Cameras have infiltrated every conceivable spatiality, each front- and backstage region bounding social activity. Teleoptic visualisation has become a prevailing condition, and the systematised magnification of spatialised activities, from arthroscopic surgery to professional soccer matches, a mundane procedure. Being watched and spectating are run-of-the-mill experiences these days. It matters not the extremity or sanctity of the milieu, it is likely that either an overtly or covertly positioned camera is maintaining a watchful vigil. Few 'free' (i.e. unmonitored or undetectable) spaces – in the libertarian sense of the phrase – remain, as more and more social activities and settings become the subject of monitoring and visibility (Cohen and Taylor 1992). Prison cells, workplaces, gymnasiums, beaches, forests, nightspots and bedrooms, even high school toilets (Taylor 2013), are now places routinely exposed to the intrusive and unrelenting stare of the camera sensor, and what once were considered sacred intimacies and sensitive recesses have become commercially and culturally reconfigured as consumable stimuli – as commodities for sharing, distributing and screening (McGrath 2004; Koskela 2004).

The transfusing of previously sub rosa phenomena is a reverberation contingent on backstage infiltration by data-capturing and data-circulating technologies (Jones 2006; Wise 2013). Intimacies (i.e. expressions of self) are rendered as mediated objects of perception, items of fascination and sources of stimulation for a globally dispersed flâneur, an anonymous televoyeur who capitalises on machine-led vicariousness to enrich her or his subjective experience. A quick browse of popular website YouTube illustrates that there are few, if any, acts from suicide and substance ingestion to self-mutilation and parturition that, as telemediated spectacles, cannot be indirectly accessed and virtually witnessed. To do so involves clicking on a few icons, perhaps registering some details, and then navigating several advertisements. Cameras are almost everywhere, and they see almost everything. This situation is influencing markedly how we perceive (and present) ourselves and how we relate to others, as embodied data repositories of sharable pleasure (Smith 2014b).

Yet, trying to determine the exact number of cameras shadowing our embodied demeanour has become an impracticable and unrealistic task – the stuff of mythos (House of Lords 2009, 20). Establishing even an approximate figure is a difficult assignment. Several factors account for this oddity. Camera unit ownership is widely distributed across public and private sectors, and the CCTV market is now global in reach and scale. Hence, there is no easy method of measurement; no systematic way to discern manufacturing or expenditure patterns. Therefore, depending on which specific agency is speculating, and for what particular end, and contingent on how one actually defines 'surveillance camera' or 'CCTV system' (does one include dummy cameras in the equation, for instance?), and where/who precisely one samples, camera quantity estimates range from the hundreds of thousands to the millions.[10] Rather than enter an arbitrary conjecture in what has become to all intents and purposes a futile, albeit intellectually and factually important, debate, suffice to say that camera numbers have increased prodigiously in the past three decades, and in a predominantly unregulated fashion (Webster 2009, 11; Lyon *et al.* 2012, 1). So universally popular have camera schemes become that, as Stephen Graham (2001) has aptly observed, they now provide a fifth utility 'safety service' to well-endowed social groups – prerogative stakeholders who possess surplus means to consume, who control machineries of production and who dwell in high-value residences. They have become an archetypal signifier of the excess and exclusivity underpinning advanced capitalism, an amenity wielded for securitising property and person, and for influencing the bearing of those whose presence and/or inclination threatens overarching circuits of wealth, ownership and civility.

Over a period of 20 years the UK government has committed immense resources from its Crime Prevention budget to install CCTV schemes in jurisdictions for which it has law and order responsibilities (Surveillance Studies Network 2006);[12] and UK council authorities between 2007 and 2011 spent in excess of £500 million on CCTV-related goods and services.[13] Certainly when one takes into account these statistics, it becomes patently evident that cameras are an extraordinarily prominent aspect of the fiduciary system, the urban ecological realm and the cultural field. Camera coverage, for instance, was predicted to grow ten-fold in the five years following 2002.[14] The UK, in fact, leads the world in terms of CCTV distribution and use (House of Lords 2009, 20). Few legal, economic or geographical restrictions exist to stultify their (diverse) introduction and usage. Not even contemporary research evidence or media negativity (and arguably waning public confidence) is capable of dislodging CCTV's primacy as a securitisation and visualisation medium, with numerous studies and media reports consistently challenging the practical efficacy of CCTV in reducing incidences of criminality.[15]

CCTV, it would seem, really has become the fifth utility. It has extremely powerful allies and serves important markets and functions. More than this, it has infused our way of seeing *and* being in the world (Finn 2012, 67). As a synoptic medium, we fathom social reality through its channels of legibility. It supplements pedagogically the formation of our identities – our value and belief systems. It provides consumable spectacles for a culture of converted scopophiles. Our dependence on CCTV stems from it being a primary method of social engagement, a means of witnessing worldly banalities and extremities, and, as we'll see a bit later, a figure of reassurance in a time of unbridled societal insecurity.

It is evident from this section that CCTV and visibility are entwined in an anomalous union. On the one hand, CCTV is a technology of visibility. It televisualises social life in intimate detail and it dispenses captured telecasts to designated audiences for profiling and categorisation. CCTV was (and still is) launched (and lauded) by its proponents in a highly visible manner. Industry trade magazine *CCTV Today*, for example, previously announced that counties with CCTV installed would be among 'the safest in Britain' (*CCTV Today*, September 1995: 48). Grand claims were made by high-profile dignitaries regarding its astonishing effectiveness in obliterating incidences of criminality[16] and improving perceptions of safety

(Norris and Armstrong 1999, 38, 64). The dividend for those exponents of CCTV was that the cameras would both dissuade the wicked and reassure the dignified. As former Prime Minister Gordon Brown stated in 2010, 'If you're going to be tough on crime and tough on the causes of crime, you need that CCTV protection ... [It] is one of the ways we keep people safe and make people feel safer in our communities'.[17] Exorbitant sums of money have been and continue to be spent on CCTV equipment and services. CCTV cameras provide a palpable reminder of a watching authority; they are intended to regulate space better and to deter wrongdoing by spreading 'anticipatory conformity' – a preventative logic that instils a discourse and repertoire of self-government (Fyfe and Bannister 1996). They extend circulations of supervision into relational circuits of sociality.

However, on the other hand, CCTV has become unvisible and/or banal (Goold *et al.* 2013, 984), its equivocal unobtrusiveness a product of carefully managed policy briefings and public relations spin, and a culture prioritising busy lifestyles (and thus inculcating attention deficiency), property ownership and mass visualism. It is indifference to CCTV that typifies the dispositions of many citizens, the technology's spatial foregrounding contrasting with its cognitive backgrounding. Few of us, for instance, register the presence of camera paraphernalia as we engage social space. Even fewer have knowledge of CCTV's component parts or have visited a camera monitoring facility. In all probability, most of us have not once pondered the role of those who sit behind the cameras observing the images that they harvest. Most of our experiences of CCTV are second hand. They accrue from indirectly accessing broadcast content on television shows and websites. CCTV is unvisible in other ways. We're not entirely sure of the amount of funds that have been – or are being – committed to these implements. We don't know what codes of conduct govern watching practices. We're not well informed about camera density – in other words, how many of these things actually sense our motions and scan the nation. We are not especially cognisant of how CCTV imagery is processed and how it affects camera operators. We do not know who is being looked at or looked for.

So the 'CCTV story', as it were, involves *politics of visibility* and *politics of unvisibility*. Let's consider these politics in slightly more detail and excavate exactly why CCTV remains simultaneously protuberant and evanescent. This entails identifying the key structural forces, institutional stakeholders and value interests responsible for cultivating an impression, certainly among the upwardly mobile, of an impending crime crisis, and for presenting CCTV as an indispensable solution to this looming calamity. It necessitates also that we accentuate some of the critical 'signal events' reinforcing societal dependency on CCTV as a superlative strategy for governing egregious segments of the population. Each factor helps expound why CCTV, and not some alternative contraption, became so revered in influential political caucuses, business circles and electoral districts, and why it is that CCTV periodically appears, but then predominantly disappears, from view.

The (un)visibility of CCTV: protecting the privileged, problematising the poor

> As a key tool in the politics of vision, cameras in the cities of the UK are helping to put into effect what can and cannot be seen on the streets.
>
> (Coleman 2004a, 301)

Perhaps unsurprisingly, given the pledges of providence that its endorsers make (see the quotation from Jack Straw, below), and its obvious resemblances with a prominent Orwellian literary metaphor, CCTV evokes in people a broad spectrum of opinions, ranging from the enthusiastic, to the indifferent, to the outright aversive (Goold et al. 2013). Attitudes differ according to various factors: one's personal contact with CCTV, and whether historical encounters have been experienced positively or negatively; one's exposure – and susceptibility – to contrasting CCTV dogmas; one's political persuasion and degree of trust in authority; one's personal wealth and social position; one's level of educative insight, and so on. However, it seems, at least according to most polls,[18] that public support for CCTV is fairly widespread and popular appetite remains for its continued expansion.[19] This sentiment, one might contend, is elicited not from experiencing CCTV operativity first hand or from studying the impact of cameras on crime rates over time. It derives instead from recurrent subjection to fear-provoking political discourses, that is, seditious slogans manufactured by a host of ideological technicians and disseminated in miscellaneous media to precipitate widespread hysteria – concern that will effectively secure compliant uptake. Criminological scholars of the media have consistently demonstrated the hegemonic effects of media representations and story distortions on audience imaginaries (Cohen 2002; Jewkes 2004a; Greer 2009). Such rhetorical hyperbole conveys escalating levels of violence and portrays a need for stringent securitisation measures (and asks for conformity with them). Popular anxieties around 'difference' and 'excess' (specifically concerning diversity and irresponsibility) get targeted and manipulated to exacerbate feelings of vulnerability and intolerance, and these sensations enable new supervisory circulations to procure legitimacy, CCTV representing a protective force field for asset safekeeping and for managing risk. Beyond intimidating would-be offenders, maximising CCTV's public profile permits authorities to broadcast their 'tough on crime' posture and to showcase their capacity for spatial management.

Neoliberal crusades: managing space, economy and belonging

> The evidence is clear. In the right context, CCTV can significantly reduce crime and disorder. It is like having permanently on the beat in particular streets or areas a number of police officers with eyes in the back of their

heads and an incontrovertible record of what they have seen. When used properly, CCTV can deter criminals, greatly assist the police and others in bringing offenders to justice, and help to reduce people's fear of crime.

(Jack Straw, UK Home Secretary, 16 March 1999)[20]

Public enchantment with CCTV is influenced by what has become a standard account expressed by a united group of self-serving and profit-driven agencies, a narrative hailing CCTV as an indispensable 'panacea' weapon in the 'war on crime', and as a gallant deliverer of public safety, order and assuredness.[21] Statements are made, such as the one by Home Secretary Jack Straw above, that sing the praises of CCTV – both as an objective record keeper and as a crime-fighting instrument. High-profile cases, where CCTV evidence has proven pivotal, are selectively drawn upon to sell the technology's utopian virtues: 'From the IRA terrorist campaign in the 1990s and the Brixton nail bomber in 1999, to the terrorist incidents in London in July 2005, CCTV released to the public led to early identification of suspects and played an important role in the subsequent prosecutions' (Gerrard *et al.* 2007, 7). Those propagating the value of CCTV either exploit and capitalise on, or reify and reflect, an age of societal insecurity – a period typified by obsessive concerns with dangerous bodies and risky futures, and by cravings for pre-emptive visualisation technologies, identification mechanisms that can assist in the governance of uncertain, but imminent, harms (Lianos 2013). However, these proponents, from politicians and industrialists to journalists and community safety groups,[22] are themselves victims of indoctrination. They have been proselytised by, and perpetuate, the mantra of neoliberalism, an ideology championing market-driven instrumentalism and penalising activities at variance with this ideal.

Neoliberalism is a system of thought and a technique of governance prioritising many things: individualism, instrumentalism, competitiveness, market liberalisation, service privatisation, globalisation and glocalisation, minimalist government, labour outsourcing and contractualism, credit growth, joined-up services, fiscal austerity, risk actuarialism, hyper-managerialism, performance measurement, and so on (Harvey 2005; Davis and Monk 2008). As such, there is considerable debate in the social sciences regarding the precise nature and facets of neoliberalism and its utility as a concept and analytic. However, and that aside, neoliberalism has become the dominant mode of systematisation in today's advanced capitalist economies. At its ideological core is a posture that: (a) seeks opportunities for unleashing enterprise, and (b) concentrates attention on appropriation and coordination of assets. These principles have, in hegemonic fashion, percolated into each facet of social life. Social spatialities, of both the physical and cognitive variety, form the diagrammatic superstructure on which neoliberal designs are erected and a neoliberal ethos is imprinted (Hall and Winlow 2006). Indeed, neoliberalism is not merely an organisational arrangement: it is also a subjectivity (a way of being) and a

The (un)visibility of CCTV: protecting the privileged, problematising the poor

> As a key tool in the politics of vision, cameras in the cities of the UK are helping to put into effect what can and cannot be seen on the streets.
>
> (Coleman 2004a, 301)

Perhaps unsurprisingly, given the pledges of providence that its endorsers make (see the quotation from Jack Straw, below), and its obvious resemblances with a prominent Orwellian literary metaphor, CCTV evokes in people a broad spectrum of opinions, ranging from the enthusiastic, to the indifferent, to the outright aversive (Goold *et al.* 2013). Attitudes differ according to various factors: one's personal contact with CCTV, and whether historical encounters have been experienced positively or negatively; one's exposure – and susceptibility – to contrasting CCTV dogmas; one's political persuasion and degree of trust in authority; one's personal wealth and social position; one's level of educative insight, and so on. However, it seems, at least according to most polls,[18] that public support for CCTV is fairly widespread and popular appetite remains for its continued expansion.[19] This sentiment, one might contend, is elicited not from experiencing CCTV operativity first hand or from studying the impact of cameras on crime rates over time. It derives instead from recurrent subjection to fear-provoking political discourses, that is, seditious slogans manufactured by a host of ideological technicians and disseminated in miscellaneous media to precipitate widespread hysteria – concern that will effectively secure compliant uptake. Criminological scholars of the media have consistently demonstrated the hegemonic effects of media representations and story distortions on audience imaginaries (Cohen 2002; Jewkes 2004a; Greer 2009). Such rhetorical hyperbole conveys escalating levels of violence and portrays a need for stringent securitisation measures (and asks for conformity with them). Popular anxieties around 'difference' and 'excess' (specifically concerning diversity and irresponsibility) get targeted and manipulated to exacerbate feelings of vulnerability and intolerance, and these sensations enable new supervisory circulations to procure legitimacy, CCTV representing a protective force field for asset safekeeping and for managing risk. Beyond intimidating would-be offenders, maximising CCTV's public profile permits authorities to broadcast their 'tough on crime' posture and to showcase their capacity for spatial management.

Neoliberal crusades: managing space, economy and belonging

> The evidence is clear. In the right context, CCTV can significantly reduce crime and disorder. It is like having permanently on the beat in particular streets or areas a number of police officers with eyes in the back of their

heads and an incontrovertible record of what they have seen. When used properly, CCTV can deter criminals, greatly assist the police and others in bringing offenders to justice, and help to reduce people's fear of crime.

(Jack Straw, UK Home Secretary, 16 March 1999)[20]

Public enchantment with CCTV is influenced by what has become a standard account expressed by a united group of self-serving and profit-driven agencies, a narrative hailing CCTV as an indispensable 'panacea' weapon in the 'war on crime', and as a gallant deliverer of public safety, order and assuredness.[21] Statements are made, such as the one by Home Secretary Jack Straw above, that sing the praises of CCTV – both as an objective record keeper and as a crime-fighting instrument. High-profile cases, where CCTV evidence has proven pivotal, are selectively drawn upon to sell the technology's utopian virtues: 'From the IRA terrorist campaign in the 1990s and the Brixton nail bomber in 1999, to the terrorist incidents in London in July 2005, CCTV released to the public led to early identification of suspects and played an important role in the subsequent prosecutions' (Gerrard *et al.* 2007, 7). Those propagating the value of CCTV either exploit and capitalise on, or reify and reflect, an age of societal insecurity – a period typified by obsessive concerns with dangerous bodies and risky futures, and by cravings for pre-emptive visualisation technologies, identification mechanisms that can assist in the governance of uncertain, but imminent, harms (Lianos 2013). However, these proponents, from politicians and industrialists to journalists and community safety groups,[22] are themselves victims of indoctrination. They have been proselytised by, and perpetuate, the mantra of neoliberalism, an ideology championing market-driven instrumentalism and penalising activities at variance with this ideal.

Neoliberalism is a system of thought and a technique of governance prioritising many things: individualism, instrumentalism, competitiveness, market liberalisation, service privatisation, globalisation and glocalisation, minimalist government, labour outsourcing and contractualism, credit growth, joined-up services, fiscal austerity, risk actuarialism, hyper-managerialism, performance measurement, and so on (Harvey 2005; Davis and Monk 2008). As such, there is considerable debate in the social sciences regarding the precise nature and facets of neoliberalism and its utility as a concept and analytic. However, and that aside, neoliberalism has become the dominant mode of systematisation in today's advanced capitalist economies. At its ideological core is a posture that: (a) seeks opportunities for unleashing enterprise, and (b) concentrates attention on appropriation and coordination of assets. These principles have, in hegemonic fashion, percolated into each facet of social life. Social spatialities, of both the physical and cognitive variety, form the diagrammatic superstructure on which neoliberal designs are erected and a neoliberal ethos is imprinted (Hall and Winlow 2006). Indeed, neoliberalism is not merely an organisational arrangement: it is also a subjectivity (a way of being) and a materialised infrastructure (an architecture). Persons and landscapes are predisposed to programming and come to embody and exhibit the values and insignia of the neoliberal perspective: they are subject to stimulation, they self-advertise and they bear alluring and perturbative features that ensure consumption practices are reproduced – and prevailing circuits of capital ownership are sustained (Thrift 2005). Space, from this doctrine, is tantamount to economy. It is a vital resource requiring careful stewardship and intensive superintendence, a place where social bodies, objects and flows converge in contrived ways to actualise and perpetuate the neoliberal project. The restructuring – or 'purification' – of urban space has been one pivotal concern for neoliberal elites (Graham 1998; Coleman 2004b; Lomell 2004). Commercial forces strive to enhance the marketability and profitability of space and to liberate it from occupying pollutants (Cohen 1985), those whose presence tarnishes – or makes less believable – the 'fantasy' aesthetic encasing the production and atmospherics of consumerism (Bauman 1998). Among such 'flawed consumers' are beggars, the homeless, prostitutes, street traders and gangs of youths, the appearance of whom, according to one urban authority, 'is a nuisance to those who want to use the streets and shopping centres in a more *conventional* way' (cited in Graham and Marvin 1996, 20, emphasis added). This motivation makes space susceptible to both privatisation and fortification processes, which act to 'massage the social space of a town centre into something more socially conducive to consumers' (Reeve 1998, 78). CCTV figures as a technological manifestation of this will for sociospatial cleansing and ordering: a technique for sterilising municipalities, governing conducts, securing properties and crafting ambiences.

During the recession-hit 1970s and 1980s, there was a popular impression that British municipalities were being overwhelmed by dangerous sections of the population, and that space was not being fully optimised and utilised, nor sufficiently controlled (Bannister *et al.* 1998; Norris and Armstrong 1999, 38–39). An intractable poor or urban underclass was emerging, a group considered to be incapable of improving their economic situation and a social menace – a source of depletion and discontent – for those taxpayers partaking in legitimate trade as self-responsible 'prosumers' (i.e. service producers and consumers). Their profaning presence was causing considerable alarm among ascendant publics.[23] As Nils Christie (2000, 66) puts it:

> Poverty has again become visible. Beggars have appeared. The homeless and drug-users are out in the streets. They hang around everywhere, dirty, abusive – provocative in their non-usefulness ... Hiding places in slums and dark corners have been replaced by heated arcades leading into glittering shopping paradises. Of course, homeless and/or unemployed persons also seek these public alternatives to the places of work and homes they are barred from. And as an equal matter of course, they are met with agitated demands to get them out of sight and out of mind.

Maliciously exaggerated media coverage was inculcating apprehensiveness among property-owning magnates of an impending 'crime crisis', a circumstance deliberately blamed on second- and third-generation immigrant groups and white disenfranchised outcasts, each of whom was deemed morally contaminated and captive to innate violent compulsions (Hall et al. 1978; Young 1999).[24] The primacy proprietors and patrons were placing on 'appearance', 'safety' and 'cleanliness' meant that the visibility of unbelonging 'outsiders' was constraining spatial innovation and related marketisation initiatives. An intimidating scourge of poverty – and concomitant threat of politically motivated extremism and psychotic barbarism – was destabilising the commercial viability of urban economies, and damaging their desirability as places to frequent. Privileged elites were shunning public transit and public life for fear of victimisation and molestation. They were seeking gated residences, reinforced SUVs and sanitised work and retail precincts (Simon 2007), sites of homogeneity and sterility where problematic expressions of difference could be entirely avoided and cognitively denied. Society was becoming ever more divided along plutocratic and ethnic lines, and this was being reflected in its spatial arrangements (Davis 2006; Wacquant 2007; Davis and Monk 2008). 'Habitation apartheid' was transpiring, ghettos populated by the indigent outcasts overlooked by shiny residential urban 'fortifications' inhabited by the affluent. It was this diagram of spatial privatisation and purification, of *exclusivity* and *segregation*, which would come to shape the redesign of civic spaces (Bannister et al. 1998; Hubbard 2004; Coleman 2004b; Crofts et al. 2013). It was in this context that CCTV had a role to play as 'a new technology transposed onto an old spatial economy which works to maintain racialized segregation in the city ... [as] a means of social defense from imagined communities of risk' (Walby 2006, 60–61).

A perception of insecurity was further accentuated by the manifestation of a dispossessed band of Irish republican paramilitaries who sought to perpetrate sustained terror attacks on the UK's major cities as part of a second wave liberation campaign.[25] An increasing supply of media stories and sensationalist television programmes like *Crimewatch UK* added discursive and semiotic fuel to sentiment being publically expressed by eminent politicians – and other 'moral entrepreneurs' (Becker 1963) – that pathological behaviours were on the rise and civil society was undergoing a sharp spurt in degradation. Such reports and broadcasts prioritised violent incursions on 'ideal victim' subjects (specifically Caucasian and middle-class women, children and the elderly) by predacious assailants (Christie 1986). The UK was seemingly in the midst of a high crime wave (Garland 2000). The egregious abduction and killing of Merseyside toddler James Bulger in February 1993 by two ten-year-old boys proved a watershed 'signal event',[26] both in terms of exacerbating unease and outrage among the public regarding the precariousness of public space, and foregrounding a national appetite for enhanced CCTV coverage (Norris 2012b, 25).[27] The repeated circulation of a CCTV still depicting an ingenuous James being led to his death appalled the nation. The grainy picture showing the infant clasping the hand of his abductor while exiting a shopping mall struck a moral nerve, as it ignited contradictory fears around child susceptibility – both in terms of being victims and perpetrators of barbarity. The felony, therefore, ruptured popular and conventional conceptions of childhood innocence and purity, and aroused disquietudes regarding the harmful effects of film violence. CCTV had participated in bringing this issue to public attention and in bringing resolution to a brutal offence. It had been launched into the national spotlight as a crime-capturing detector and as a textual source for the construction of collective consciousness (Norris 2012b; Goold *et al.* 2013, 981) - binding together *us* and demonising and Othering *them*.

Although the cameras did nothing to prevent James's murder, the images they captured assisted the police in detecting his attackers and ensuring that they were swiftly brought to justice. As with the David Copeland case (1999),[28] the 7/7 suicide attacks in London (2005) and the UK riots (2011) years later, CCTV was deemed a success; a capable guardian in times of hostility and barbarity (Kroener 2013, 132). It had played a pivotal role in solving a gruesome act. State, police, industry, media and community representatives were quick to praise – and promote – CCTV's investigative capabilities, and demand its continued augmentation. As Norris and Armstrong (1999, 37) note, '[t]he public mood in the wake of the killing, as evidenced in the newspapers of the time, made those who tried to raise objections to CCTV seem either callous or too concerned with the rights of criminals'. In the same vein, Simon Davies (1998, 244) points out the symbolism concomitant on this signal event: 'Put bluntly, an argument against CCTV was interpreted as an argument in favour of baby killers.'

Signal events assimilating CCTV footage actualise six things. One, they delineate atrocities in meticulous detail and they indicate an unbridled viciousness ('them') lurking within societal fissures. Two, they bind together a moral majority ('us') that is undergoing shock, distress and indignation.[29] Three, they symbolise the inevitability of crime and tend to foreground the public's proximity to it.[30] Four, they accentuate failures in preventive policing, and exhibit the police's inability to free communities from villainy. Five, they exhibit the effectiveness of CCTV as a detector and consolidate a public outlook that these technologies are *sine qua non*. Last, they sediment trepidation and panic in those who have the most to lose from expressions of deviance and the most to gain from extravagant securitisation measures. In other words, signal events implant concern about external threats and they imbue receptivity to the exercise of social control – especially when aimed at curtailing 'problem others'. They ensure that politicised articulations – and point scoring – on 'system failings' can be promulgated, audiences abide in a state of perpetual trepidation and security industry vendors capitalise on yet another multimillion-pound securitisation contract (Newburn 2001).

At a time when it seemed the police were losing the 'war on crime', town and city nuclei were also losing desirable patrons to 'socially exclusive' hypersecuritised retail parks on the suburban margins, where conceptions of security could be more easily manipulated, and space more decisively regulated (Reeve 1998, 84; Norris and Armstrong 1999). Undesirable bodies were liable to banishment in places owned by, and ergo under the jurisdictional authority of, business corporations (McCahill 2002). They could be subject to legally enforceable banning and dispersal orders and had limited recourse to legislative protections. In the face of stiff competition, local authorities had to do something radical to galvanise urban cores, to revitalise their functionality as employment, retail and leisure hubs. An intervention was sought to appease business owners and community electorates: to entice a return of investors and purchasers to the high street. It came in the form of policymaking and spatial redesign, an 'urban renaissance' via regeneration logics, a central goal of which was to rejuvenate the reputation, and resuscitate the prosperity, of downtown areas (Atkinson and Helms 2007). To make, in other words, these unruly and decaying places more environmentally attractive, competitive and vibrant, and to encourage further the occurrence of legitimate (i.e. taxable) enterprise. This entailed liberalising premise opening hours, enhancing transportation services, renovating and gentrifying dilapidated thoroughfares, and enhancing natural surveillance through improved street lighting, architectural innovation and increased population density. It principally involved reclaiming space from the fear-inducing clutches of inhabitant 'abusers', and dispossessing them of their 'right' to occupy the city, and thus to tarnish its emerging recreational texture. Newfangled policies were introduced, a series of tough bills criminalising conducts adjudged to taint the city's prosperous façade and endowing law enforcers with extensive new powers. Town Centre Management (TCM) quangos were also formulated alongside 'Safer Cities' Partnerships, committees that comprised professional representatives from enterprise, district councils, health services and police constabularies. These initiatives were charged with securing the high street's fiscal and ecological sustainability. Part of their remit focused on liberalising markets, that is to say, on designing in buoyant new economies, the night time economy being the obvious exemplar. The other part focused on aesthetics and regulation, and entailed the wielding of numerous securitisation measures to purge manifestations of destitution, non-productivity and non-consumption – specifically begging, sex work, unlicensed trading and drug peddling (Bauman 1998; Coaffee *et al.* 2009). As Coleman (2004a, 301) observes:

> As surveillance cameras routinely monitor the street prohibitions of the neoliberal city, they also reinforce the moral codes, intolerances and normative prescriptions of its creators … [with] certain forms of culture increasingly subject to oppressive monitoring and curtailment.

It was in this context that CCTV, a hi-tech military technology, advanced from deployment in combat zones to application in civil milieu. It had proven its worth in thwarting political adversaries from *without* and could now be deployed in thwarting problem adversaries from *within*. The diminishing significance of Cold War animosities meant a declining emporium for many surveillance technology manufacturers. The answer was surprisingly simple: annexation of the civilian marketplace. British society was enduring considerable social disobedience associated with paradigmatic ideological transformations, specifically the transition to a post-industrial neoliberal economy. The dismantling of welfarism and trade unionism by the Thatcher-led Conservative government was generating a swarm of discontents, as was their proposal to outsource labour from cheaper global regions and to privatise public-owned facilities and services. A society prioritising individualism, consumption, enterprise and wealth accumulation, and punishing unionism and benefit dependency, was sparking belligerence among those either left behind or Left-leaning in their political penchants. Conflict (and unemployment) was on the rise and a symbolic saviour was needed to quell the struggles (or at least to manage them better), an imposing monitor that could assist urban planners and authorities in identifying dissidents, in governing problematic and anti-social behaviours and in realising spatial aspirations. CCTV had this very reputation as a combative tool with an impressive track record and with an influential lobby. It could suppress complications associated with regime realignment. It could, once again, ensure *and* insure the capitalist order from those that threaten its integrity. What's more, it was readily available for recruitment. A campaign was needed to convince primary voters that CCTV could remedy the ills of market excess and service commercialism, and this manoeuvre, of course, would not prove difficult given that prominent members of the public were already imbued with unease and courting governmental solutions. Thus, fear of crime – and attendant vulnerability – became judicious sentiments on which CCTV crusaders of both the political and industrial strains could engrave the merits of the technology while mutually actualising their own dogmatic and material interests.

CCTV arrived at an opportune historical moment in the unfolding of advanced urbanism. It reflected an emerging policy framework that sought to incentivise local inter-agency partnerships and to embrace risk-aversive principles (Fussey 2008). It was painted as the quintessential control measure for managing the poor, for managing perceptions of authority, for managing impressions of safety, for managing subversive publics, for managing declining markets and for managing dwindling police outlay. In accordance with voguish actuarial logics, it could deter the rational offender and reduce opportunities for offending (Feeley and Simon 1994). It could streamline the prosecution process, enlighten criminal justice agencies and inform the institution of law enforcement. Indeed, as Norris (2012b, 34) remarks, the popularity of CCTV resided in its ability to create 'an objective record of events … [and to] capture the past in perpetuity'. It could, in other words, produce specialist knowledge that would aid the identification and governance of problem communities, and systematise how intelligence-led and preventative policing was delivered.

Neoliberalised city technocrats were, for these and other reasons, encouraged to compete with one another for centralised CCTV funding totalling hundreds of millions of pounds. The upshot was a considerable swell in 'public' space, but privately made (and often operated), camera schemes. CCTV proliferation, therefore, flourished within conditions of urban renewal and in accordance with changing dynasties in the management of street usage (Coaffee *et al.* 2009). A neoliberal infused agenda sought to transform city centres by putting them under the custodianship of multi-agency stakeholders and by exposing them to a multitude of regeneration statutes and 'target hardening' programs. The aims were to accumulate sustainable income streams from the unleashing of a consumer-driven order, and to erect 'pacified' hubs where shoppers and workers alike could inhabit clean, crime-free and poverty-clear spaces, without feeling wealth guilt or assault apprehension. Manipulating perception became a central directive of the revitalisation project, the installation of CCTV cameras helping establish a perceptual representation of sterility that would foster desirable comportment and magnify the feel-good factor – and reverie – associated with transcendental consumption pursuits (Coleman and Sim 2000). CCTV mediums would lower insurance premiums for retailers (thereby attracting their *métier*), cultivate civilities and cleanse urban marginality. 'Flawed consumers', i.e. those not possessing the means to consume appropriately, and other such undesirables, rapidly became the targets of these machineries and the subjects of disciplinary ordinances designed to prohibit them from congregating in, and thus profaning, the sanctity of shopping precincts (McCahill 2002). As Norris and Armstrong (1999, 201) reveal:

> The gaze of the cameras does not fall equally on all users of the street but on those who are stereotypically predefined as potentially deviant, or through appearance and demeanour are singled out by operators as unrespectable. In this way youth, particularly those already socially and economically marginal, may be subject to even greater levels of authoritative intervention and official stigmatisation, and rather than contributing to social justice through the reduction of victimisation, CCTV will merely become a tool of injustice through the amplification of differential and discriminatory policing.

The CCTV revolution was initiated by the 'neoliberal turn' and boosted by an absence of regulatory frameworks that could have inhibited its subsequent sprawl. Urban authorities across the UK invested heavily in CCTV camera networks not because of their proven efficacy, but rather to mitigate against any displacement effects generated by nearby systems and to remain competitive players in the 'safety politics' and 'safety dividends' of entrepreneurial urbanism. As we have seen, symbolism and 'keeping up with the Joneses' are important facets of the CCTV story. Yet camera augmentation would not have occurred but for the consensualism of some powerful rhetorical technicians and wherewithal financiers. Supporters of CCTV provision predominantly include the likes of politicians (at the national, regional and municipal levels), law enforcers and judiciaries, security industrialists, insurers, business executives, journalists and members of the property-owning classes. Each stakeholder benefits from CCTV proliferation, whether as a recipient of political kudos, enhanced detection and evidence means, heightened sales and profits, or personal protection. Notwithstanding an assortment of, at times, competing rationales, several key institutions, with monopolies on the means of communication and the means of expenditure, especially gain from endorsing CCTV diffusion. The state has an interest in championing the CCTV cause for reasons previously outlined (i.e. being visibly 'tough on crime' and rolling out a new political economic order) and to demonstrate that it takes seriously public concerns regarding criminality and its contractual obligations as paramount guarantor of security provision. CCTV makes for good media, as both a newsworthy story and a visual medium with appended entertainment value (Jewkes 2004a, 56; Barnard-Wills 2011). The security industry is, of course, a significant proponent of CCTV as it acquires profits from hardware manufacturing, goods merchandising, and installation and training services. Policing agencies approve CCTV dispersal for operational, evidential and liability purposes, but also for its ability to counteract the effects of dwindling staffing budgets. Business owners derive distinct advantages from CCTV multiplication, in that cameras combat stock shrinkage, reduce insurance costs and foster environmental ambiences conducive to worker productivity and client expending. Property owning citizens typically acquiesce with mushrooming CCTV coverage for its apparent capacity to retrench the onslaught of a property-less (and desperate) underclass. Moreover, and drawing on the cultural analysis of Finn (2012), Goold et al. (2013, 983) observe that a further factor explaining CCTV's continued acceptability is the conditioning of citizens to 'see like cameras'. A remarkable escalation in image capturing technologies and practices has occurred in recent times, civil members now inhabiting and experiencing a social world organised around data sharing and data analysis principles. CCTV is but one brick in a much larger 'wall of visualism' (see Smith 2014a), a structure valorising visibility while trivialising the means of its emergence. The cultural banality or legitimacy of CCTV stems from it being but one of many information-rendering means, its ends as a 'security comfort blanket' (Goold et al. 2013, 987) and 'synoptic platform' (Mathiesen 1997) considered to outweigh its expedience as a potentially invasive or exclusionary lever.

Under the lens: research on CCTV

Camera (in)effectiveness?

Research on CCTV has been predominantly evaluative in nature and concerned with statistically measuring its effectiveness, as a crime-reducing technique, as a crime-detecting implement, as a prosecutorial vehicle, as a attitudinal manipulator, and as a public or private resource expenditure. It would take another book to review the findings from this corpus and to reflect on their respective methodological dimensions: their design flaws and merits. Suffice to say here that, just like trying to tally camera numbers, attempting to determine camera utility is a notoriously tricky task – dependent as much on assumption and extrapolation as on the measuring instrument itself. All manner of facets, probabilities and controls need be taken into consideration when critically assessing the multi-functionality of CCTV. For instance, choice of sample will undoubtedly influence the results, as each area reviewed will have its own pre-existing glocal contingencies and circumstances, in terms of demography, ecology, economy and criminality. One needs to account for processes like displacement and for fluctuating seasonal trends. Moreover, how does the inquirer know, when drawing inferences about camera potency, that a camera system – and not some other variable (i.e. another 'capable guardian') – was responsible for deterring a crime? How would this be established? Does the fact finder need to quantify public awareness of CCTV and examine chronologically the issue's degree of mediatisation? Are offenders' views on CCTV required to assess its preventive properties? Trying to establish CCTV's impact on fear of crime is a further complexity to gauge. In addition, how does the researcher sufficiently rationalise rises in recorded crime that are the outcome of prolific career criminals, transformations in spatial economies and camera systems capturing more illegality? Should types of offences be graded against a threshold of severity? For example, CCTV captures some perceptible crimes but not others (e.g. corruption and white collar crime). Beyond these difficulties, how does the researcher explicate structural differences between and among systems in terms of operational procedures, operating staff, operations capital and camera density/technical specifications? What role does chance play in all of this? Calculating CCTV efficacy, therefore, involves conducting longitudinal and comparative research, and it requires that a multitude of factors are recognised, tested and manipulated.

These important metrical problems aside, it is evident that an ambiguous picture has emerged from subjecting CCTV to external appraisal and to contrasting systems of mensuration (see Welsh and Farrington 2002; Armitage 2002). There are those who maintain that it has a positive effect on reducing specific expressions of criminality (like vehicle crime, vandalism and theft, e.g. Tilley 1993; Skinns 1998), there are others who contend that it has a negligible or detrimental effect on offending patterns, and there are some who claim its effects are neutral (Gill and Spriggs 2005). Similarly, there are those who argue that CCTV lessens fear of crime (Sarno *et al.* 1999), and there are others who insist that it either has no detectable effect or in fact raises levels of alarm by signalling the actuality of disorder in a given locale (Ditton 1998; Gill and Spriggs 2005, 60). Likewise, there are debates around whether or not CCTV deters offending (Armitage 2002). From an in-depth evaluation of 13 separate CCTV systems as part of Home Office-commissioned research, Gill and Spriggs (2005, 43, 58) found:

that the CCTV schemes that have been assessed had little overall effect on crime levels. Even where changes have been noted, with the exception of those relating to car parks, very few are larger than could be due to chance alone and all could in fact represent either chance variation or confounding factors ... Although there is some evidence that there was a reduction in fear of crime following the installation of CCTV, there is little to suggest that this is attributable to CCTV ... All systems [sampled] aimed to reduce crime, yet this study suggests that CCTV has generally failed to achieve this. Although police-recorded crime has decreased in six out of the 13 systems for which data were available, in only three cases might this decrease be attributable to CCTV, and in only two areas was there a significant decrease compared with the control.

The pair conclude:

[T]he majority of the schemes evaluated did not reduce crime and even where there was a reduction this was mostly not due to CCTV; nor did CCTV schemes make people feel safer, much less change their behaviour.
(Gill and Spriggs 2005, 115)

Correspondingly, research on CCTV usefulness in Australia discovered:

The effectiveness of CCTV as a crime prevention tool is questionable. From this research, it appears CCTV is effective at *detecting* violent crime and/or may result in increased reporting as opposed to *preventing* any type of crime.
(Wells *et al.* 2006, iii, original emphasis)

What is patently clear from the oeuvre of this international research is that the initial claims made by dignitaries and industrialists regarding CCTV effectiveness were the stuff of mythos, being founded on suspect motivations, dubious research designs and iffy evidence bases (Groombridge 2008; Webster 2009, 17–19). So, too, were declarations that CCTV made (or would make) a 'significant' impact on decreasing public fears of crime. Indeed, the faith with which successive authorities advanced the CCTV campaign was grossly misplaced (if, of course, the frontstage narrative was at all congruent with the backstage agenda), especially when juxtaposed with its actual operating record and outlay (Groombridge 2008, 74). It is, as Goold *et al.* (2013, 981) remark, perturbing to contemplate the scale of public resources that were pledged for CCTV 'services' without proportionate or compelling evidence concerning operational practicability. This kind of unsystematic and irresponsible approach to governing in all probability does little to inspire public confidence and trust, specifically in terms of the sovereign state delivering on core contractual obligations around security provision and service delivery. These issues aside, it appears that we can draw three firm conclusions from applied studies of CCTV efficacy to date: one, that this form of analysis is methodologically demanding (Germain *et al.* 2013, 136); two, that if CCTV does have an influence on criminality and public perceptions of safety, it is an extremely infinitesimal one – and one conditional on a profusion of components; and three, that the leverage CCTV does wield over crime rates falls well short of the monies that have been, and continue to be, spent on these visual circuitries.

Camera usage: operating procedures

Another major strand of research has concentrated on CCTV's operational dimensions, specifically as these relate to how camera operators normatively source object 'targets', how CCTV footage is used as evidence in court (and beyond), privacy issues contingent on CCTV creep, and how CCTV systems effect policing cultures and professional working relations between watchers and watched.[31] This research has drawn attention to the formal and informal features of CCTV application, and to its wider socio-cultural effects on occupational practices and institutional processes. A prominent rationality has been to uncover the degree of discretionary discrimination that occurs behind the screens as camera operators profile populations and select bodies for inordinate scrutiny (Norris and Armstrong 1999; Dubbeld 2003; Smith 2004; Lomell 2004; Walby 2005a). Findings from CCTV monitoring observations have consistently demonstrated that the gaze cast upon the street is determined less by objective markers of disorder and more by cultural stereotypes and subjective prejudices.[32] It is activated less by suspicious behaviours and offbeat gait, and more by how operators perceive social groups in terms of their assumed desirability or dangerousness; whether they *belong* or *unbelong* within a normative spatial ecology (Norris and Armstrong 1999, 140). Criteria such as appearance, group affiliation and non-consumption become decisive in deciding a person's degree of (un)visibility. As Norris (2003, 265) puts it, '[operators] rely on a set of normatively based, contextual rules to draw their attention to any behaviour that disrupts the "normal"'. Bodily traits, like skin colour, gender and age, and surmised class affiliation, materialise as categorical signifiers for gauging disreputableness. These studies have collectively accentuated the potential for ethnocultural minorities to experience disproportionately higher levels of CCTV supervision in urban precincts than that received by the (white) majority (Fiske 1998; Norris and Armstrong 1999, 119). Put another way, they have shown the disciplinary stare of the camera unit to be instructed less by situational factors than by pre-existent colour-coded and class-coded intolerances. This circumstance undoubtedly reflects individualised hostilities but it also evinces the 'pressures of the organizational complex which oblige the CCTV operator to produce deliverance through the camera' (Walby 2006, 59). Interesting policy ramifications emanate from this research in terms of its identifying a requirement for stricter camera operator recruitment and training protocols, operational codes of practice, and compliance and accountability procedures. It alerts the public and regulators to endemic system misuse and underlines the need for tougher legal directives and enforceable sanctions to avert CCTV technologies from being simply appropriated as tools of oppression.

Insightful and critical as it is, the research on CCTV reviewed above merely tells us: why it emerged; how it gained political and popular traction; why it is or is not (cost) effective; and how systemised watching is normatively biased and influences things on the street. What it seldom excavates are expressions of lived experience – sentiments divulged from the perceptual and phenomenological realm. That is to say, studies of CCTV tend either to bypass or disconnect the accounts and practices of those responsible for initiating the circuitries and for monitoring them on a recurrent basis (Fussey 2007). However, by abstracting a system of visibility from its operating context and by exalting power asymmetries as the predominant unit of analysis, sensing procedures get detached from processes of social mediation and meaning-making. Those doing sensing work are effectively silenced and spectacle rendering is reduced to mere instrumentalism. So if we are to engage better the compositional nature of supervisory circulations in general and visibility-visuality alternations in particular, and elucidate their relational connectivity, then it is precisely the voices and actions of system designers and camera operators that need to be sourced, heard and observed. It is their in situ verbalisations and activities that demand detailed documentation and close analysis. This necessitates adoption of an ethnographic research approach and sustained fieldwork so that these lines of inquiry can be empirically probed and conceptually arranged. It involves addressing the following research questions:

- What socio-historical contexts and policy frameworks govern a camera scheme's mode of operation and how do these temporal circumstances interface with spatial transformations?
- What forms of sociality and sociability do camera mediums co-produce in terms of relational exchanges between watchers and watched?
- What role do camera operators play in determining visibility-visuality reticulations and what role do camera images play in determining the dispositions of their primary audience? How, in other words, might the remote watching of street life be shaped by, and structure, selfhood?

It is, therefore, to a consideration of how these styles of question were practically operationalised – and an overview of the study's general method and methodology – that I now turn.

Contacting supervisory lifeworlds: issues and techniques

Few ethnographic studies concerned with the process of camera watching have been performed. Considering the prevalence of CCTV surveillance in city spaces across Europe and North America, ethnographic studies of

CCTV control rooms should serve as an important site of sociological/ criminological research in the future.

(Walby 2006, 62)

It is evident from both the research problems identified above, and the quotation delineated here, that CCTV monitoring stations provide a rich, albeit relatively neglected, context for those interested in the structural mechanics and microphysics of supervisory relations. However, how exactly does one go about researching supervisory circulations of the 'closed circuit' species? What methodological challenges attend to accessing supervisory lifeworlds and engaging their relational lifebloods? How was research for *Opening the Black Box* executed? Which methods were applied, what sample was observed and for what duration? These critical questions are what inform the remainder of this chapter.

Opening black boxes: closed circuitries and chains of watching

Systems of visibility are in the business of rendering things visible. Yet the operating realities of these machineries are, more often than not, shrouded in opaqueness, black boxed by secrecy prohibitions and data protection codes (Monahan and Regan 2012). The knowledge surfacing from personal information collection and processing, as well as the data-accretion techniques themselves, are treasured organisational assets, not chattels to be shared with strangers or with sociological snoopers.[33] Boundaries to operational cores are thus protected by judicial statutes, spatial barricades and sanctioned gatekeepers; by a raft of measures designed to proscribe outsiders from gaining admittance to – and scrutinising – internal processes. This, of course, makes accessing backstage 'screening chambers', and exposing them to extended observation, a tough assignment for the social inquirer (Ball and Haggerty 2005). CCTV monitoring facilities are a fine exemplar of such 'closed' environs. It is exceedingly onerous to research these enclosures via ethnographic means. They tend to be located in publicly unreachable premises and subject to the discretionary jurisdiction of their operations managers, licensees eager to cite compliance stipulations as rationale for inhibiting sensing sanctities from being externally scrutinised. Moreover, as with all research locales, the actual objects of inquiry – the CCTV camera operators – wield volitional capabilities in terms of determining what degree of ingress to subjectivity and social practice is permitted. They can, with some artistry, make fieldwork an awkward undertaking. An irony lurks here. CCTV circuitries facilitate intensive monitoring of public bodies and spaces from afar, and yet it is exceedingly difficult to annex this watching chain by placing camera observers under sociological regard. Thus, data mining procedures and conditions of access are the dominion of the institution to which the system of visibility principally serves. This power asymmetry has played a decisive role in the scarcity of independent and heuristically-informed research on monitoring lifeworlds.

Penetrating the material barriers enclosing processing stations, and unveiling operational protocols to the wider public, is an arduous undertaking and perseverance test. It takes considerable negotiation, and demands that the inquirer exercise fortitude and recoup serendipity. In the instance of this research project, it took many months of letter writing, impression-managed campaigning and system-participant deliberation before I secured a sustainable means of entry into the research field. Even when formal approval is granted to initiate research, by a gatekeeping authority, a right to study the sample population must then be informally earned. This involves differing assimilation appraisals, maintaining integrity in the face of occupational politics, enduring long shifts and ensuring that participant confidences are never breached.[34] Indeed, it became patently clear to me that in exchange for gifting access, many of the operations managers perceived me as a 'nark' who could, through the veil of independence, report back on camera operator practices and perceptions. Likewise, camera operators viewed me (and my alliance to management) as a piece of political ammunition in their struggle for better working conditions and as a source of information for confirming or allaying their suspicions. Other camera operators saw me as an impartial intimate to whom they could vent frustrations regarding the job and deride other colleagues, willing me to side with them on matters of conflict.

Notwithstanding these inconveniences, the specific nature of my research problem and questions necessitated that I negotiate the field defences circumscribing the CCTV lifeworld, and adopt a research method capable of engaging the personal experiences and embodied repertoires of camera operators in situ as they interfaced with visibility-visuality confluences. This entailed conducting a detailed ethnography of CCTV operation where the contextualised watching practices and sense-making reasoning of camera operators – the social meanings these workers ascribe to their labour – could be detected first hand. It invited an empirically grounded approach to data collection and textual analysis, where proximate situation and collaborative dialogue with those operating the technologies over a prolonged spell could progressively reveal the social dimensions structuring and influencing this particular field of practice. An enriched qualitative understanding (or *verstehen* as it was famously termed by Max Weber) of supervisory relations and circulations would involve sustained immersion in an 'operating theatre' and exercise of participatory means (i.e. participant observation and interviewing) to derive informative ends (i.e. linguistic codes, perceptions and tacit operating assumptions) (May 1997, 14). It would also demand that textual materials be sourced and deconstructed analytically as instruments of insight evincing 'how actors and institutions represent themselves and others' (Atkinson *et al.* 2001, 4–5).

The empirical research for *Opening the Black Box* was conducted over a 24-month period and included the study of 13 CCTV monitoring stations for a total duration of approximately 320 hours (equivalent to forty eight-hour shifts). The observatories analysed overlooked, and were responsible for, a range of

52 *Problematising and contextualising watching practices*

spatialities, from public thoroughfares, housing estates and underground/ overground railway premises, to retail malls and outlets, sport stadiums and international airport terminals. They were chosen mostly out of necessity, but also for their variances in terms of *operating priorities* (what it was they were charged with protecting/managing) and *organisational ownership* (who it was that set the operating rules/agenda). Sample diversity provided comparative nuances but also opportunities to accrete more comprehensive insight on operational commonalities and disparities as these materialised from hub to hub. Ephemeral observations, visits lasting less than several hours, occurred in the majority of the locales contacted, as a consequence of time limitations, access restrictions, seasonal constraints, geographical complications and staffing issues. Fieldnote excerpts derived from informal interviews and observations and predominantly taken from two open-street municipal CCTV schemes feature prominently in the chapters that follow, as these sites had round-the-clock monitoring services and supervised, in real time, two thriving, albeit contrasting, socio-economic metropolitan precincts. This meant that each arrangement had liabilities for telecasting and teleordering both the day- and night-time economies, and was systemically subsumed as a visual thread within wider webs of supervisory control. They employed professional and, for the most part, experienced CCTV operators, and their operating parameters coalesced with my thematic interests in telegovernance and (dis)orderly interfacing. Of these two supervisory circuitries, one became the principal object of inquiry and primary source of knowledge. Covering the major streets and landmarks of a city that I shall term 'Newborough',[35] this police-run CCTV network of 84 cameras provided ample resources for effectuating project aspirations. Its executive directorate, for example, bestowed on me unconditional access to the operating theatre and liberty to disseminate results,[36] its team of camera operators were, on the whole, welcoming and forthcoming,[37] and its manager of operations was extremely obliging in terms of information supply (both historical and contemporaneous) on system ecology and ergonomics. It was for these pivotal factors that the site hosted a significant chunk of the fieldwork. General observations and chats were supplemented with additional methods of inquiry. Documentary analysis[38] was conducted, along with a small attitudinal survey of camera operators, each procedure complementing the ethnographic component by providing extra particularities on certain matters. All in all, some 40 camera operators participated in the research as well as manifold system managers and contributors. Each of the fieldnote excerpts (which appear in *italics*) and respondent narrations used in this book were derived either from 'shadowing' the camera operators in situ (i.e. sitting alongside them and observing their work practices) and documenting notable sequences, or from conversational interviews with them at particular moments during the ethnography. Most of the 'interviews' were relatively unstructured in format, and emerged organically from informal discussions where key sentiment was discreetly noted down and then written up more fully when an opportunity arose. A formal interview with the CCTV working group secretary occurred via telephone and was tape-recorded and transcribed. Selected extracts from this exchange appear later in the book. Similarly, several tape-recorded interviews were conducted with the Newborough CCTV manager and with CCTV manager 2. Passages from these interviews surface at various points in the subsequent chapters.

Role transitions: intersubjective experience as the object and instrument of research

> The idea that 'rigorous research' involves the separation of researchers from the subject of their research simply reflects the idea that reason and emotion must be separated. Instead of seeing people in the research process as simply sources of data, feminists argue that research is a two-way process. Frequently, however, textbooks speak of not becoming 'over involved' with participants ... The researcher should be detached and hence objective. According to feminists, this is not only a mythical aim, but also an undesirable one which disguises the myriad of ways in which the researcher is affected by the context of the research or the people who are a part of it.
>
> (May 1997, 20)

The observational role I adopted in the field transformed considerably over time, reflecting changes in my epistemological perspective and thematic concerns. I commenced the research in a systematic fashion inspecting and documenting the commentaries and behaviours of the operators in meticulous detail. I surmised naively that content validity would stem from my being relationally detached. I tried to chronicle exhaustively the points of intersectionality where three spatially separate, but organisationally interconnected, realities converged: the camera operators' embodied actions and verbalisations; the telemediated occurrences on the monitor screens; and the communicative signals being relayed across the radio network. The sheer volume of visual, aural, sensory, semiotic and symbolic information in circulation makes these operating theatres stimulating places to inhabit, but methodologically burdensome to scrutinise in any methodical process. It became quickly apparent that my initial approach to data collection – i.e. trying to describe everything from an impassive position – had been tainted by a normative reading of camera work as being morally disreputable by virtue of inherent power asymmetries and privacy incursions contingent on this type of activity. It had also been influenced by positivist sentiment that emphasises methodological objectivity and puritanical evidence gathering. My inceptive data-gathering role was unsustainable on practical and theoretical grounds: pragmatically, in terms of it encumbering me with information overload and ergo analytical blindness; substantively, in terms of it wielding an uncompassionate disregard for the camera operators' subjective experiences, and thereby an obliviousness to their tacit perceptions and interior struggles. Realising that intersubjective experience was both the object *and* the instrument of the research enabled me to become more embedded in the cultural contours of the surroundings and to better detect their structural patterns and affective tonalities.

By increasing my participation in the operators' workaday discussions and by concentrating attention on the typologies of labour that they had to perform, I began to appreciate more their predicament, specifically the thrilling, tedious and distressing dimensions of their daily duties and routines. My being indirectly exposed to scenes of suffering, as the camera operators and I overlooked persons being beaten unconscious on a street corner or struck by oncoming traffic, prompted several restless nights, and these personally endured incidents informed and sharpened my analytical understanding of CCTV operation, particularly the extent to which visceral disturbances and self-management are determining features of the lifeworld. As May (1997, 21) aptly observes:

> Personal experience is frequently devalued as being too subjective, while science is objective ... [Yet] researchers should be aware of the ways in which their own biography is a fundamental part of the research process. It is both the experiences of the researched and researchers which are important.

Collection means and dissemination ends

Rather than execute a case study approach to data presentation (i.e. where one compares and contrasts dynamics in the locales researched), the substantive chapters that follow are, as per the principles of grounded theory, arranged around key relational themes. Empirical evidence, selectively drawn from the totality of the data set, is employed non-sequentially as a means to concretise and to problematise certain issues, and to elucidate critical reflections on the lived dimensions and practice of CCTV operation. All of the ethnographic excerpts produced in this book were the product of engaging particular camera operators from a qualitative perspective, noting down what they talked about, what they looked at and how they dealt with situations and described their job. Owing to the camera operators' understandable suspicion about my presence and role in 'their' domain, observations and comments were logged as shorthand notes in an A5-sized jotter and then subsequently transcribed at the first available opportunity. The confined (and operationally sensitive) nature of the settings researched meant that I was often in close physical proximity to the operators as they remotely monitored the outside world. It seemed respectful and prudent to, at times, refrain from writing notes. On such occasions, I would take mental notes, silently reciting memorable happenings or quotes repeatedly until I could jot them down in shorthand on impromptu toilet breaks or at moments when the camera operators were involved in an incident. Documenting events and impressions in this fashion, of course, has some limitations for the accuracy and reliability of the research findings presented. It is, for instance, facile to lose a sense of wider context in such narrow abbreviation (i.e. 'thin description'), or to compromise descriptive richness (i.e. 'thick description'), and consequently to undermine central pillars of the ethnographic canon (Geertz 1973). In order to rectify this shortcoming, bolster findings validity, and pursue novel lines of inquiry, a profusion of conversational interviews were effectuated with CCTV operators, and with circuitry supervisors, managers and maintainers. Such dialogues occurred in a range of locations, some in the monitoring rooms and catering facilities on-site, and others in public conveyances, residences, cafeterias, public houses and thoroughfares off-site. As per standard ethical protocol, I have disguised any distinguishing features or details that might betray the confidentiality of the research participants or the research sites.

Overture to Part II and to Chapter 3

Part II proceeds to place empirical flesh upon the conceptual bones and contextual skin specified in Part I. It conveys the reader from the formative margins of supervisory circuitry design and assemblage to the operational nucleus of supervisory circulations in terms of viewing habits, conducts and experiences. In Chapter 3, 'Instigating circuitries: inception and reception', we contemplate genealogically the activities of a municipal committee responsible for instigating the Newborough camera network. Content analysis of historical documents evinces the rationalities and strategies that helped cement a CCTV circuitry in this district and it elucidates how historicised decision making continues to wield a structural influence over the system's present-day arrangement. Empirical evidence demonstrates the camera operators' ambivalent attitude toward the socio-technical structure they previously inherited and now inhabit, and it illuminates the contradictions emanating from what is identified as a 'fusion of agency': that is to say, aspirations from the past mingled with desiderata in the present.

Notes

1 See: www.youtube.com/watch?v=lWam4EWI48M (accessed 7 February 2014).
2 See: news.bbc.co.uk/2/hi/uk_news/politics/election_2010/8648357.stm (accessed 7 February 2014).
3 See for instance: Norris and Armstrong (1999); McCahill (2002); Coleman (2004b); Goold (2004); Norris et al. (2004); Fussey (2007); Webster (2009); Doyle et al. (2012); Norris (2012a, 2012b); Germain et al. (2013); Goold et al. (2013).
4 I have previously (see Smith 2012a) presented an argument prophesying the imminent decline of CCTV, its defenestration as a 'disciplinary mannequin' being an outcome of precisely the same market imperatives and fiscal rationalities that, some 30 years earlier, had prompted its notable rise. However, for the purposes of this particular narrative, I will attend exclusively to the items accountable for the CCTV 'spurt'.
5 For example, the following observation is made in the National CCTV Strategy report: 'The introduction of digital CCTV systems could provide opportunities for

real benefits if the technology is harnessed correctly ... Improving the quality of CCTV images will support the development of current, complimentary technologies such as Automatic Number Plate Recognition (ANPR) and future technologies such as facial recognition' (Gerrard et al. 2007, 8).
6 'Riskscaping' refers to the process of identifying and managing risky flows as they are categorised by a given ordering system.
7 By the phrase *significant otherness*, I refer to the formative ideas of Donna Harraway (2003) that focus attention on the pervasiveness and variance of non-human actors (like canines, technological platforms or food items), which, as material-semiotic presences exert, in often subtle ways, a co-producing influence over our subjective inclinations and procedural routines.
8 At the time of writing, the footage had been viewed on YouTube over 4.3 million times.
9 I am referring here to the steady stream of publically available CCTV sequences that depict citizens and celebrities in all manner of distressing and compromising situations.
10 See: www.telegraph.co.uk/technology/10172298/One-surveillance-camera-for-every-11-people-in-Britain-says-CCTV-survey.html (accessed 24 December 2013); and www.cctvusergroup.com/art.php?art=130&cat=132 (accessed 7 February 2014).
11 See: www.bbc.co.uk/news/uk-england-12726789 (accessed 7 February 2014).
12 The Home Office ran a 'CCTV Challenge Competition' during the mid-to-late 1990s and committed £38.5 million to help secure 585 schemes nationwide (Gerrard et al. 2007, 7). Its subsequent Crime Reduction Programme (CRP) made available £170 million of capital funding for local authority CCTV bids and, 'as a result of this funding, more than 680 CCTV schemes were installed in town centres and other public spaces' (Gerrard et al. 2007, 7). In fact, during the 1990s over three quarters of the total Home Office crime prevention budget was invested in CCTV services and an additional £500 million of public money was spent on CCTV in the decade up to 2006 (House of Lords 2009, 20). In addition, it is estimated that during this same period some £4.5 billion of private funding was spent on the installation and maintenance of CCTV (Norris et al. 2004). The extraordinary confidence with which policy makers backed CCTV is all the more astonishing given how little they actually knew about it both from an operations and evaluative perspective. Indeed, detailed independent and longitudinal research on CCTV generally came *after* the contracts had been signed and the resources duly pledged (Norris and Armstrong 1999, 63–67; Norris 2012b, 29), and despite the unfavourable findings much of this research was broadcasting, that CCTV was not a cost-effective solution to crime management and was susceptible to misuse, policy officials continued to disburse CCTV monies. They do so even to this day (see: www.abc.net.au/news/2012-10-08/coalition-promises-2450m-for-security-cameras/4300642 (accessed 7 February 2014)).
13 Cited from: www.bbc.co.uk/news/uk-england-17116526 (accessed 24 December 2013).
14 Cited from: news.bbc.co.uk/1/hi/sci/tech/1789157.stm (accessed 6 December 2014).
15 Perhaps the most prominent of these, research actually commissioned by the Metropolitan Police Service in 2008, discovered that only one crime had been solved for every 1,000 cameras operating in London: www.telegraph.co.uk/news/uknews/crime/6081549/One-crime-solved-for-every-1000-CCTV-cameras-senior-officer-claims.html (accessed 7 February 2014).
16 For instance, police chiefs in Airdrie reported in 1993 that since installing cameras, they had experienced a 74% reduction in crime. Based on dubious measuring techniques, this mythical statistic nevertheless was extensively reported in the national media, and was cited as 'evidence' by senior political figures, and sparked a surge in requests for CCTV uptake: www.independent.co.uk/life-

style/long-lens-of-the-law-big-brother-is-watching-you-it-started-in-a-small-scottish-town-paul-greengrass-report-1411876.html (accessed 7 February 2014).
17 Cited in: news.bbc.co.uk/2/hi/uk_news/politics/election_2010/8648357.stm (accessed 7 February 2014).
18 It is worth noting that few of these attitudinal surveys provide sufficient input from members of the 'watched' classes, i.e. youths, ethnic minorities and the urban poor. Moreover, the majority of censuses have been designed and operationalised by partisan practitioners whose views of CCTV are either sympathetic or antagonistic (Norris and Armstrong 1999). The truth of the matter is that we simply do not possess a satisfactory understanding of how CCTV makes people act and feel in everyday contexts (Goold et al. 2013).
19 See: www.cctvusergroup.com/art.php?art=143 (accessed 7 February 2014). This contention accords with my participation in media calls and interviews which have each revealed a desire among the public for more, not less, CCTV coverage. Not that I am, of course, claiming for one moment that listeners of the radio or website audiences are representative of the general populations of the UK or Australia.
20 Cited in Goold et al. (2013, 981).
21 As we shall see later, these assertions are derived from an unreliable evidence base. After completing one of the largest ever evaluations of CCTV effectiveness, Welsh and Farrington (2008, 18–19), for instance, claimed: 'The studies included in this systematic review indicate that CCTV has a modest but significant desirable effect on crime, is most effective in reducing crime in car parks, is most effective when targeted at vehicle crimes.'
22 See Norris and Armstrong (1999, 60–88) for an informative overview of CCTV beneficiaries.
23 The exclusion of this dispossessed population from both the means and ends of legitimate consumption processes constitutes, at least in the minds of the cumulatively advantaged, a point of difference for the imposition of moral denigration and scapegoating. However, it also elicits a visceral unease; a perturbation that the actions of this group pose a significant risk to personal welfare and to status symbolising properties: and, thereby, a conviction that the so-called dangerous classes need be 'managed' via punitive interventions (Feeley and Simon 1992; Wacquant 2009a).
24 For Wacquant (2009b), these transformations in ideology and 'problem' representation correlate with a retrenchment in welfare expenditure, and the concomitant emergence of state penalism and governmental narratives from the centre-right lambasting benefit dependency (see also Rose 2000).
25 See: news.bbc.co.uk/2/hi/uk_news/1201738.stm (accessed 10 February 2014).
26 Comprising similar properties to moral panics, 'signal events' are exceptional occurrences – e.g. acts of terrorism – that have a profound and dramatic impact on societal sensibilities and present opportunities for disproportionate long-term responses (Innes 2004). They function to: (a) indicate the existence of some latent abomination; (b) prompt moral revulsion; and (c) simulate a need for excessive corrective solutions.
27 Indeed, Norris (2012b, 25) notes that there were no more than ten open-street CCTV schemes in the UK preceding the James Bulger murder. By 1999, the figure had risen to 500 (Armitage 2002).
28 David Copeland was convicted in 2000 for carrying out the London nail bombings.
29 This 'Othering' process is akin to Durkheim's observation that crime functions as a text on which society engraves its morality.
30 Consider how media coverage of signal events solicits the bystander perspective and stresses the immediacy of the occurrence. As Jewkes (2004a, 56) puts it, 'Combining the mundane ordinariness of everyday life with the grim inevitability of what is about to unfold, CCTV footage – played out by the media on a

58 *Problematising and contextualising watching practices*

seemingly endless loop appeals to the voyeuristic elements in all of us, whilst at the same time reinforcing our sense of horror, revulsion and powerlessness'.
31 See Davies (1998); Norris and Armstrong (1999); Coleman and Sim (2000); Newburn and Hayman (2001); McCahill (2002); Goold (2004); Neyland (2004); Walby (2005a); Neyland (2006); Norris and McCahill (2006); Lippert and Wilkinson (2012); Doyle *et al.* (2012); Edmond and San Roque (2013); Taylor (2013).
32 Norris and Armstrong (1999) found in their now classic observational study of three open-street systems that 93% of targeted surveillances were directed toward males, 85% of whom were in their teens or twenties, usually sporting particular forms of clothing such as baseball caps, shell suits and 'hoodies'. They claim that such practices reflected the operators' negative attitude to male youth in general, and black youth in particular.
33 A snooper being someone who might appropriate classified personal information or reveal operational mechanics to a rival audience.
34 The following fieldnote excerpts provide an apposite illustration of the challenges associated with the acceptance process:

> *There is a conversation between two camera operators regarding the management's unjust treatment of staff members. I listen intently to the discussion, taking brief notes as and when possible. As an operator recites a story about being rebuked for taking a break with another colleague, the site manager walks in and the colloquy abruptly ends. The atmosphere quickly turns tense. The manager courteously asks how the afternoon is panning out and the operators utter a few pleasantries, before turning to me and saying, 'Fancy grabbing a coffee?' I am torn between a desire to decline (thus saving face with the operators who have just been lambasting this individual) and a wish to preserve cordial relations with him. I decide to go, sensing the operators' acrimony ... The manager is keen to find out how I am getting on with the operators and whether or not they are being forthcoming. He also wishes to know how I think they are performing. I respond to his inquisition in a positive manner, giving nothing conclusive away. On returning to the monitoring room, several spiteful comments are made, before a stony silence falls upon the milieu for the rest of the shift. I note that such behaviour reflects the informal power of camera operators to control access to the operating lifeworld – specifically its experiential contours and interactional order.*

> I am intentionally committing to long shifts both to observe more and to procure the camera operators' respect. This strategy is clearly impressing some of them, particularly given that they are cognisant of my being an unpaid volunteer: 'Wow, you still here, I'm impressed!' (Camera Operator 11); 'What the hell are you doing here at this time? I didn't think students got up 'til the afternoon?!'
>
> (Camera Operator 9)

> *On arrival I sense a discomfiting atmosphere in the monitoring room. I am unsure whether the shift is like this normally or whether it correlates with my being present. As soon as I enter the facility Camera Operator 15 asks brusquely, 'How long will you be staying today, then?' For the next few hours scarcely a word passes between the operators and myself. Formal responsibilities, of course, may account for this circumstance. But given the shortage of 'problem' activity occurring on the screens, I discern the awkwardness to be an outcome of my intrusiveness. The camera operators have their backs to me the whole time, a gesture symbolising their lack of willingness to engage, and*

preventing my seeing what it is that they are observing. Silence prevails for the remainder of the shift.

35 'Newborough' is a medium-size UK city positioned on several waterways. Its population has expanded exponentially in the past 40 years, as a direct result of industrial augmentation. This sector accounts for Newborough's buoyant financial system and for surges in overseas migrants. Leisure economies have emerged in the downtown and promenade districts. Each locality comprises a diverse mix of facilities to cater for diurnal and nocturnal consumption trends. The local police estimate that up to 20,000 revellers descend on the entertainment precinct each Friday and Saturday evening, creating a policing quandary for an immeasurably outnumbered cluster of social control agents. Although organisationally and spatially distinct, these behavioural regulators find themselves connected communicatively and professionally via a shared 'public order' brief.

36 This meant that I could alternate the days, times and even seasons when I conducted my observations, enabling me to build up a detailed impression of the contrasting sequences that were encountered by the camera operators in the course of their work.

37 I would, of course, always seek their explicit permission before commencing research observations. Many of the camera operators were implicitly or explicitly uncomfortable with being tape-recorded or having their actions systematically registered, so much of what follows in terms of camera operator activities and commentaries are based on shorthand jottings that were later transcribed as full fieldnotes.

38 Discourse, in other words, that was generated *by* the field of inquiry (via organisational documents and policies), and *about* the field of inquiry (via newspaper articles, Internet pages, television programmes, films etc.).

Part II
Engaging the means of watching

3 Instigating circuitries
Inception and reception

> The institutional world is objectivated human activity ... In other words, despite the objectivity that marks the social world in human experience, it does not thereby acquire an ontological status apart from the human activity that produced it ... It is important to emphasize that the relationship between man, the producer, and the social world, his product, is and remains a dialectical one ... The product acts back upon the producer.
>
> (Berger and Luckmann 1966, 78)

The above epigraph accentuates the dialectical nature of structures, in terms of their being formulated *by* individuals and formative *of* individuals. It provides, therefore, a useful theoretical framework for understanding relational processes of CCTV circuitry inception (product making) and reception (product usage). It points to the historical (often latent) activity responsible for producing contexts which then act to structure contemporary experiences. It shows that each sociomateriality is perched on a lineage of antecedent decision making, a fact that we are often programmed to forget. CCTV provision is a case in point. It is facile to discern a CCTV circuitry as being a stable and rigid entity. It is just as possible to dismiss that existent arrangements did not appear instantaneously and nor did they materialise out of thin air. As a consequence of perceiving only its front-end materiality and receiving second-hand accounts regarding its back-end operativity (often via biased media reportage, governmental discourse and industry rhetorics), CCTV is easily fetishised, and ascribed an ahistorical invariability. Owing to this process, camera networks are often disconnected and dislodged from the contextual messiness of their localised origins, their initial logics and their contingent means of unfolding. In reality, supervisory circuitries are socially induced products generative of newfangled socialities. They emerge in processual phylogenesis from earlier flows of social interactivity. As David Lyon (2007, 165) puts it, 'surveillance is not a static, relentless or unyielding process. Rather, in many contexts it is dynamic and amenable to modification. It is malleable, flexible, and the product of game-like processes in which, though the overall rules may stay the same, the outcomes are far from determined in advance'. As such, the structural silhouettes of supervisory machineries bear the volitions, assumptions and aspirations of those whose precursor actions and provisions inspired their initial instigation. However, despite their prominence and sway on systemic orientation, little is known about the circumstantial ancestries (the 'genetic' substructures) that underlie the supervisory circuitries we commonly regard and analyse. Indeed, as Pete Fussey (2007, 232) notes, 'investigations into the implementation of public surveillance cameras constitute an under-populated region in the burgeoning field of surveillance studies'. Similarly, few empirical studies measure the effects of bygone decision making (or 'sedimented agency') on the present desiderata of those with liabilities for supervisory action. How do these structures enable and constrain contemporary activity?

Seeking to redress these lacunae, this chapter excavates in brief the social history of Newborough's CCTV circuitry. Evidence derived from documentary analysis and qualitative interviewing is delineated so as to map the genealogical evolution of the system, from inception to objectivation. This approach actualises two discrete rationales. One, it renders legible the source of power orchestrating the formation of supervisory circuitries like the Newborough CCTV network. Two, it situates in a wider structural context the camera operators' relational affinities with the system they oversee. Chapter 3, therefore, provides crucial empirical grounding for the thematic issues surfacing in this chapter, and in the ones to follow. It makes evident how distanced imaginaries and past decisions imbue supervisory circuitries with distinctive traits, and how they sediment into types of socio-material 'inflexibility' and 'fragility'. It shows how, in true dialectical fashion, these products start to act back upon their recipients in often unintended ways by influencing how monitoring practices are – and can be – conducted. The purpose of this chapter is to illustrate empirically how objectivated human activity affects not only supervisory circuitry practicalities but also the phenomenology of CCTV operation itself. The contention here is that in order to understand adequately the lived experiences of CCTV operators and daily operationalisations of supervision, it is essential to analyse the broader socio-historical contexts from which both have sprung.

Sedimenting inflexibility: instigating circuitries

Spanning a 15-year period (1993–2008), included in the following dissection is a critical synopsis of the key events and reasoning responsible for the instigation of the Newborough CCTV circuitry. Attention focuses on the logics that effectively governed the contours and tonalities of this supervisory initiative, and which determined the nature of its composition, positioning, representation, implementation, operativity and resiliency. The analysis attends to the exclusive and privileged nature of the working group initiated to bring CCTV coverage to the streets of Newborough and it reviews their surmising and decision-making protocols. Foregrounded also are the disjunctions between intention and outcome, power and knowledge, policy and practice, and operational issues transpiring from these inconsistencies. While the majority of evidence presented below came from anatomising the meeting minutes of the Newborough CCTV Working Group (CCTVWG hereafter) and other official documents, background interviews were also conducted with the working group secretary, with the operations manager and with an operator who was employed when the system was launched. The archives of two local newspapers were also consulted to accumulate further detail and to obtain an appreciation of how the district media characterised the emerging system and how reportage might have framed public opinion – and thus the legitimacy of the unfolding project. Ethnographic excerpts derived from the observational study of the Newborough monitoring room are selectively availed for their capacity to demonstrate correlative effect. These strategies were adopted to better discern how historical interactivity influences contemporary practices, how designs from the past impinge on procedures in the present. They reinforce David Lyon's (2007, 82) point that 'there is a frequent assumption that surveillance systems are all-powerful, after an Orwellian fashion, rather than contingent, fluid and unpredictable'. They point to the intricate relational chains of interdependencies that typify the occupational and operating cultures of supervisory networks.

The case of Newborough: germination and background

The original idea to inaugurate a CCTVWG to probe the feasibility of establishing an open-street camera network in the city by means of a public-private sector collaboration was motioned by a municipal councillor at a Newborough Regional Council Public Protection Committee (PPC hereafter) convention in April 1993:

> My recollection was that a councillor tabled a motion that Newborough should look at the use of CCTV. I think this was following some publicity in the media that highlighted the success of what was then described as the most modern CCTV system at that time – King's Lynn. The councillor felt that we should not necessarily take the lead but certainly move more speedily down the avenue of exploring the usage of CCTV rather than play catch-up with the big boys at a later stage. The deputy chief constable at the time was an individual who had a good technological background ... and so he was quite comfortable with the concept ... I was the force's architectural liaison officer and I was pulled [into the project] quite quickly as an aide and a guide ... because I had a good rapport with a number of the council officials and a number of private enterprises that were looking quite seriously at ways in which they could encourage crime reduction within the design concept of their developments. I became secretary to the working group and was tasked with moving the concept forward on behalf of the group. The group would come up with the ideas [and] with what they perceived to be the best way forward and then I was tasked with going away and either making that concept work or alternatively investigating whether there was a better way of going about the implementation. When completed, our system was to be the biggest city centre CCTV system in Western Europe: that was the accolade; that was the flag that we were going to be flying.
>
> (CCTVWG Secretary)

Requesting that the Finance and General Purposes Committee (FGPC hereafter) approve initial funding of £2,000, and canvassing membership from local authority and business representatives, the PPC set the first CCTVWG meeting on 15 November 1993.[1] In total, the group convened 22 times before it was supposed to transform into a post-implementation CCTV liaison committee – a steering group that would manage the proposed system's ongoing development. This action, however, never materialised and the operationalisation and future ontogenesis of the system ended up becoming the sole responsibility of the local police force, a situation that created (and still generates) heated disputes among city councillors and police officials around asset ownership rights, and maintenance and operating overheads.

The formation of a public-private quango to steer the Newborough project reflects the fiscal-orientated principles (cost minimisation and capital maximisation) and collaborative (risk and burden sharing) ideals of a neoliberal paradigm. The orchestration of urban planning and governance, although sharply influenced by national guidelines and priorities, is now legally determined by circumscribed local public-private sector partnerships that comprise a consortium of district officials (e.g. emergency services staff, councillors and civil servants), business leaders and community members. Emergent 'community safety partnerships' (CSPs), much like the CCTVWG, coalesce around proximate issues of concern, such as crime patterns, enterprise opportunities, urban marginality, traffic congestion and environmental degradation. Devolution of service supply and 'joined-up government' are the pivotal rationales behind these committees, motivations reflecting the sovereign state's transition in role and purpose: from its being a utility monopoliser and asset guardian to its becoming a brokerage of knowledge, a facilitator of alliances, a manager of fiduciary, a regulator of mobility and a penal enterprise (Garland 1996). However, their formation also corresponds with radical transformations in social problem epistemology: from a system of thought that regarded cause as identifiable and treatable, to one that now gauges actuarial correlations among variables and locates strategies for the temporary managing out (not eradication) of expressions of disobedience (Feeley and Simon 1992). Social problems have come to be defined in terms of their inherent complexity and interconnectedness (Dillon and Lobo-Guerrero 2009). They are best addressed, it is contended, by pooling assets, and by multi-agency collaborations that can share the burden with regards financial costs and organisational risks. It is CSPs that have now constitutional responsibilities and legislative powers for envisaging cities in terms of their design, for responding to their lived arrangements and for delivering key provisions (Coleman 2004b). The CCTVWG, in terms of composition and directives, is an apposite exemplar of this kind of fiscal body. Driven by a mandate to make Newborough more commercially attractive, economically viable, visually legible and ecologically governable, its scope was not to foster social inclusiveness but rather to enhance business opportunism and policing capacity. Its resource-rich membership is endowed with political, economic and practical leverages to execute reasonably dramatic social and spatial projects.

Working group membership: ideology, structure and strategy

It is apparent from the inaugural meeting minutes that 'copycatting' was the major project driver, evidence of the group's inculcating governmental narratives on CCTV effectiveness and desire to maintain a competitive edge over nearby retail hubs in terms of managing public safety perceptions – and thereby assuring enterprise communities that ongoing and future investment would yield profitable returns. Another noticeable theme was the primacy the CCTVWG placed on securing provisions from registered traders:

> Police representatives offered to provide crime statistics for Newborough city centre at the next meeting and 'stressed the value of a CCTV system, not only as a tool for crime solving, but for crime prevention'. Discussion turned to how the proposed project should be funded, including the suggestion of a surcharge or supplement to non-domestic rates. A decision was taken to approach a 'number of other organisations to ascertain their willingness to take part in future meetings, including public and private transport companies, public utilities, licensed trade organisations, finance houses, insurance companies, and the Roads and Finance departments of Newborough Regional Council.
>
> (CCTVWG minutes)

The organisational structure and orientation of the CCTVWG membership is especially intriguing. The police had the highest proportion of representation on the committee, the other core bodies being local authority officials, public servants and delegates from commerce. It is evident from the minutes that the key priorities and drivers for the proposed supervisory circuitry were prevention and detection of crime (two objectives for which the system remains legally registered), spatial control and redesign, economy buttressing and public perception manipulation.[2] There was a premium placed on devising strategies for responsibilising the business sector in order to (a) fulfil national policy goals, and (b) obtain the necessary financial revenue for funding the proposal. There was precedence put on employing operating staff from AssistUK, an organisation that finds work for disabled persons, less for ethical motives and more for accruing a government subsidy that was granted to employers who had reached specified employment quotas. As we shall later discover, this decision prompted some unintended consequences when the circuitry was operationalised as certain recruits were neither physically nor mentally capable of performing the job effectively. Thus, right from inception to delivery, the proposed camera network was being shaped by political and economic incentives, and by convictions that these measures could effectively 'design out' crime and 'design in' prosperity. Evident here is CCTV's symbolism, as a signifier of neoliberal collaborative governance and as a marker of urban progressiveness. Yet, although sharing a common concern (i.e. the construction of an open-street CCTV network), the stakeholders possessed

68 *Engaging the means of watching*

differing organisational interests. They each had motivations that would prove troublesome to reconcile. This created, as we shall see later, a set of tensions around how the system should be staffed and directed, how it should be financed and where precisely the cameras and monitoring facility should be positioned.

Not only is it imperative to discern the types of individuals *involved* in the instigation process itself, but it is perhaps of greater significance to regard those whose voices and representation were systematically *excluded* from the 'consultations' altogether. Indeed, the CCTVWG conversation left little room for deliberation and parley, occurring in publicly inaccessible spaces and featuring limited civic participation. Although meetings were attended by approximately 20 invited 'members' from the Newborough legislative body, there were no women in the core caucus and no affiliates from ethnic minorities were represented. It was a homogeneous and gendered enterprise exclusively populated by white, masculine, bourgeois and authoritarian values – a factor that perhaps elucidates the preoccupation with (a) spatial control and discipline via technical measures, (b) cost saving and capital gains, and (c) non-consultative means of achieving desired ends. There were, for example, no representatives incorporated from the voluntary and not-for-profit sectors, and nor did any CCTVWG discussions include groups that might have voiced dissent, challenged the ethical and legal status of the proposals or questioned their pragmatic merits.[3] That is to say, the CCTVWG had the capacity to dictate who would and would not be involved in the project, and what concerns would and would not be heard. It used this juridical power instrumentally to ensure that its motions encountered nugatory external resistance, that its controversial aspects were not publically broadcast nor debated. The CCTVWG did commission a small-scale survey of public attitudes on CCTV provision, but the design only included two (possibly leading) questions and did not specify the number of individuals measured nor their demographic attributes. As the following excerpt indicates, the questionnaire schedule was far from rigorous in its scope, appearing formulated in a way that would merely reinforce the committee's pro-CCTV sentiment:

> The Chairperson of the Finance Group stated that the Newborough City Centre Project had 'recently carried out a survey which included two questions; one on the potential use of CCTV systems and one on the usage of the City Centre at night by the public. The poll revealed that over 80% of the general public were in favour of and would welcome a CCTV system in Newborough.' A further survey was deemed unnecessary. A member proposed that 'the opinion of the Finance Group be respected and no further public attitude survey be implemented.' This was accepted.
>
> (CCTVWG minutes)

This was the first and last concerted effort by the CCTVWG to engage and source public opinion on the proposed initiative.

Notwithstanding the immoderate legislative privileges possessed by the CCTVWG, a topic dominating meeting agendas was how the proposed CCTV plan should be framed and presented, so as to secure embryonic, and then ongoing, support from multiple publics. Because the initiative was entirely dependent on favourable publicity and patronage for its political and economic viability, project symbolism and representation required attentive stewardship. It was important for the group to expend effort in public relations, to control the flow of information and to seize each opportunity, each communicative medium, for spinning the proposal in decidedly positive terms:

> You have got to manage it very carefully and as a result we had to bring in a number of personnel from organisations and agencies working within the area so they could also sell the message to their client base.
> (CCTVWG Secretary)

> [It was] again stressed to the members that the concept of the partnership approach could not be over-emphasised to the public, and this was the underlying theme that the CCTVWG was striving to achieve in this project.
> (CCTVWG minutes)

> The chairman suggested that thought be given to approaching the local television broadcaster with the request that they again highlight the project – the fact that it would be the largest in Europe – and to emphasise the good experiences achieved by other initiatives.
> (CCTVWG minutes)

There was great precedence placed on *impression management* (Goffman 1959), on manipulating the 'scope' and 'sale' of the plan to prospective investors and to influential communities (e.g. planning officials and heritage wardens), convincing each segment that buy-in would return orderly dividends and productivity bounties. The committee was acutely aware that circuitry materialisation would only succeed with significant private revenue financing and multi-level municipal coalescence.[4] Sourcing monies and procuring legitimation involved artful and careful manoeuvring of the discourse privately rehearsed and publicly released, specifically ensuring that the worthiness and indispensability of the idea was never doubted or questioned. It was framed in purely positive terms and tones, with sentiment strategically orientated to the propitious ends that camera schemes serve. Senior police officers – or outside 'experts' – were enlisted by the group's directorate to impress upon peripheral associates in commerce the unquestionable effectiveness of CCTV units and to present statistics that indicated endemic unruliness in the city centre – a problem demanding a technical solution:

> The Newborough city centre commander then outlined the crime rate in the city centre: '1090 crimes of theft by shoplifting from the main shopping areas have been reported between January and October 1993,

compared to 1413 in the same period the previous year' ... With regards to assault and robbery, breach of the peace and other disorderly behaviour, possession of a dangerous weapon, vandalism and theft from motor vehicles, there were 980 crimes recorded between January and October 1993. The commander acknowledged that these figures were for reported crime only, and that 'doubtless the true figure would be higher'.

(CCTVWG minutes)

Such dignitaries were purposefully enrolled in the project to diagnose authoritatively the existent 'problem', boost the scheme's credibility and to reassure the CCTVWG business members that the camera network would make a positive impact on the city landscape by transforming its social demography, ethos and dynamic. These non-objective, and arguably non-qualified, advocates were keen to stress that CCTV was both operationally cost effective, and was a prudent investment and political enterprise. It is telling that the CCTVWG, a resource-rich cluster of uninformed urban managers, selectively sought an evidence base derived not from independent sources that might refute the proposal or from critical inquiry that might elicit doubts, but from partisan policing practitioners and security industry envoys: informants who would of course merely reify their conception, values and strategy.

The systematised management of details was a purposeful technique that the CCTVWG used internally (on itself) but it was also a procedure that it employed for manipulating the frames of reference of external audiences:

> The Chairman requested that, on occasions a press release was made, information to that effect, including the content of such releases, be circulated to him and others as necessary. This was to ensure continuity in the progress of the initiative via the media.
>
> (CCTVWG minutes)

> Long before the system was working properly, when we had people coming in to view it, what they [the CCTVWG executive] did was to make sure there were pictures on every monitor. But six of the pictures displayed were taken from the same camera; you know, so it looked really good to the media.
>
> (Camera Operator 7)

> It was again emphasised that camera locations be treated as confidential, especially as far as the media was concerned.
>
> (CCTVWG minutes)

A 'publicity subgroup' was effectuated by the CCTVWG fairly early on in the endeavour, with a designated 'spin doctor' appointed from each of the partner organisations. This specialisation in the group's communicative modus operandi, and sagacious unleashing of technology valorising dogma, was initiated so that 'an organised approach be considered to publicity' (CCTVWG minutes).

This was to ensure that the information disseminated publically and promotionally was consistent in its content, idiosyncratic or specialised queries were addressed by the appropriate 'expert' commentator and the system was uniformly depicted in a providential light (through cautiously engineered 'sound bites'). The restricted number of discussants involved ensured that the following mantra was perpetually uttered and broadcast: *that CCTV will lower crime and will consequently stimulate a feel-good factor within the populace; that the local authority are addressing crime concerns through the appropriation of vanguard technology; that the system will be operated professionally and justly; that support for the scheme is widespread; that finances are being well managed; and that implementation of the scheme not only makes 'business sense' for the city of Newborough, in terms of increased footfall and lower insurance premiums, but should also be a source of civic pride.* These unambiguous and emotive 'legitimacy discourses' were chiefly designed to cultivate uptake appetite within the business sector, so that inception funds would be forthcoming and a cascade effect would transpire. But they were also manufactured to incentivise public conformity and obedience.

Additional methods of persuasion included: the penning of two marketing letters encompassing statistics and pleas in a bid to lobby and responsibilise local business owners; the showing of a propagandistic video detailing CCTV's panacea qualities; and the recruitment of a high-profile (and respected) local businessman to champion and incentivise the cause among the vacillators, and to exert pressure on recalcitrant companies/business owners either unconvinced or unwilling to contribute endowments. Thus the intentional structuring and tenacious promotion of a 'value for money', 'effectiveness' and 'renaissance' narrative constituted a major aspect of the group's deliberative exchanges, with broader opinion framing a key objective:

> [Sure,] there was resentment at the early stages, but again, it was working with the people saying: 'You really cannot see the value of it just now, so we need work with you.' So it just took a little more hard work and a bit more time to bring them around to our way of thinking.
>
> (CCTVWG Secretary)

> The [marketing] letter should state that there will be no significant on-cost following the installation of the scheme and highlight the benefits of reduced insurance premiums. It was agreed to continue personal approaches to organisations in addition to the letter.
>
> (CCTVWG minutes)

> In order to hard 'sell' the idea to his fellow traders, a commerce member indicated that he would show a pro-CCTV video made by the police inspector who had presented previously. The chairman encouraged others to consider similar methods to ensure support of their groups.
>
> (CCTVWG minutes)

72 *Engaging the means of watching*

It is patently evident that at the 'idea' or feasibility stage of CCTV deployment, the 'discursive audience', as symbolised by local journalists, industrialists, benefactors, regulators and citizenries, became the distinguished coordinates of an ideological management campaign. Emphasising the emblematic potential of CCTV circuitries and the political economic benefits concomitant on camera coverage were the two pivotal rhetorics exploited to fashion external consent and credibility, and to accumulate the desired wherewithal. Of course, the intention to condition audiences was, in all probability, not the stuff of deceit or illiberality. It instead reflected the group's certitude that CCTV was an indispensable tool – a disciplinary pivot that could obliterate disobedience and deliver safer cities. It was this truth, this undoubted fact, as testified by professional crime controllers, that needed to be conveyed and registered.

Dependency fragilities

As it turned out, convincing people of CCTV's merit, and getting scheme approval, proved a far from straightforward task. Indeed, for all its executive potency the CCTVWG, and its elaborate and fanciful scheme, remained predominantly fettered to the agency of external others. The wider legal frameworks governing local authority practices, and dependencies on those contracted to design and furnish the system, made the implementation stages burdensome. The Environmental and Heritage authority, for instance, exercised constitutionally ascribed jurisdiction to influence planning direction, so too numerous other agencies:

> It was the opinion that individual planning applications would be necessary [for each camera], the reason for this being:
>
> - so that the public were fully and precisely aware of the proposals;
> - should one planning application be submitted, then one objection to any location would prohibit the application being further progressed.
>
> The chairman questioned whether in law, any procedure was available for such a CCTV scheme to be implemented without planning approval. He was advised that a planning application was both essential and a legal obligation.
>
> (CCTVWG minutes)

> We had to satisfy a number of external organisations like Environmental Planning and Heritage. Quite a lot of the buildings within our catchment area were listed buildings ... So we had to liaise with them and say: 'this is the colour of the cabling that we are using, this is the route that the cabling will take, this is the location on the building, this is the casing that we are going to be using, this is the colour we are going to be using

for the camera cover itself.' All who lived, worked and used that venue for entertainment purposes had to be consulted, too, by way of the planning process so it was not a case of just turning around and saying, 'we are going to erect 53 cameras, this is where they are going to be', there was statutory consultation that had to be done under the planning legislation itself. We had to consider that each camera has to have an electrical supply to it, where do you put the control boxes? The control box may have to be located on a building nearby so we had to get planning permissions, we had to get 'way-leaves', we had to get the owner's consent not only to fit the camera onto perhaps the side of a building but also out of good grace and favour to supply that camera with a token contribution of electrical supply from a nearby source ... so we were asking people to contribute a financial cost towards it.

(CCTVWG Secretary)

Other lateral legal bodies wielded prerogatives that could (and did) restrict the scope and actualisation of the initiative. The regional council Finance and Resource committee had discretion over capital dispensation. Individual businesses had the capacity to refrain from contributing, an action with associated repercussions for the project's viability and sustainability. Moreover, other intermediaries induced practical and financial headaches, as illustrated in the following extracts:

The project manager reported that difficulties had been experienced with the national rail operating company whereby a 15-week delay was inevitable in order to obtain the relevant possession order [so that work could commence].

Practical difficulties were being experienced at the remaining two camera sites, one involving the installation of a pole and the other concerning planning permission.

(CCTVWG minutes)

You had to satisfy those occupiers ... that the camera operators were not able to peer into bedroom windows or bathroom areas. Very quickly the group agreed ... that it [the monitoring facility] would have to be within the police control for the capture of the images and the usage. But you had one or two of the key players who sat around the table saying, 'Well we are contributing vast sums of money [and] we also want to derive some form of control over the cameras for our organisation's purposes'. Therefore, you had potential conflict. Let's use the bus company as an example; they wanted to view the length and breadth of River Street to find out why there were delays on certain bus routes. Now, if they suddenly were able to take control of a camera, while an operator within the CCTV control room was overseeing some form of ongoing incident, and that camera was then relocated or resighted as far as its view was concerned, you could lose valuable information, so there had to be quite tight protocol arrangements developed at an early stage.

(CCTVWG Secretary)

In addition, the local media, on the back of tainted relationships with certain police chiefs, seized their power of narration and conveyance to represent the system in antipathetic terminology, as a spying ring, as an absurdity and as an extravagance, and to influence public (and worse, financier) attitudes, a scenario with potentially dire ramifications for the scheme's reputation and accomplishment:

> I have to say that some of the media did not particularly support us because they continually referred to it [i.e. the scheme] as: 'The Spy Camera System for Newborough', so that did not help either. That went back historically to frictions between the local media and police because of individuals within each organisation, and it was taken perhaps to extremes in that respect. So, we were finding that we were not getting 100% support from every source, and those that you may well have expected to have been supportive towards us, for personal reasons, let's say, went against the conception principle right from day one, which certainly did not help with going forward.

(CCTVWG Secretary)

Newborough scheme already misses out on Government cash for camera system

The spy camera system will miss out on Government cash aimed at encouraging such projects.

(*Newborough Express*, 2 March 1996, 6)

Cable problems may pull the plug on CCTV

Delays in laying a key cable over a railway bridge threaten to pull the plug on most of Newborough city centre's crime-busting cameras. The hitch could leave two thirds of the system blank at this month's official switch on ... [and] would add £3,000 to installation costs.

(*Newborough Express*, 2 March 1996, 6)

Spy camera controversy flares again

The simmering unrest between Newborough councils blew up again yesterday over who should switch on the city's new spy cameras.

(*Newborough Daily*, 23 February 1996, 3)

The chairman began business by intimating to the members that 'the feature article appearing in the [local newspaper] that morning was inaccurate in its content and that the status quo remained with regard to the implementation of the CCTV system' ... Another member remarked that a similar type feature had been portrayed on a local television station broadcast.
(CCTVWG minutes)

During the cursory consultation process, civic members availed civil powers to contest the proposed camera locations and the legal standing of the submission:

There was one particular woman who took great umbrage [to the proposed system]. She just felt that this was Big Brother spying and she was on the community council and she used that to good advantage, rightly or wrongly, in the consultation process to get some of the cameras moved. So there were concerns, one or two where we had just to eat humble pie and get second best location purely and simply because we could not appease or satisfy the individual objectors ... A number of city centre occupiers were of a view that they were paying substantial sums of money already on high levies of rates and taxes so there was a reluctance right across all the organisations to fund it ...
(CCTVWG Secretary)

Small-scale businesses, voluntary sector enterprises and individual tenants could thereby shape the terms of CCTV provision in their own wilful fashion. Each of these agents had the capability to determine whether or not they were prepared to lease their physical assets for use as camera mounts and/or to provide electricity supplies. Even after camera assembly, situationally derived resources could be exploited to subvert the system's functionality, camera maintainers and controllers both possessing the means to destabilise the network via exorbitant repair invoices and the issuing of authoritative prescriptions:

The extension has further exacerbated the [tense operational] situation by the fact that Deep-Sea Electronics are responsible for the maintenance of the cabling but not the connections to the cameras which are under the remit of Central Securities. A considerable degree of conflict has arisen with each suggesting the other party is responsible for the maintenance.
(Newborough Police Force CCTV Report, 2004)

I think that CCTV should be left to do what it was meant to do – not scanning or catching cars, but following individuals on foot. We're forever being told where to point the cameras.
(Camera Operator 12)

76   *Engaging the means of watching*

As the CCTVWG secretary percipiently put it, and as further attested in the newspaper report below:

> When you start working with 'partner' organisations everything is great until you come to the first step; and then you suddenly realise that to get the first step achieved, there are about 20 paces in between that you have got to develop and build upon.
>
> (CCTVWG Secretary)

CCTV rap for bus company

> Newborough Buses has been accused of behaving like a schoolchild by withholding £50k from a new security camera scheme in Newborough ... [A] regional councillor accused the firm of arrogance in attempting to secure control of cameras in return for cash. He said: 'This is reminiscent of the schoolboy who takes his football away because he cannot play.'
>
> (*Newborough Express*, 29 March 1996, 16)

Notwithstanding all of the above turbulence, delays and strains, the CCTVWG persevered with its project and eventually succeeded in instituting a full-blown open-street CCTV circuitry (initially comprising 56 cameras) in Newborough in 1996. The committee's dogged determination, legislative forcefulness and elite membership, when combined with the period's fertile and favourable social and cultural conditions for CCTV dispersal, were pivotal in progressing the scheme, from imagined concept to material actuality. In spite of their struggle to market the proposal, canvass allies, solicit patrons, suppress critics, source equipment and execute the installation in a timely fashion, the steering body's rhetoric and resourcefulness had proven paramount in bringing to bear a socio-spatial transformation in the governance of Newborough. What had been a fanciful crusade had become a socio-technical assemblage – an objectivated structure with a reality above and beyond the group out of which it germinated. The product that the CCTVWG occasioned was now a wired infrastructure, a place of work, a source of justice and a tool for managing perceived risks and the excess and extremities associated with consumer culture: a palpable expedient for visualised others to wield. They had formulated a system of monitoring that would come to influence the lives of those beneath the cameras, as much as it touched the souls of those behind the screens. But exactly how it affected things – spatial theatrics and the course of criminal justice – was not the province of the CCTVWG. It was instead the responsibility of those employed in the work of watching. It became the custodial concern of the camera operator, whose key duties appear in the box opposite.

Box 3.1 Original Newborough CCTV camera operator duties, 1996

CCTV camera operator duties

- The monitoring of at least 17 camera positions
- Keeping a daily incident log
- Insertion/removal of tapes from video recorders
- Storing/withdrawing tapes from correct areas
- Keeping an individual tape log
- Numbering of video tapes
- Production of still prints
- Recording and logging of still print records
- General administrative work
- Viewing of incidents, assessing their priority of importance and relaying messages to Force Dispatch Room
- Responding to requests for monitoring from dispatch inspector
- Monitoring radio transmissions
- Future keyboard entries on computer system
- Requirement to attend court as a witness

The socio-material sedimentation of expedience: structural and operational solidity

The operator has many tasks. The main one being the monitoring of public space to locate ongoing/developing incidents, and to liaise with operational officers/force dispatchers to organise an appropriate response. We are also here to support the work of retail and licensed premises staff in monitoring potential offenders and arranging police assistance as and when required. We also check tapes for incidents that have perhaps been caught on camera at a previous time. We log 'known' persons who are seen on camera and also respond to police, ShopSafe and PubSafe requests[5] which are many and varied. We also make footage available for court via videotape and download DVD footage of cellblock and van requests.

(Camera Operator 14)

Actualising precursory dreams: formalised functionalism

The powers and actions of the CCTVWG crafted a socio-material and networked contrivance for governing perceptual impressions and behavioural expressions within the new urbanism. Sedimented within the contours of this structure were both the aspirational, and the negotiated, attributes of a three-year undertaking to cleanse the streets through teleoptic means, to regulate conduct through enhanced visibility and to manage out perceived threats to the social order and to private property ownership. It is undoubtedly the

78 *Engaging the means of watching*

case that the Newborough camera circuitry embodies, serves and extends these foundational aspirations. As disruption detectors and as conduits of information, the camera operators are primarily responsible for detecting suspicious motions or actual disturbances, capturing these occurrences as evidential compilations and alerting the appropriate authority so that a physical response can be actioned. This obligation to sense disorder entails that camera operators proactively and perpetually 'riskscape' (i.e. scan for categorical indicators of risk as these relate to typologies of behaviour), react to incoming information circulated by mobile authorities (be they police officers, security staff, etc.), and register events in fine detail so that antecedent actions can be retrospectively reconstructed, instigators can be identified and footage used for prosecutions. The camera operators are assisted in these tasks by virtue of the communicative technologies they have at their disposal. The camera produced visualisations furnish them with vicarious vision, mobility and input, the Police National Computer (PNC) presents itemised intelligence, and the telecommunication terminals afford audio feeds to be relayed and absorbed. CCTV viewing stations are places of knowledge production and consumption or stimuli 'prosumption', and are imbued by flows of visual, verbal and visceral data. Because order preservation is a common priority for diverse street authorities, and the conveyance channels of these external stakeholders are integrated into the CCTV circuitry, it can prompt fairly elaborate multi-agent collaborations:

> *A message comes across the radio from a music vendor alerting all Shop-Safe users and CCTV that they are currently chasing a young male who has been seen stealing a red box set CD. Camera Operator 10 immediately contacts the police dispatch centre to alert them of the situation and to request a police unit: 'Hi CCTV here, we've got a chase occurring on Grange Street. Moosic have reported having some property stolen and wish to make a complaint.' Meanwhile, Camera Operator 17 has proficiently located the culprit and is switching from camera to camera tracking the chase, which now involves a security guard from another retailer. The dispatcher confirms that a police unit is on its way and asks CCTV to liaise with the unit directly over the police radio system. She also asks whether or not the security guard will be able to handle the situation for a few minutes until the unit arrives, to which Camera Operator 10 responds, 'Yes, as he now has back up from another store'. Camera Operator 17 is keeping up with the pursuit until the youth gets apprehended. Within a few seconds the other two guards arrive and have the young male's arms held firm. Camera Operator 10 has meanwhile been informing the arriving unit about incident details ... As the police car pulls up, two women begin a protest in response to the young man's treatment. Seeing this, Camera Operator 10 retorts toward the screen: 'I hate these "do gooder" members of the public; I know he's young, but tough, he's getting lifted. It's his own fault. He shouldn't have shoplifted in the first place.' The police search the boy and recover a red box set album from his trousers, all captured by Camera Operator 17. Evidently*

distressed, the male is then taken away in the police car. The security guard thanks CCTV for their assistance over the ShopSafe radio, and Camera Operators 17 and 10 resume general screen scanning duties.

The time is 11:45pm and a radio message is relayed by a police dispatcher requesting the attendance of police units to an ongoing disturbance in Fraser Court. A description of the alleged antagonist is provided, the dispatcher also indicating that the male in question is well known, and has a record of domestic violence. She suggests to the units attending the call that the sought suspect may now be 'clear of the flat' and to be on the lookout for him. Camera Operators 6 and 16 immediately begin searching the area with proximate cameras in an attempt to locate the male. Camera Operator 6 spots a man walking briskly away from a block of flats. Although the camera operator does not know the man in question, the observed male's behaviour and his whereabouts prompts her to maintain focus as he makes his way briskly along the street. She phones the police dispatch centre and relays the information back that she has picked up a male matching the description supplied but has now lost him to view. The dispatch centre update the police units attending, and ask the operator to call over the police radio should she find the male again. Intuitively taking control of a camera overlooking the Bishopsfield area, the camera operator again spots the same male as he strides in the direction of Grange Street while keeping the police unit informed. The male heads in the direction of Fraser Court again. Camera Operator 16 directs the arriving police unit to the man: 'Yes, that's him on your right now Alpha Bravo 35.'

When functioning to capacity as a unified entity the circuitry is experienced and perceived by its principal users as a highly efficacious apparatus:

The role CCTV plays in crime detection and intelligence gathering is so underplayed. If you think of the last four or five big cases in the city, all of them have been directly aided, if not solved, by CCTV footage. The lad who was stabbed to death in a supermarket car park; his killer was caught on camera six driving his car on his way to the shop just shortly before the fight. Also, the poor girl that was killed in that accident down at the beach. The camera clearly showed the off-duty officer jumping a red light and smashing into the girl's car. The youth worker murder case was also solved directly thanks to CCTV, as we got the killer trying to withdraw money from the victim's bank account. We also managed to get the last sighting of the poor lad who was killed in the hit and run on East Street. We traced his last movements and also got a chance to see on the East Street camera all the possible cars that were in the area around the time of his death. CCTV footage also led to the prosecution of the boy who kicked to death the lad outside the bar on Grange Street on Boxing Day. We also managed to get those boys for the racist attack on the two

80   *Engaging the means of watching*

> foreign lads on Frank Street ... So you can't underestimate the importance of the cameras after offences have taken place, especially major crimes with lots of detectives on the case ... CCTV is often used to prove or disprove allegations that are made against the police or other members of the public. You'd be surprised how often the cameras disprove false allegations, some of them fairly serious. It's a great tool for all that.
>
> (Camera Operator 7)

> The cameras have helped to reduce the number of recorded incidents in the city centre by around 10% in the first year of operation and have provided evidence which has led to 700 detentions. A total of 2140 incidents have been recorded on camera of which the majority relate to breach of the peace, suspicious persons and drunk and incapables. In addition there were 54 drugs incidents, 97 assaults, 11 housebreakings, 125 thefts, 66 vandalisms and 700 alarm calls. On a more human note, 85 medical incidents were observed which resulted in a prompt response from the emergency services. The cameras were also used to monitor parades, the dispersal of football crowds and to police the New Year party.
>
> (Newborough Police Force 1998)

While entirely reliant on the intervention of embodied social agents ('spiders') for the *physical* apprehension of miscreants, the entangling of 'prey' within the virtual confines of the visibility 'web' is often down to the observational prowess, tacit acumen and interpretive faculties of the principal 'thread spinners'. It is the camera operators who often determine the fodder to be captured and the threads to be spun:

> I mean you take the pizza shop robbery man we managed to get done. We'd heard that there had been an armed robbery in a takeaway earlier on in the evening and so we were looking for a bloke dressed in particular clothing. Just by chance, I was flicking through the cameras and saw this boy disappearing down an alleyway. Now, normally, on a Friday night this is common practice among males who need relief, so I didn't think much of it. But when I saw him coming back out of the alleyway wearing a different t-shirt I immediately alerted the police dispatch room with the bloke's description and they got a unit dispatched quick smart as my description matched the geezer who they were looking for. He ended up getting picked up and sent down for five years, all because I'd noticed him going into an alleyway wearing one thing and then re-emerging wearing something else. I guess you could put it down to a bit of luck and skill, and I 'spose that's how CCTV works really.
>
> (Camera Operator 2)

Camera operator duties transfigure as the circuitry expands in coverage and mutability and as social relations and connections get formulated and re-formulated, their attentive energies and technical skills being expended in the

Instigating circuitries 81

accomplishment of diverse inter-organisational objectives. Some of these tasks *excite* the watchers while other requests merely *incite* them:

> Last week I was asked by cops on the ground to find an old biddy her coach, as she'd got lost while shopping! We frequently help people find their cars when they can't remember where they've parked.
> (Camera Operator 14)

> *Camera Operator 7 tells me about some of the more 'informal' tasks the operators are asked to do: 'Well, when some of the cops get new cars they often ask us to position a camera on where they have parked, you know, to keep an eye on their car.'*

> The purpose of the system has always been the prevention and reduction of crime, but it serves other functions ... We see people who have been injured or knocked down and we can react quicker than somebody picking up a phone; we can get an ambulance there quicker, so it works to that benefit. It does other things, too, like traffic monitoring for the local radio station. We find children missing from shopping centres, old people who are missing, patients missing from the mental hospital; just anything and everything, really. All of that adds to the day, I quite enjoy it; it gives you something to do rather than sitting here being bored ... The police dispatch facility upstairs will constantly ask us about whether we have cameras in certain areas and whether we can check things out. We do things like crowd control at the football matches, New Year celebrations and concerts. We can see where trouble is starting and you can get units into that area and you can actually channel the people to where you want them to go and not where they think they want to go. We do intelligence work for the undercover cops.
> (Camera Operator 1)

> We're forever getting asked to do things that we're not meant to be doing, like taking down the details of illegally parked cars and checking that their owners are disabled or checking the numbers of buildings for cops. It just means we're distracted from what we should be doing which is proactively monitoring the cameras in order to locate 'dodgers' and deal with ongoing situations.
> (Camera Operator 18)

As evinced earlier, the origins of the Newborough circuitry date back to those technocratic and legislative technicians responsible for producing its symbolic criterion and material infrastructure. Even after introducing independent and autonomous components, in this case the camera operators, designer values endure as a set of sedimented operating principles. The embodied practices of the overseers now assigned operational prerogatives perpetuate such codes in a space-time 'fusion of agency' (i.e. where past and present actions coalesce to form systemic reifications). This is particularly evident in terms of the latent instrumentalism and discrimination influencing visibility work. Note the significance of metrics contained in the camera operators' musings in the following passages:

> Oh you really should have been here last night. We got two drunk drivers stopped and arrested and got a guy in custody for a robbery; we've had a really good week.
>
> (Camera Operator 3)

Looking through the list of incidents recorded in the SIB [sightings and incidents book] during the day, Camera Operator 3 proclaims that: 'We've got to get more sightings for the book or we'll get into trouble!' This is an interesting comment as it indicates the degree to which camera operators are externally supervised and are subjected to performance metrics. It seems as if the watched are perceived as point scoring 'targets' for statistical accumulation. Camera Operator 2 replies, 'Well, a good little scan of the harbour area [a district populated by prostitutes] should boost the numbers up a bit, plenty of scummers out on Grange Street begging as well'. This has been the fifth time today that the camera operators have searched for homeless individuals in the town centre and logged details. None of the individuals sighted are wanted by the police [under warrant] which seems to disappoint the operators.

> I hope he's wanted for ten offences so we can get him lifted.
>
> (Camera Operator 9)

It turns out from Camera Operator 10's PNC check that the individual on camera is in fact wanted by the police for a minor pre-existing offence. Similar to how a crowd celebrate goal scoring in a football match, Camera Operator 10 punches the air and exclaims: 'Oh yes, you beauty ... Got you! That's my second lift of the day!'

For all the faith and capital invested by the CCTVWG in instigating the circuitry, and for all its operational power in governing the conduct of the public and influencing the ends of justice, the Newborough camera matrix magnetises destructive turbulence. Its fragility is predominantly a symptom of the committee's defective long-term planning and deficient acuity, but it also arises from: (a) failures to integrate disparate organisational nodes; (b) strains associated with compelled viewing and positional impotence (see Chapter 5); and (c) the complex chains of reciprocity on which supervisory superstructures are precariously dependent. Indeed, as a result of the subjective propulsions constituting their historical foundation, and the multiplex sets of transitioning interrelationalities on which they are dialectically contingent, supervisory circulations are especially susceptible to operational incapacitations. It is to an overview of these that I now turn.

The socio-material sedimentation of improvidence: structural and operational fragility

It's shite. And it always has been shite.
(Camera Operator 7, commenting on the perceived utility of the Newborough CCTV system)

For all its resources and legislative potency, the CCTVWG comprised a staff of policy officials, law enforcers, legal practitioners and business tycoons who had: (a) limited understanding of specialist fields like CCTV ergonomics and economics; (b) a scarcity of technical knowledge and operational expertise in the CCTV field; (c) little inclination to commit long-term funds and labour pools for ensuing developmental supplementations; and (d) problems specifying a defined operativity schedule and assigning proprietary rights and responsibilities. Scant attention was paid to ownership and enterprise issues, a corollary being that there was no firm legal nor coherent financial blueprint agreed for making the venture sustainable in the long term. A singular fixation on how revenue could be amassed to install, *but not preserve*, the system was the CCTVWG's core focus. Moreover, technocratic reasoning (i.e. a belief that technological interventions can mitigate social problems regardless of complexity) prevailed in discussions around system operation,[6] with staffing issues and occupational protocol[7] all but absent from confabulation. When the committee did review operational matters, how and where to attain 'discounted' – not specialised – labour, and how to exercise dominion over the appointed workers (via an operational code of practice), were the main topics of concern. As such, insufficient regard was assigned to heuristic affairs, specifically recognition of camera operator needs and their organisational significance in bringing to bear supervisory circulations – in animating these relational circuitries with meaning and rendering them into objectivated realities. These historical oversights were to have major concequences for how the system came to be experienced by its 'secondary recipients', the camera operators inheriting the structure post-inauguration and whose embodied practices effectively determine its end points. Indeed, my contention is precisely that the socio-material sedimentation of improvidence – and related contradictions – have now come as structural impediments to exert considerable force over the system's projected functionalism, refiguring its parameters of attainment and ergo its prospective aspirations. Just like any other social system, a CCTV network is part dependent on the historical conditions that fashioned its 'structural' arrangement and part dependent on the desiderata subsequently expended by those generative of its 'cultural' lifeworld. The objective in the section that follows is to re-connect analytically these 'dependency' relationalities (i.e. *archival actions* and *present livedness*), in order to demonstrate the countless ways in which bygone injudiciousness exerts constraints on systemic *being* (on what can be achieved by the supervisory circuitry now) and imperils the scope of its future *becoming* (on what could be achieved in an ensuing iteration).

Staffing fragilities

> A CCTV system is only as good as the people operating it – without them it is just a collection of mechanical and electrical components.
>
> (CCTV Manager 8)[8]

It is evident that members of the CCTVWG perceived the camera network in purely technological terms as an automated physical entity of control rather than construing it in social terms as a complex system of relational exchange and interactivity. Thus, the multiplicity of actors whose practices constitute the system's everyday operativity, were interpreted one-dimensionally as 'plug-in' cogs within a larger machinery of mechanisation rather than as subjective agents with capacities to impose their distinct energies upon the equipment and to subvert operating principles. In other words, there was a preoccupation given to the mechanical ends as opposed to the human means of supervisory circulations. It was assumed that once installed and operational, the cameras would automatically and autonomously function in desired and anticipated fashions. An understanding of the intricacies of human agency and the complexities of workplace culture was plainly absent, with technology interpreted as a social glue that would integrate and bind together a diverse assortment of occupational hierarchies and institutionally affiliated actors. The CCTVWG's obsessive application of instrumental rationality and corollary desire to implement a cost-effective CCTV system is perfectly illustrated in their recruitment directive. Certain members felt it an astute idea to acquire monitoring staff from a disabled employment provider, AssistUK, as a special government subsidy for hiring registered individuals meant reduced labour costs:

> Newborough police in an effort to reduce costs entered into a contract with AssistUK who would provide the civilian staff to operate the unit. The AssistUK employees are all Registered Disabled people requiring sheltered conditions of employment and therefore qualify for a government subsidy which currently stands at 30%.
>
> (Newborough Police Force 1997)

This decision, however, was not without operational reverberations. Certain recruits, for instance, were unsuited physically, psychologically and socially to the multiple demands and pressures of CCTV work. They found the need to focus sustained attention on the screens, and the obligation to communicate proficiently with the scheme's various partner entities, such as police officers and public house door staff on the ground, a challenging demand. They also found processing scenes of social disorder, and interfacing with egregious spectacles, an arduous expectation. Many appointees, for instance, had poor eyesight, concentration problems, communicational difficulties, restricted mobility and long-term health issues, impairments seriously inhibiting their ability to control the system in an effective fashion:

Camera Operator 3 mentions how little work Camera Operator 12 does and how the individual suffers from a medically defined 'concentration problem' – 'I mean, why oh why would you employ someone like that to monitor CCTV cameras for ten hours?' She then goes on to talk about Camera Operator 9 who, she tells me, has always had health issues: 'He was another of the ones they got in through AssistUK. I mean it's a shame and all that about his health, but the thing is that he can't speak properly because of a stroke he had and so can't communicate over the radio effectively which causes us serious problems. Not only that, his condition means that he suffers from serious mood swings and he always leaves the cameras in the wrong positions after his shift and it's so annoying. I've told him so many times about it. He hasn't got much camera ability, put it that way.' I find out from Camera Operator 3 that the team leader for her shift, another AssistUK recruit, is off sick with a long-term illness, so 'we're down to two [camera operators in the team] for the next six months anyway'.

The majority of the initial staff appointed have visual impairments. My concern is that the ability to handle and process visual information is not only dependent upon visual acuity and thus an eyesight test alone cannot guarantee that individuals will pick up things on the small screens and react appropriately ... I am further concerned with:

- The lack of opportunity to rest the eyes periodically on a relatively plain surface to help reduce eye fatigue
- The opportunity for regular breaks away from the screens to help reduce fatigue
- Difficulties with regard to wheelchair access
- Potential problems arising for the wheelchair bound employee in achieving a comfortable working position
- The ability of individuals with physical disabilities to access cupboards and shelves

(Letter from Newborough Police Force Medical Adviser, 1995)

Based upon discussions with senior police officers it is understood that there are concerns as to the standards of work performance of two camera operators. In respect of Camera Operator 15, it is apparent that whilst being of a pleasant disposition she is unsuited to her current post, to such a degree that she is more of a liability than an asset ... In respect of Camera Operator 17, it is understood that he needs to adopt an improved attitude and therefore some form of official warning should be issued.

(Newborough Police Force memorandum, 1996)

Despite often being physiologically and psychologically incompatible with the job requirements, such workers were protected legally by way of their AssistUK registered status, in effect meaning that if wishing to terminate their employment,

86 *Engaging the means of watching*

Newborough police force had either to 'buy them out' of their existing contracts or find them another suitable occupational position within the broader organisation:

> Whatever happens they cannot simply terminate our contracts, unless of course we accept a voluntary redundancy offer. One of the key clauses of our present contract is that the police have either to pay us off, or find us suitable employment elsewhere for a year, should our jobs be suddenly axed.
> (Camera Operator 1)

Such contractual indemnity enabled those with little interest in the job (but who were compelled to be in work as a condition of their benefit allowances) to 'hide' and earn 'easy money', and it lumped further pressure on the shoulders of other shift operators. This situation created a hostile workspace fraught with accusations of underperformance and allegations of harassment. It produced a series of divisions among the workforce and became a source of much frustration and a point of recurrent vengeance:

> You had guys who were like, 'this is a nice easy number', guys who would stick paper on the door there [to cover the glass partition] and then sit here with their feet up doing nothing. One of them would, as soon as he came on duty, just disappear. He would be downstairs in the cell block playing card games on the computer. We had another, a super guy, he would come in and he would actually physically fall asleep in the chair! So he would fall asleep and I would deliberately move his joystick so the machine wouldn't actually go off. And he would be asleep for 40 minutes and he would wake up and say, 'Oh, I nearly fell asleep there'.
> (Camera Operator 5)

> Half the guys that work in here are a bunch of nuggets. They've either got no brains or can't be arsed being here – what I call 'hiders'. That's what happens when you pay people peanuts; you get a load of monkeys!
> (Camera Operator 27)

> *Camera Operator 15 is incessantly yawning, sniffing and coughing. With each yawn he seems continually to proclaim how tired he is and how he 'can't be bothered with this place'* ... *'Oh please roll on two o'clock'. This prompts Camera Operator 12 to derisively ask the despondent camera operative: 'Are you happy in your work?' Camera Operator 15 replies, 'No'. Camera Operator 12 then responds by sarcastically uttering, 'Oh really? You'd never guess it'.*

> I was kind of pushed into the job by the disability service.
> (Camera Operator 1)

> I'm tired all the time in here. I just can't be bothered being here. It's such a crap place to work, but it pays the bills and you can get away with doing fuck all which is quite good, but my god it can be boring.
> (Camera Operator 6)

Instigating circuitries 87

Perhaps unsurprisingly, the behaviours and (in)actions of those above created all manner of intra-organisational tensions and interpersonal conflicts. These quarrels had the effect of disuniting team members from one another and isolating certain camera operators. They precluded discrete staff members from working on the same shift. In a context where turbulence and trepidation are familiar companions in terms of watching scenes of distress unfold on screen, situating this reality within an environment already infused in personality disputes made for unpleasant viewing conditions:

> You've got Camera Operator 39 [a new recruit], she might drive you mad, but as an operator she's a thousand times better than at least three people I could mention. She gets a bit over excited with the radio, and you're like, 'Calm down, just calm down'. But Camera Operator 11 is coming back next month and so Camera Operator 39 will be out of a job. But again, why lose her? You've got so many people on long-term illness, why not keep her on a monthly contract? I have told the CCTV manager on many occasions but I have no say on the matter. I don't stir the shit, I never have, but if somebody asks me something or something annoys me, I will actually say something about it. There are plenty operators who shouldn't be in here and I have told them personally. I don't know why they [their police service employers] are just too scared to get rid of them … Even for somebody like Camera Operator 18, who hasn't been here a particularly long time, even she knows who the wasters are. We have known who the wasters are for years and years and years; people who are just getting paid for nothing. I don't have personally anything against the other operators as people, but I really get so annoyed, especially when it's persons like Camera Operator 13. In the last four years, she has probably got a year's wages for zilch, because she hasn't been here. Have the courage to actually say, 'I'm sorry Camera Operator 13, but you haven't been at your work for X amount of time and whether she has got a doctor behind her or not … ' [conversation abruptly ends as the CCTV manager enters the room]
> (Camera Operator 7)

One of the camera operators has acquired a reputation for avoiding work. It seems he is not held in high regard by any of his colleagues. In fact, he is frequently talked about by the other shifts and referred to in derogatory terms. Camera Operator 13 tells Camera Operator 3 in some detail about how this person 'went mental' on her recently, accusing her of 'being a grass'. He claimed that she had reported to management his recurrent absences and his inaccurate recording of hours worked. Camera Operator 3 mentions that the operator is frequently taking the day off to attend funerals, 'He must have been at about 40 funerals this year. I mean going to one or two is fair enough but 40, well, that's just blatant taking the piss if you ask me … Not only that, he's been off sick so many times this year,

88 *Engaging the means of watching*

and was even using the excuse that his son was off ill from school so that he could take the day off. I mean it's just the fact that he lets the whole team down doing that, and it's not fair on the rest of us who are constantly having to cover so that he can get out of coming in' ... Camera Operator 3 goes onto say, 'This is the worst place in the world to work, there is so much bitchiness between the shifts. There is just so much politics going on in here'.

A further example of operational negligence in terms of how the system prepared and disciplined its staff concerns how the original recruits were trained. Despite talk in the minutes of a comprehensive training programme being established and administered so that operators would be informed and briefed about technical and operational protocol, the reality, as captured in the following juxtaposition, was to prove somewhat less efficacious:

A two week training programme incorporating the geography of the camera area; legislation; evidence and court procedures; and operation of the system, would be conducted.
(CCTVWG minutes)

We all sat round one monitor and had shots and that was our training. We went round Markies [Marks & Spencer] and the shopping centre to see exactly what their systems were like, but there was no basic training ... [it was more like] 'there it is, have a shot'. There was only one monitor that was plugged in. It was like a fight [for control of it], 'I'm using it, no I'm using it'.
(Camera Operator 7)

One day we're told, 'We're moving to Airwaves [transmission]'[9] and we were like, 'Oh, really, nice of you to ask us about it'. So we got this pathetic introduction one day and we've just had to make it up as we go along, just like we do with most of the things we get given. I'm forever pressing the wrong buttons, though!
(Camera Operator 16)

The circuitry was officially launched in January 1996, with the explicit terms and parameters of the system encapsulated in a paraphrased internal memorandum:

Operators begin Monday 8 January 1996 (training consists of a visit to a major retailer and a local shopping centre). 24 hour coverage commences 15 January 1996 with only 4 cameras operational. One member of staff resigns in the first week. The operators, who are employees of Interwork (a faction of AssistUK), are contracted to work a 40 hour week averaged over a 7 week period and must sign the Official Secrets Act (OSA) as part of their terms of service. Interwork are responsible for all administrative matters including payment of wages, with the total annual salary, including shift allowance and weekend working enhancement, standing at £10,400.

Annual leave is 20 days per annum excluding statutory public holidays. The monitor room will be strictly 'out of bounds' to unauthorised personnel, but when a substantial number of the cameras are implemented and the monitor room staff have become familiar with the operation of the equipment, conducted visits will be arranged for police staff to view the facilities.

This narrative is particularly insightful in that it outlines the general structure of the occupation as perceived by management. It also draws attention to the meagre salaries that the camera operators get paid (reflecting their symbolic positioning at the very bottom of the public policing hierarchy), the long hours they have to work and the inadequate levels of instruction they received. It points to the 'controlled' and isolating nature of their duties, the fact that they must sign the OSA and refrain from sharing viewing experiences, and corresponding feelings of shock, grief and distress, with any external parties or familial confidants. But the prohibition on sharing details about the job – on expressing feelings and on communicating retentions regarding the intimacies vicariously witnessed in the course of monitoring riskscapes through the medium of the camera – meant that camera operators were predominantly left to deal with trauma in their own personalised ways, a scenario that produced severe health and cultural complications (see Chapter 5). In other words, system designers evidently perceived the camera operators one-dimensionally, as cheap, exploitable and expandable resources – labour capital that was dispassionate in its enterprise and infinitely capable in its emotional intelligence. We will regard later the degree to which these core assumptions were intrinsically uninformed by context and flawed by economy.

Material fragilities

As has become patently evident, system designers were motivated by fiscal concerns and embodied a fervent technocratic consciousness. Their social positionality and access to symbolic and material resources permitted them first to envision and then assemble a public space CCTV network, operations room and set of operational parameters. Yet what the group possessed in terms of legislative authority, they lacked in technical competence and operational proficiency. While they unquestionably established a system of visibility capable of altering the sociality and course of justice on the street, its relative inflexibility as an infrastuctural arrangement started to spawn feelings of anger, frustration and apathy among those with responsibilities for camera manoeuvring. Indeed, notwithstanding the prodigious effort expended in securing finances and legitimacy for the CCTV network in Newborough, it is perhaps a touch ironic to learn how camera sites were unmethodically elected. Rather than avail geometric spatial mapping techniques/technologies or utilise computerised crime data, a police architectural liaison officer was instead dispatched to the city limits with a paper telescope to envisage how and what a camera might see from a particular vantage point:

We knew where concerns were … so armed with that sort of information [we would walk the sites] and basically put a mark against a corner of a building and say 'if I imagined myself as being a camera at this location, how good a view would I get?'

(CCTVWG Secretary)

The extraordinary lack of precision in determining the project's most critical deliverable reveals the extent of specialist incompetence within the CCTVWG. It exposes their inability to think spatially and temporally, to exercise clairvoyance in terms of prospective economic markets, and, to reflect in advance upon probable ecological and demographic contingencies. It underlines the extent to which this initiative was couched in 'policy', rather than in 'practical', terms. It displays, in other words, the primacy placed by the CCTVWG on camera supply symbolism (on getting the system up swiftly) rather than on camera supply materialism (on managing the chattel as an enduring entity). It reveals the committee's obvious deficiencies in problem visualisation, in critical thinking and in comprehending the socio-material repercussions ensuing from particular decisions. Where and how you site cameras *really* matters, and it requires considerable and meticulous planning; not spur-of-the-moment propulsions by individuals attempting to be proxy cameras. Indeed, ensuring a rigorous scientific basis for determining the placement of detector points (i.e. why they are necessary), and guaranteeing their capacity to sense (i.e. how they are situated), are perhaps the most crucial dimensions of circuitry instigation. It requires foresight of likely crime transitions and a longitudinal affinity – and familiarisation – with the space in question. The objectivated arrangement of cameras via the means of paper telescope and notepad was, perhaps not unsurprisingly, to have significant consequences for the scheme's subsequent operability and (in)effectiveness:

Camera four has been in the same spot for donkey's years, just a waste – all it needed was, what, ten yards up the road and, at that time, you would have been able to see the bar, into the harbour and you would still see exactly the same as what you've got plus extra; and yet there wasn't any thought in it. They wanted to move a camera at the theatre for ages and yet the council wouldn't allow it, because it was going to be on a pole with a large box at the bottom. And they said, 'You can't have that; some kid will stand behind it and run onto the road'. So that's why they didn't move it … Of course, they [the CCTVWG] were not going to know how much drugs activity would change and stuff. We've been here for 12 and a half years and they were thinking of it how many years before that? So they were never going to know what was going to develop[10] … From going about then with a paper telescope, I mean, they wouldn't do that now, they actually have common sense. People in charge really should speak to the people who use the cameras day-in, day-out before putting any new ones in.

(Camera Operator 7)

Most of the camera positions are crap and if we had been consulted during the process we would have asked for them to be put in different locations. As operators, surely we are in the best position to suggest sites? I mean, look at cameras nine and ten – they're virtually touching one another; you've got to ask yourself, why on earth did they put two cameras in such close proximity to one another? I'd much rather they move camera ten into one of our blind spots, surely that would make more sense? It's the same as camera forty-seven in the multi-storey car park; we don't get any use of it as ... it can't see out either left or right due to the wall it's been fixed to. It's such a waste of resources.

(Camera Operator 2)

Beyond the encumbrance of perplexing and arcane camera emplacement, camera operator vision was also persistently impeded by the obstructive dimensions of several either unwieldy or disinclined urban actants:

Bus shelters, buses and the 'To Let' or retail premise signs in the city centre are the biggest nightmare. They piss us right off as they prevent us from seeing what is going on half the time on the street when an incident takes place; which in turn means that you don't know who did what, and you've got no evidence on tape for the police. It's even worse when there is a festival on in the city and they've got all the banners and flags up, or at Christmas time with the lights and decorations across the main street; the banners and the glare off the lights seriously obstruct what we can see ... I appreciate the council have a remit to make the city attractive to visitors, but they have to realise that they are seriously impacting on the job that we can do in here and people's general safety in the process.

(Camera Operator 15)

Camera Operator 7 discusses how the glare emanating from city centre streetlights makes viewing, and retrieving conclusive evidence, difficult. This is because the lights either blur the image that is seen or are so dim that the picture is in complete darkness. He also shows me the problems operators have with tree leaves and branches. According to the camera operator the council perceives the cameras as, 'secondary to making the place look pretty'.

Thirty-one cameras obtain their power on a grace and favour basis from business or private premises. Several cameras have had to be switched off or moved due to development work. One has been disabled due to the removal of consent, and one may be in the near future, as the owner is claiming the running costs. This equates to £9300 per annum for all thirty-one cameras should claims be pursued. One camera has been out of commission for at least three years. This is because the site was developed after installation.

(Newborough Police Force 2005)

It's just an absolute joke. They've [Traffic Division] taken away some of our key cameras and are using them in a pointless exercise to scan [the registration licence plate of] moving vehicles. I mean, surely we need them more than the traffic cops do? What a waste of resources, it pisses us right off. What will happen when someone gets murdered in the area and there is no CCTV evidence to go on? I mean the thing is that, even if the system registers a suspicious car, by the time someone responds, it has more than likely already left the city or whatever. It's like trying to find a needle in a haystack.

(Camera Operator 9)

These examples provide insight into the depth of frustration camera operators experience as they attempt to manage a far from perfect architecture of visibility. They expose the alternative priorities of 'partner' constituents and the fact that camera workers must labour under conditions not of their choosing – circumstances that impinge on their capacities to provide a gaze that will deliver public goods. A further technical problem wielding constraints on systemic functionality – and camera operator autonomy – concerned the camera technology itself. The CCTVWG's inability to factor in an achievable and enduring budget for maintenance services meant that certain cameras were either of limited technical sophistication or were fast becoming unfit for purpose. The poor manoeuvrability of certain cameras and substandard picture quality proved major hindrances to operativity stipulations:

The cameras have now been going for twelve and a half years non-stop and are basically obsolete. Getting replacement parts for them now is difficult. As I say, digital would be brilliant, but, like most things, it's down to money. But you've really got to look at what you're seeing in front of you. Look how many cameras are actually steamed up or are white out or are showing no image at all [I am shown various screens on which there is no image being relayed]. There is nothing more depressing then actually following somebody and then losing them because you don't have a camera to follow them on or it's broken.

(Camera Operator 7)

The life of cameras and equipment is 5–10 years, therefore much of the equipment is reaching the end of the design life and the accommodation is dated. Failure of components is commonplace. Deterioration of front-end equipment is exacerbated by the environment ... Replacement of the system seems to have been delayed to a point where equipment failures are reaching a high level and the equipment is in the main beyond its design life. The control room and review facilities have suffered from a lack of investment [and] are barely adequate and complaints are made by staff regarding the ergonomics.

(Newborough Police Force 2005)

Look at how many cameras are steamed up. Look at this camera, that is as fast as it goes [the camera's zoom and rotation is painfully slow]. It's been like that for four or five months. Yet you report it however many times and nothing is ever done.

(Camera Operator 18)

Again, these extracts unveil the fragility of the system in a technical sense, but they also capture the sentiment of despair felt and voiced by the camera operators in that they are not provided with the sufficient tools required to satisfy the demand placed on them as projectors of a protective gaze and as custodians of the social order. The ergonomic features of the monitoring room also impacted significantly on the camera operators' ability to execute assigned duties in a competent and efficacious manner. An architectural blunder in the design of the operations desk meant that the bottom row of 'spotter screens' on the back wall was obscured from view. Moreover, because the spotter monitors were only 15 inches in diameter, the images they did display were effectively indecipherable to the naked eye. Perhaps unsurprisingly, this situation, when coupled with other construction defects, induced plentiful discontent. It instilled a sense of dissatisfaction in that the arrangement of the means of visibility was perceived to have irrevocable defects – problems that would ultimately act to disadvantage and persecute the camera operators themselves:

This place has been so craply set up. I don't know who the architect was but they ought to be out of a job. None of us can see over the desk so all the bottom spotter screens are lost to view, and it's virtually impossible to make out what is happening on the screens we can see, as they're just too small. This [design flaw] might mean that we end up missing something important.

(Camera Operator 6)

The cameras are here because of the terrorist threat and because the government can't afford to have something happen and then have someone turn round and say: 'Why was there no CCTV?' It's all for show. It's just to make the public feel safer. The effectiveness of the cameras is another matter. I mean, take this system for instance, how can three, sometimes two, guys really monitor it effectively? We've got about 140 cameras and three pairs of eyes for the most part, so that's one guy to watch 47 cameras, and they're talking of bringing in more. It's just a joke.

(Camera Operator 37)

Camera Operator 9 tells me that there is no logical sequence correlating the camera numbers. So, for example, camera one is not necessarily in propinquity to camera two. Indeed, cameras fourteen and fifteen are at opposite ends of the city: 'It takes a while to get your head around and I still get confused with it to be honest; especially when the pressure is on

94 *Engaging the means of watching*

and everything is kicking off. Surely it would have made more sense to organise them by proximity rather than by cluster?'

Despite the fact that poor monitoring ergonomics was an issue officially recognised by a consultant medical adviser in a police document dating back to 1996, it seems that a decade on, little has improved in terms of operational usability:

> The principal area of concern relates to the brightness and degree of flicker associated with the small monitors ... The flicker when all the monitors are on will potentially lead to a degree of fatigue in the operator ... The atmosphere is relatively dry and I wonder how effective the current humidifier is, given its location and the ventilation arrangements ... There are, on occasions, quite significant background noise levels arising from the area between the Unit and the Public Office which is likely to contribute to overall stress levels in situations where operators are having to concentrate or where the radio is being used.
> (Newborough Police Force 1996)

> There's just no fucking room in here or space to move about, especially if you're in a wheelchair or have mobility issues. It would all just be so much easier if we were to get our digital system.
> (Camera Operator 2)

Notwithstanding the existing cluttering of fittings and equipment in the monitoring room, management frequently introduced new monitory 'gimmicks' into the setting with limited justification or explanation regarding object nature and purpose. These additions were either technological (e.g. supplementary cameras or recording systems), or procedural (e.g. novel monitoring rules or shift adjustments). The camera operators were expected to subsume passively such adaptations into their working rhythms, often without training, usually without due consultation and certainly without registering any dissent. A good illustration of this transmutation process was when Newborough police elected to replace its traditional radio system with a digital communication terminal:

> Basically the police just told us one day that they were getting a new mobile communications technology to replace the radio system that we've had since this place opened and that was it. The only brief we got was an email giving us the dates that it would be installed; we didn't even get an opportunity to ask questions about it or see it working in practice. I'm just sick of the way they just introduce gimmicks in here without even having the politeness to ask our opinions or get our views, even to educate us regarding how these things work. We're just expected to know how everything works and cope with everything we have to do. There's times when I just think I can't be done with this job any more.
> (Camera Operator 2)

The introduction of novel procedures and technologies in this non-collaborative fashion ensured that the stable working patterns and conventions the operators followed were ruptured, a scenario undermining their trust and respect for the system managers. It left them in a state of perpetual concern in terms of their being displaced and dispossessed from their vocational role as urban order custodians by the introduction of automated systems of oversight.

Positional fragilities

It is not only the material properties of the system that create problems for social operativity. The intra-organisational demands of the workplace also influence the coherency or discord of the wider system of visibility. Most of the researched camera operators, for example, complained about shift lengths and schedules, and the alternating times that they were obliged to work, claiming that such labour was having negative physiological and psychological affects on them both inside and outside the workplace:

> It can be pretty tough spending ten hours cooped up in a box, my eyes are really hurting now; they're really sore. It's just far too difficult trying to concentrate for a ten-hour shift ... I don't feel like I've any time for anything once I go home after dayshift and the backshift, you're just so tired when you get out of here.
> (Camera Operator 13)

> Last night I ended up falling asleep twice and missed three dispatch radio messages. It wasn't until the phone rang that I woke up! I was like 'where am I, what's going on?!' I don't know, it gets to about 4am and I just can't keep my eyes open. They [the police dispatch centre] weren't too happy with me like, but what can you do? I'm well known for falling asleep during nightshifts. Last Friday night we had the divisional inspector through here saying to Camera Operator 15: 'Oh, so you're a man down tonight then, eh? You better keep an eye on him 'cos otherwise he'll be falling asleep again!' I just wish they had made this desk out of foam or something as it's pretty sore when your head whacks against a plywood table top!
> (Camera Operator 14)

> *The time is 4:42am and Camera Operators 17 and 18 are both lapsing in and out of consciousness with neither alert enough to proactively monitor the cameras. Silence engulfs the room. When awake, both operators stare blankly at the same camera view: 'I'd be much better in my bed. I mean, I'm awake, but I'm not; my brain just kind of shuts down' (Camera Operator 17) ... I do notice, however, that the operators fracture the time with a number of informal rests – i.e. through sleeping, tea breaks and toilet stops, walking stoppages, the checking of emails on the computer,*

personal phone calls and text messaging, perusing the holiday and shift rotas for the coming weeks and through trivial conversation etc.

A further strain on the camera operators was their subordinate position in a convoluted communication structure and lack of jurisdictional command over police and security units dispersed across the city. Because the watchers had no legislative power or juridical authority to dispatch police personnel or to instruct security staff, and because they had to share communications systems with multiple other policing agents, there were abundant instances when camera operators experienced exasperation with transmission delays and with having their contributions or perspectives disregarded:

> If we see an incident and can tell from experience that it's going to erupt into something and we want to try and stop it from happening, all we can do is flag it up in the hope that the dispatcher has a unit to send. It can be very frustrating for staff if they [dispatch] disagree with our judgement or have missed the start of it ... all the time there is a delay, the etiquette of the system is such that we can't tell the police to get there unless it is an absolute emergency; we've got to go through the force dispatch centre as they control the deployment of police resources. Unless it's an emergency we can't just say, 'get your arses down there'. And that's another frustrating thing from our point of view, you know, you'll be polite on the radio to them but the moment your finger is off the button you're cursing and swearing because we know it's [the incident] going to be bad or we know it was bad; does make you think it's just a lottery when you contact the police.
> (Camera Operator 20)

> ... Knowing that the individual is wanted for two previous offences, Camera Operator 15 tries to alert the dispatch centre via the radio. This is not possible, however, as the dispatch inspector's lengthy instructional exchange with a police unit on the ground is effectively blocking the airwaves. Camera Operator 15 is clearly angered by the duration of time it is taking for the inspector to relay the message: 'Oh shut the fuck up. He's a right fucking idiot, just loves the sound of his voice far too much.' The dispatch centre is eventually contacted and a unit is sent ... A short time later, the police unit asks CCTV for 'an update on the male's present location'. Just as the camera operator attempts to respond, the dispatch inspector interrupts the transmission demanding an update on the situation from the unit, effectively preventing Camera Operator 15 from being able to transmit situational specifications. Throwing the radio handset down in disgust, Camera Operator 15 angrily proclaims: 'God he's such an interfering cunt. I wish he would just shut up and let us get on with it.'

It was not only struggles for airwave utilisation that generated problems for the camera operators. Indeed, both the quantity and quality of relays between 'partner' components, and the forms of information 'shared', also induced frustrations. While one might anticipate that those tasked with maintaining order in the city would engage proficiently in precise forms of communicative protocol, and follow similar repertoires to those of rationalised military units, what flowed across the airwaves instead were many instances of non-professionalised communicative ambiguity:

> Camera Operator 2 takes a message from a doorman on Victoria Street. The doorman has a strong foreign accent making what he is broadcasting on the radio difficult to comprehend. Despite giving me a bemused glance and a shrug of the shoulders, and asserting, 'What the hell was that all about?!', Camera Operator 2 responds to the doorman, 'Yes, roger that'. He then turns to me and says: 'It's really difficult to make out half of what the Paki boys say on the radio. You should hear some of them. I mean, I didn't understand a word of that. The bars really need to get some more local guys working on the doors, so that we can actually understand what they're saying.' Choosing to ignore the doorman's instructions, Camera Operator 2 resumes general monitoring duties.

> Camera Operator 1 proceeds to apprise ShopSafe security personnel to be on the lookout for DT and to 'alert CCTV immediately if the individual is spotted. We do not have a description of what he is wearing or if he is with anyone, but those who know him please keep an eye out.' Just to show a perfect example of the levels of error and misinterpretation that can exist between the camera operators in the monitoring room and those positioned on the streets, around 15 minutes later a call comes in from a security guard of a major retailer asking CCTV to confirm what the FR guy looks like, and what he is wearing. Camera Operator 1 replies sharply that the 'wanted male's name is DT, not FR, and we do not have a description of what he is wearing.'

> ... Because the police are communicating on different radio channels, the information being passed around the parties is variable ... After the incident, Camera Operator 3 turns to me and says, 'I bet you're really shocked at how badly the police handled the whole incident? It's probably opened your eyes to a lot of stuff. The communication between us is just so bad sometimes, though we're not entirely blameless, like. We should have tried to tell them more, I just thought Camera Operator 6 [who has temporarily left the room] had told them [police dispatch] that he had actually seen the two running away from the crime scene.'

> Yet another erroneous description of MB is verbalised prompting Camera Operator 15 to retort: 'Fuck's sake, why do we bother.' This time, though, he chooses not to correct the description. Information passing between stores is like a game of telephone, with each description altering to the point where the observed person either assumes a new identity or an entirely different outfit!

Frictions in terms of how Newborough had been spatially divided by its order stewards into contested territories of concern were commonplace. Each of the respective parties had differing perceptions regarding what constituted legitimate risks. They had also contrasting understandings of spatial and occupational responsibilities as the following excerpt evidently indicates:

> *Camera Operator 12 starts talking about pub and club door staff's use of CCTV and the PubSafe radio system. She is annoyed with how the door workers contact the CCTV operators 'every five minutes' to report incidents occurring within their premises. According to Camera Operator 12, some of the doormen work on the false assumption that it's the CCTV camera operators who should be calling out ambulances and police units to attend those injured inside the pubs and clubs, prompting her to proclaim: 'We are a "public space system" and not a "private space system". What happens within the bars and clubs really is not our responsibility. It's only when it spills outside onto the streets that it becomes our concern.'*

Despite being employed as social order custodians, the camera operators at times chose to incorporate guardianship and devotion duties exceeding those demanded by the external municipality. The following example beautifully illustrates how social factors and filters – in this case, animal welfarism and enchantment – mediate the informal ends to which the system is directed:

> *A short while later, around 9:50pm, one of the Newborough police support staff (i.e. those who work behind the public office desk) brings a dog into the CCTV suite on a leash of rope. The dog had been tied to a tree for an excessive duration and then subsequently released by a concerned member of the public. The animal is in an understandably frenzied state, chaotically darting around the room before periodically stopping to greet Camera Operators 11 and 7, and myself. It eventually takes shelter underneath the main operations desk. Camera Operator 7 takes a shine to the animal and leaves his terminal to further mollycoddle it. He then takes the dog for a walk along the police station corridors. Camera Operator 11 is left for a number of minutes to operate the entire system on her own. Camera Operator 7 and the dog return to the room shortly after 10pm and the dog, evidently bewildered, yet keyed up by the new surroundings and attention it is receiving, abruptly defecates on the floor. Camera Operator 11 leaves her terminal to clean it up with blue roll, before spraying the carpet with an air freshener: 'Ah it's just another day in CCTV!' I learn later from Camera Operator 8 that having a dog in the CCTV suite is not something out of the ordinary: 'I remember when we had a Labrador in here with us on one shift. It just sat under the desk and slept for most of the shift. Getting dogs in here that have been dumped by their owners is not a rare thing in this place.'*

It is perhaps revealing that a site, the apparent operational sterility and legal sanctity of which is prohibited to the outside public, can be breached, blemished and disturbed in this way by abandoned canines. The fact that this banal interruption effectively precluded urban street monitoring from occurring for a significant duration elucidates the susceptibility of supervisory watchers to incidental, yet consequential, disruptions. It reveals the informality of relations that wield influence over the organisational parameters of the operating lifeworld. It testifies to the curious structuring of supervisory arrangements and experiences.

Proprietary fragilities

Structures are sedimented as much from actor activity as from actor inactivity. In the case of the CCTVWG, a lack of managerial foresight in the consultation period generated all manner of subsequent problems, quandaries that cumulatively constrain the operating capacity of the current Newborough camera network. Although a motion to create a liaison committee to oversee the maturational unfolding of the Newborough system was initially agreed, this entity never materialised. Indeed, management of the camera network became the responsibility of a police sergeant who had no interest or personal stake in the long-term viability of the scheme:

> Well, when I came to the post it appeared that nothing had been done to the system in the last ten years ... The problem was that the post had previously been filled by a retiring sergeant, or somebody late in service, who did not really have a lot of push [i.e. desire] to keep CCTV going. He was just seeing out his time [before retiring], I think, so there was no forward planning. All the gaps were filled ... with the monitors and there seemed to be nowhere to put additional cameras. But they never took in the possibility of putting more than one camera on a screen, sequencing it – the technological knowledge wasn't there ... Stagnate is the word. I think the staff were managed and the maintenance was done when required but there was no forward thinking involved.
> (Newborough CCTV Manager)

The fact that no legal documentation existed to indicate who owned, and was therefore responsible for, system hardware and associated operating costs, prompted the newly elected municipal authority to refuse liability:

> The CCTVWG had no real legal recourse, if you like, because it wasn't defined, it wasn't identified, the remit wasn't agreed other than within the remit of the group itself. It wasn't taken a stage beyond that and put into some form of legal document that made it quite clear as far as the future was concerned. And I think that was a shortfall, that certainly was a big learning outcome as far as the project was concerned ... Perhaps we did

not appreciate how big a beast, how big a project it was going to be, and at an earlier stage we should have given thought to getting these protocol documents and agreements in place. Because by the time that it came round to thinking about the need for them, the project was actually up and running and we [the police] had committed ourselves to the spending, to the maintenance, to the ongoing upkeep of the system without giving proper thought as to who was going to be responsible if the bubble burst in any way, shape or fashion. Who owns it? The entity owns it but there is no legal definition of who the entity are or what the entity is. The ducts, and some of the cable running through, are owned by the local council, some are owned by the entity, because we got civil engineers to put in new ducts in areas where they didn't exist, rather than using existing ducts which had the potential of rental agreements coming into being.

(CCTVWG Secretary)

An attendant lack of annual investment from the private sector (prompted by the finance subgroup's original decision to collect only a 'one-off' contribution) meant that the system was left to deteriorate and to badly fragment, with no agency willing or able to part with the funds required to service ailing hardware components:

There was no maintenance cost [factored in], no kind of forward planning in terms of, 'Each year we will need X amount from you', which everyone is finding throughout the UK now, because there has been no strategic planning for securing future funding. No disrespect to them because it was a brand new thing, but there was no foresight that we need to get each year a guarantee that they [business corporations and local authorities] are going to contribute something towards the cameras. I would have made sure that the agreements were better and that there was a bit more strategic planning for the future. Of course, technology is moving forward so much more quickly now and it is very difficult to plan for; you're looking at two years then systems will be out of date.

(Newborough CCTV Manager)

A liaison group was intended, [but] it kind of fell to the wayside. There was a change of heart in a number of individuals once the project was up and running because ... they were continually putting their hands into their pockets to feed this beast and, as a result, there was a bit of friction in one or two of the organisations. It ended up with the police for a period of time having to meet all costs of the system and that perhaps didn't go down well from both points of view and, as a result, the friction that was there became a red hot fire and quite a number of things were said and done that, with hindsight, could have been resolved, better handled. And as a result, the overseeing group didn't come into being.

(CCTVWG Secretary)

Instigating circuitries 101

Hence, the failure of the CCTVWG to craft a legally binding constitutional agreement detailing ownership rights, and maintenance and operation responsibilities, provoked a lengthy and heated dispute between the council and the police service, a disagreement which has frosted relations between the two agencies on this matter, and fostered the system's gradual degeneration. By failing to exercise foresight and identify potential risks (processes, ironically, that are synonymous with contemporary supervisory applications), the CCTVWG unintentionally made their property and facility vulnerable to the volatility of an impending economic recession.

CCTV circuitries, therefore, are both materially 'durable' (non-negotiable in terms of their physical structures) and socially 'fragile' (negotiated in terms of their interactional orders). They embody a multiplicity of contrasting logics, interests and subjectivities and proceed in indeterminable directions after being exposed to the competing grammars and turbulences of everyday interrelations. They are established structurally and maintained operationally by multiplex agents and reflect in their arrangement the distinctive volitions and values of guarantors at specific points in space-time. They are formulated in the course of history and transition in its progressive and continuous unfolding. Although neoliberalism spawned the CCTV surge and provided conducive fiscal, policy and spatial contexts for the technology's rapid proliferation, its prioritisation of evidence-based measurement and economic rationalism might as easily bring about the decommissioning of this iconic 1990s policy intervention. As austerity and cost saving increasingly exert influence on municipal and federal authority decision making, medium- and large-scale public CCTV networks, with only the immaterial, imperceptible and transitory commodities of order[11] and safety to trade as justification for their continued existence, have themselves become considerable financial burdens and sources of political risk (Webster 2009). Having surpassed its historical apex, and having attracted unwanted condemnation from multiple commentators, CCTV seems destined for a rocky ride henceforth. A 'politics of diminution' may soon supplant the 'politics of expansion' emphasised in Chapter 2. Where previous accounts of CCTV have foregrounded the factors responsible for its growth and creep, future studies may conceivably need to focus on the factors inducing its impending decline (Smith 2012a). The requisite for asking differing epistemological questions about supervisory circulations, in terms of their comprising seemingly inevitable ontologies of escalation in the hyper-security era, in a recession plagued political economic environment is crystallised in the following excerpt:

> There need be a drive for greater integration, modernisation and expansion of systems so that long term cost savings can be acquired. This necessitates a 'joined up' partnership approach, making sure that the right policies are in place, legal requirements are met, shared facilities are developed and a long term sustainable financial plan is implemented … Using a business approach to the operation of systems will enable the

identification of revenue opportunities and income generation ... There may be funding streams available from the issue of fixed penalties for crimes and offences such as: Detection of Litter Offences; Detection of Dog Fouling; Detection of Road Traffic Offences; Detection of Minor Crime such as Breach of the Peace; Detection of Graffiti Damage ... Systems can be used as an effective operational tool to manage and free up [police] resources thus producing efficiency ... savings. There is a need to embrace new technology which will, in the long term, be more cost effective than employing additional staff ... The existing accommodation is cramped, dated, unfit for future expansion and borderline fit for purpose. If this current proposal is not implemented in one of the identified forms, Newborough police and its partners will potentially lose a significant investigative tool.

(Newborough Police Force 2008)

This insightful operational planning document conveys the cautionary sentiment alluded to previously. It suggests that these visual measures face an uncertain future, with systemic innovation in terms of revenue generation via camera system realignment proposed as the optimum solution to an inexorable problem of technological decay and fragmentation.

Chapter 3 synopsis

This chapter has sought to excavate the socio-historical genesis of CCTV circuitry design and execution. It has endeavoured to position supervisory circulations in a broader longitudinal context and to illuminate their evolutionary interconnectedness – their situation within fields of social relations. As symbolic texts (i.e. value-laden discursive ideas) and lived entities (palpable work environments and policing hubs), CCTV arrangements are the objectivated products of historicised courses of action. Focusing attention on those liable for instituting the Newborough CCTV scheme, and juxtaposing their precursory decision making with present-day protocols and situational pressures, has made possible the analytical reconnection of detached temporal and spatial sequences. It was apparent that the project initiators were guided by a technocratic consciousness and enthusiasm that prioritised systemic and fiscal matters, and that repudiated social and operational details. The CCTVWG's practical incompetence, aspirational dissension, dubious labour recruitment methods and ecological myopia, precipitated a disjointed operating culture and unsustainable material infrastructure. Accordingly, this dissection has evinced how oversights made in formulation can linger as intractable flaws, impinging on the delivery of supervisory services.

Overture to Chapter 4

Chapter 4, 'Construing circuitries: supervisory projection', focuses on the camera operators' phenomenological experiences of gazing and their multi-dimensional relations with simulacra visualised through the CCTV circuitry.

It seeks to show how the camera mediums function as para-social contact points, positioning watchers and watched in circumscribed interactional entanglements. It also illuminates the social meanings and narrations that camera operators ascribe to the social bodies, spaces and events they indirectly encounter. The chapter demonstrates how the impersonal nature of telemediated rhythms makes camera operators adopt strategies of personalisation and familiarisation, techniques of construal that reflect subjective orientations rather than the formalised determinations set by those in charge of the system's operating protocol.

Notes

1 The police force took an administrative lead on the project from this moment onwards.
2 A perceptual motive was behind this initiative, the CCTVWG presuming that camera coverage alone would inculcate in the public consciousness perceptions of safety and palliation – affects that would, it was thought, enhance the attractiveness of the day- and night-time economies and increase civic satisfaction with the ruling municipality.
3 The group did receive correspondence from a local charity, Drugs Action, and a young offenders organisation, highlighting concern as to the positioning of several cameras:

> *Drugs Action depends heavily on anonymity and confidentiality in order to allow free access to anyone who has a problem regarding drugs ... Consistent feedback we have is that people only come here if they feel sure they are not being watched. A camera ... recording people walking into the project is quite alarming, [and] if the scheme went ahead with cameras able to film the doorway ... it would seriously damage the service we provide.*

> It has come to my attention that a camera is to be sited ... which may cover [our] premises. This is a matter of some concern as it could potentially threaten the confidentiality of the services provided by [us]. Our offices are visited regularly by offenders and it is important to both our clients and the organisation that their identities remain confidential. Also, given the history of our clients' contact with the police, it is particularly important that they do not feel that in having contact [with us] they can be identified by the police.
> (CCTVWG minutes)

The group decided that a letter of reply signed by the committee chairman would be issued, thanking each agency for their comments, but highlighting that anything filmed would be treated with the utmost confidentiality and would most certainly not be used to the detriment of any individual or organisation. As we shall see later, however, these promises ended up being factually glib, service users receiving disproportionate monitoring:

> *Camera Operator 15 has the camera focused on the entrance to the young offenders building. I ask him why he is interested in the site: 'It's a good place to get sightings as there are always dodgers coming and going from here, and you also get to learn the [problem] faces of tomorrow.'*

104 *Engaging the means of watching*

4 The pre-eminence placed by the CCTVWG on marketing and acquiring external monies to the value of £200,000 is discernible in the following excerpt:

> The finance secretary emphasised during his telephone call that the scheme was dependent on financial support from the private sector and could not progress without it. It was suggested by a member that 'an approach be made to General Accident [insurers] as they had recently announced that discount could be available to customers located within a CCTV system area.' This was agreed by the members.
>
> (CCTVWG minutes)

5 ShopSafe and PubSafe are the names of the radio terminals and frequencies linking the camera operators with leisure economy security staff e.g. retail and tavern security.
6 Discussion centred on issues such as camera numbers, camera placement, camera type, radio communications possibilities and the whereabouts of the monitoring facility.
7 In terms of recruitment, training and mentorship etc.
8 Cited in: www.salisbury.gov.uk/news/2004/display-press-release.htm?id=2004-07-13-a.asp (accessed 19 February 2013).
9 For more information, see: www.airwavesolutions.co.uk (accessed 19 February 2014).
10 Evidently aware of both the fragility of decision making (i.e. its historical context and unintended consequences), and the durability of its outcomes (i.e. circuitry intransigence), the camera operator acknowledges that spatial usages change with time, so that new (deviant) behaviours and leisure hubs emerge and old ones decline, the inevitable reality being a visibility architecture pervaded by transience and blind spots.
11 Social order, of course, is an extremely precarious and ephemeral condition in the frictional and polarised anatomy of the urban metropolis.

4 Construing circuitries
Supervisory projection

> Surveillance researchers should focus on the text-mediated interactions made between surveillance agents and surveillance subjects at various points of contact in the surveillance circuit.
>
> (Walby 2005b, 170)

Kevin Walby (2005b) draws attention in the epigraph to the importance of watcher-watched intersectionalities and interrelationalities. His proposal highlights the primacy of engaging the moments and places where supervisors and supervisees relationally converge, and analysing how mediation (e.g. social, technological and organisational) impacts such encounters. My purpose in this chapter, following the instruction provided above, is to analyse a set of *contact points* and *text-mediated interactions* where supervisors and supervisees of human and/or non-human distinction interface in a program of remote encounters. I want to illustrate how camera circuitries get annexed by their users and rendered into mediums of para-sociality. I also wish to elucidate how camera operators profile and process a sequence of telemediated realities, how they assimilate such exposure and how such exposure assimilates them. The latter section of Chapter 3 considered camera operators' impressions of the structural circuitry they inherited and the range of relational interactions occurring between supervisory nodes in the wider visibility reticulation. This chapter anatomises the camera operator gaze, dissecting some of its projective and speculative dimensions. We discovered earlier that previous empirical research on CCTV operation accentuated the discriminatory and discretionary attributes of camera operator monitoring conducts, showing that it was minority populations and stigmatised subgroups who were disproportionately scrutinised. Camera operators, it seemed, were neoliberalised conduits whose observations merely perpetuated wider social prejudices. But are 'diagrams of aversion' the only parameters of gaze orientation? Might other factors (e.g. the social positioning of the camera operator) mediate what and who becomes legible? Further, is the gaze purely asymmetrical in tone or does it encompass dialectical properties, that is to say, reflective aspects that *direct*, *subject* and *affect* its projector?

The chapter attends to these questions by engaging both the embodied practices and verbalised narratives of camera operators to ascertain what it is they perceive and how it is they decipher, and whether the tactile bonds watchers forge with telemediated points of perception exceed mere antipathy and indifference. It shows that as para-social mediums, CCTV circuitries foster and circumscribe particular types of interactional exchange. They render distanced objects into textual points of construal, discursive items that can be recited as tales of the city; stories that encapsulate its ponderable ecologies. They fasten watchers and watched things in curious relational associations. They enable the former to sometimes influence the course of justice on the streets and the latter to sometimes direct the course of monitoring. The depersonalised nature of unidirectional observation, one-dimensionality of mediated phenomena and decontextualised character of witnessed episodes induce camera operators to creatively imbue (and supplement) with fictional narration what they indirectly regard – attributing conjectural discourses to that which is intimately visualised. Camera operators partake in scanning rituals, with viewings informing diagnostic readings of social grammars and reflecting their instinctive dispositions. It is evident that being a professional watcher is not dissimilar to being an avid television spectator, some protagonists and storylines enthralling attention and demanding definition, others eliciting indifference and inducing disregard.

Overall, the chapter elucidates how supervisory actions involve mutual processes of *visibility making* and *visuality processing*. Camera operators are formally contracted to *produce* visibilities by casting a gaze and by magnifying captivating phenomena, but they are also professionally obliged to *construe* what they witness and to *endure* what they see. As such, they need literacy in the pre-emptive decoding and reading of social comportment. They require sensorial capital for disturbance sensing and they need tacit knowledge of behavioural dynamics for formulating assessments and making risk-based decisions. They exploit capturing competencies to ensure that disorderly sequences are recorded in scrupulosity, and in perpetuity, on both material cartridges and cognitional receptacles. It is the subjective experiences of these visibility-visuality alternations that are to be our prime focus in this chapter and in the next.

CCTV struggles: strategies and tactics

> Behind the 'monotheism' of the dominant panoptical procedures, we might expect the existence and survival of a 'polytheism' of concealed and disseminated practices.
>
> (de Certeau 1984, 188)

> I love car chases in the city, when you're trying to anticipate where the boy might come out. It's like a game of chess or cat and mouse, but at great speed. Us on the cameras, against him in the motor. I can be anywhere in the city at the touch of a button. It's great.
>
> (Camera Operator 2)

Construing circuitries 107

As was outlined in Chapter 2, scholars have typically conceived CCTV circuitries as socio-material manifestations of a neoliberal agenda that strives to cleanse the city of nonconformist pollutants. CCTV tends to be regarded as a lever of social exclusion and social exclusivity, purging out the undesirables and enticing in the worthy. It is conceptualised as a spatial leverage intended to prise open problematic blockages in the aesthetics of the street. CCTV networks are a core provision in the recasting of public space to a mould where consumption rituals are prioritised and can be best maximised. The aim of this section is to appraise this perspective, and its corollary set of assumptions, by explicating whether or not CCTV operation adheres to such an explicit plan. Do the ethics of the market completely infuse its daily operativity or do other variables figure in dictating lines of sight? That is to say, is the relationship between watcher and watched, and between spectator and spectacle, characterised by greater complexity than the hierarchical asymmetry and unidirectionality presupposed in current thought? It is here that the ideas of French cultural populist Michel de Certeau (1984) become pertinent and irradiate insight, specifically the distinction he draws between 'strategies' of ruling and 'tactics' of desistance. They offer a valuable framework for comprehending the relational complexities concomitant on 'visibility dialectics', that is, acts of involuntary *exposure* and acts of voluntary *revealing*. The former instance refers to situations where an object is rendered visible via compulsion, whereas the latter episode refers to situations where an object volitionally opts to situate itself within a field of visibility, to either court audience attention or evince/project a concealed detail.

De Certeau defines strategies as the various ideological designs and material measures through which the established power elite attempt to govern specific populations and to reproduce circuits of capital and structures of privilege. CCTV systems, public-private security groundsmen, radio transmitters, exceptional by-laws, bomb-proof litter bins, fences and intelligence databases are each enrolled in managing the order of urbanism. Although designed to engineer desired outcomes and to manipulate conformity, to *act on* territories of self and space as disciplinary constraints, strategies, when operationalised, can elicit a range of contingencies. This is because strategies are tantamount to geometric diagrams. They are legislative maps imprinted upon motional environments to instigate certain ends. However, for all their vigour and resourcing, strategies remain dependent on relational interplays: they embody the interests of a few spatial technicians but are implicated in the lives of many. As such, claims de Certeau, strategies tend to intersect with tactics, with a nuanced set of heterogeneous demands. As with any flow of energy, strategies occasion repertoires of resistance. They arouse countervailing recalcitrance and creative bricolage, defiant and enterprising practices eventuating from the artful or spontaneous ways in which social bodies consciously and subconsciously respond to technologies of domination or grids of legibility: and *act on* strategies for subversive gains. Emergent tactics comprise all manner of cunning. Actors might comply with a directive for an imperceptible end. They might accidentally evade, or deliberately manoeuvre around, the pressurising attributes of a targeted intervention. They may appropriate an authoritative measure and opportunistically exploit its materiality for alternative purposes (de Certeau 1984, 96). Young people using street furniture inventively for skateboarding pursuits would be a germane instance. For de Certeau, both 'street life' and 'work life' position interest-driven and desire-ingrained individuals in a perpetual struggle with the institutional fields of power that seek to influence their behaviour. Thus, de Certeau's analytical conceptualisation of domination *attempts* and resistive *potential* provides the forthcoming discussion with a useful analytical lens and terminology for contextualising relations between watchers and watched. It indicates how these two entities mutually construct and co-produce one another, and are mutually affected by one another's actions – and by the intermediary system facilitating their contact.

Contact points: supervisory circuitries as para-social mediums

CCTV circuitries are para-social mediums that conjoin and position watchers and watched in curious relational entanglements. Curious insofar as such remote connectivity can relate to both banal and severe circumstances, and can occur without either actor ever personally or physically experiencing proximity or having any actual embodied contact. Notwithstanding such spatialised separation, and the fact that one party cannot discern the anatomy of the other (only her or his presence as conveyed in the camera's motion), watchers and watched can each engage in communicative interchanges – co-produced theatrics and reciprocal patterns of social action. They can share situated experiences and concerns. The fields of vision and visibility permit this type of interactivity, this species of interpersonal exchange. What they do not allow, of course, is the possibility for each to experience co-presence in a direct or immediate sense – there is an asymmetrical dimension to this interactional order. The veil of the camera transmitter precludes an embodied and sensorial experience of togetherness. We saw previously how the CCTV circuitry functions as a visual and aural conduit for conveying multiplex risk informatics concerning the order of the street. It hosts instructive inputs and delivers heuristic outputs. It acts as an intermediary node connecting virtually a multitude of discrete authorities and their various subjugators. Camera operators, for instance, can indirectly involve themselves in the mitigation of potential problems and the management of disorderly behaviours via the teleoptic and telecommunicational apparatuses they have at their disposal. These technologies are utilised to keep track of risky flows as they converge on city premises and to alert various grounded officials about existing or impending threats to property or contractual integrity:

> *Camera Operator 2 suddenly notices a young male running out of a shopping mall chased by a guard in uniform and another male, presumably an*

Construing circuitries 109

undercover store detective, dressed in a shirt, tie and black jacket. Just as he picks the incident up a message is blurted across the ShopSafe radio from one of the guards stating: 'CCTV ... We're chasing a guy along Henley Street at the moment, can you please send a unit immediately?' Camera Operator 2 instantly replies: 'Yeah, we've got you on camera. Unit will be on its way shortly.' In unison with Camera Operator 2 who is locating the chase, Camera Operator 3 alerts the police dispatch centre on the radio, asking whether a police unit deployed for a nearby incident could be used to apprehend the male. This request is granted and Camera Operators 2, 3 and 5 track the chase on a mix of cameras as the man runs along Henley Street into Charles Street. Despite the fact that the male has now run beyond camera coverage, radio dialogue with one of the exhausted guards, is enough for Camera Operator 2 to accurately pinpoint the offender's precise location and direct the unit to him. The male is arrested shortly after.

We get asked to make sure that licence holders are shutting down at the times specified on their contract while doormen are shouting on us to deal with stuff. It's the same with helping traffic division out with doing PNC checks; even though we're short staffed, we're busy sat on a computer checking numberplate details for them meaning we can't be monitoring the cameras and responding to calls. We can't do everything!

(Camera Operator 14)

The para-social interactivity stemming from CCTV circuitries is appositely demonstrated when contributors circulate personal information feeds regarding the details of suspicious persons or updates as these relate to ongoing incidents or generalised intelligence sourcing. This process of collaborative sharing between a plurality of spatially detached agents of social control via the supervisory infrastructure is illustratively captured in the following excerpts:

Camera Operator 3 has a camera focused on three scruffily dressed males, two of whom are wearing hats, standing at a bus stop outside a supermarket on Grange Street ... She recognises two of the men, noting down their names in the SIB, but cannot identify the third man, despite requesting this detail from each of the other camera operators. She contacts the security guard at the store via the ShopSafe radio, asking him if he knows the male's identity to which he replies: 'Yeah it's JH, and they're all banned from here.' The camera operator jots down the identified individual's name and continues to monitor the trio for the next few minutes.

'Dempseys to CCTV.' 'Yes, go ahead Dempseys' (Camera Operator 4). 'You got any idea who those two are just coming out of our front doors?' 'Roger. That would be FG and LT, both known for shoplifting and not the sort of clientele you would want in your store' (Camera Operator 4).

110   *Engaging the means of watching*

Yet, camera circuitries are appropriated and reappropriated by their users in ways that far surpass the dialogical formalities cited above. Informal usages of the medium for relational, comical and intimidatory ends produce interesting interplays between projections of curiosity (watching impetuses) and objects of perception (watched stimuli). Camera operators, for instance, are not averse to bobbing the cameras up and down in a 'We're Watching You' motion, a signification of an authoritative monologue with a targeted item. Likewise, it is not uncommon for the consciously visualised to manifest a range of camera-induced responses, to indicate via gesticulation a sentiment evoked from the experience of being subjected to scrutiny. The following fieldnote extracts appositely encapsulate the nuanced variances in symbolic interactivity that manifest from camera hardware being annexed for interactional pursuits and informalised reciprocities:

Camera Operator 1 watches a male who is sitting speaking to a scruffily dressed female on the steps outside a local authority homeless centre. The man appears agitated and unable to remain still for any duration of time. He seems to acknowledge that the camera is regarding him as he initially sticks a thumb up to the camera, before making an 'o' shape with his thumb and forefinger (i.e. presumably gesturing some sort of responsive salutation). The camera operator proceeds to move the camera body up and down to signal to the male that he is the object of observation. The observed male then sticks up his middle finger: 'Charming', says Camera Operator 1, 'Fuck off to you too, mate.' The man starts to 'mouth off' and wave his fist at the camera for a further few moments before sitting down, head in hands, on the steps again.

... the observed male has noticed that the camera overhead is focused on him. He reacts by waving his middle finger angrily toward the camera lens. The camera operator watching the male responds by sticking his two fingers up at the screen and proclaiming: 'Same to you.'

I notice one of the camera operators focusing on a group of three scruffily dressed individuals standing in an alcove. Two are male and one is female. All three appear acutely aware that the CCTV camera is monitoring them, with the female quite attentive to her visibility. One of the males sardonically waves at the camera prompting the operator to return the gesture.

Camera Operator 2 follows a 'known' individual as he makes his way along the street ... Interestingly, the man, who evidently is aware of his being tracked on camera, suddenly stops and begins pouring his can of lager down a street drain. He turns to the camera, smiles derisively and gesticulates with a thumb up gesture. The camera operator waves at the monitor screen and says sarcastically: 'Oh what a good boy! Can't say I've ever seen him do that before, he usually doesn't waste his drink.' Shortly after, the male deposits his now empty can in a nearby council bin. Again, the camera operator laughs derisively and mockingly claps the man for being such a 'good citizen'.

An interesting set of interactions were also witnessed between watchers and watched in schemes where cameras were supplemented with audio appendages. Attached microphones added a means of communicative efficacy in the projective expression of telegovernance, equipping camera operators with capacities to scan visually and address verbally the watched as they became the subjects of attention:

Camera Operator 17 notices two young males kicking a football to each other along a station platform. He presses the tannoy button enabling him to verbally address the two: 'Stop kicking that football about!' Evidently shocked at the disembodied oral command, one of the boys picks up the football while the other sticks two fingers up at the camera.

We're frequently using the audio address system to tell people, especially groups of kids or school children, to get away from the edge of the platform. Usually it's enough just to say that they are being watched and videoed on CCTV, but some of them just deliberately ignore us. What I normally do then is inform them that the police are on their way and that they will get picked up if they don't do as they're told.

(Camera Operator 33)

A number of school children are capering near the platform edge, prompting a camera operator to announce over the speaker: 'Please get back from the line, or we will call British Transport Police.' The children swiftly recede and station order is restored.

Although camera operators are detached physically from the objects of their gaze, it is apparent that this distancing does not debar them from forging relatively meaningful attachments with what is intimately magnified. The interpersonal reciprocations contingent on monitoring and street practices are particularly perceptible when the playful games of cat and mouse enacted between watchers and watched are analytically contemplated. The following narratives and episodes pertinently evince the *relational* character of supervisory circulations as catalysed by the camera medium:

If they [known miscreants] see us looking at them [through the cameras], they'll often wave back at us, or gesticulate ... It's all in good humour. Sometimes when they're pissed off that we've spotted them, we'll deliberately follow them from camera to camera until they see the funny side and cheer up! Passes the time, you know.

(Camera Operator 3)

Flicking through the cameras, Camera Operator 3 recognises an individual notorious for shoplifting and other property offences, and tells me affectionately that she likes this particular male because, 'He's harmless and he commits so many shoplifting offences every day, that he often doesn't know what he's wanted for! So we follow him on the cameras until he sees them move and gets paranoid thinking that the police are after him and tries to hide ... I've seen him run all the way up the street in tears ... It amuses us!'

Where's Benny been hiding? Haven't seen him for a while. Kinda miss not having him around, trying to get one over us. We used to play hide and seek games with him around the graveyard as he tried to either dump or pick up stolen items.

(Camera Operator 9)

Yeah he's a real character, we always get a laugh with him.

(Camera Operator 6)

He's ['Neil'] one of those who loves to think he's important [i.e. notorious] and often plays hide and seeks games with us on the cameras. He really gets off on thinking that we're following him all the time on the cameras, and that we're interested in him. I suppose it makes him feel important. I think he likes boasting to his mates that he's made a name for himself among the police and is 'well known' and 'respected' in the city [by criminals] when in actual fact, he's just a bloody pest, who starts crying every time he's picked up.

(Camera Operator 5)

I much prefer dayshift as there is generally much more going on even if it maybe isn't so explosive. I mean, I quite enjoy trying to locate and follow the shoplifters and all the games we play with them. It's quite good fun.

(Camera Operator 4)

You do get some interesting requests when you're working in here. I remember once when I got this hysterical woman who called us to say that she had left her baby on the train by accident. I got the train stopped at the next station and there was no child found on the train after a detailed search – it turned out that her baby was actually safe and well with relatives. I think when she said 'baby' she was referring to her boyfriend as the police ended up escorting some fella off! Don't think the other passengers were too amused, as they ended up being delayed by half an hour!

(Camera Operator 34)

It is apparent in each of the above empirical examples that the camera circuitry functions as a para-social contact point for watchers and watched to engage in telemediated interaction rituals. These rituals, of course, are circumscribed and encompass a disparity in terms of who is seen and who is unseen, who is spectacle and who is spectator, and what is known and what is unknown. Although some of these sequences transpire only in the imagination and consciousness of the individual camera operators, they nevertheless elucidate the personalisation of visibility-visuality interfacing, the social meanings and reciprocations attendant on watching practices and experiences. Far from being inanimate things, CCTV circuitries are steeped in relations of sociality. They act as vicarious 'contact points' that inspire normative, albeit contextually restricted, instances of social action. They imbue the theatre of the street with a spectra of socially situated perceptions and meanings. They bind categories of discrete publics into intricate relational entanglements, composite social entwinements that have a resonance transcendent of the insentient infrastructures that provide the conditions for their becoming. It is evident that the experience of watching – and of being watched – is generative of affective states, symbolic labels and expressive behaviours. It embodies opportunities for complex quasi-relationships to emerge between a watched performer and a watching audience, for impressions of visibility to marinate the interiorised territories of both. While the camera mechanism patently distorts conventional face-to-face social protocol, it nonetheless facilitates other types of attention seeking, attention evasion and attention responsiveness. It acts as a point of mediation for the co-production of behavioural repertoires and interpretive renditions. It extends a further ambivalence to characterisations of street life from above and from below.

Spectacle enchantment: the seduction of watching

Contact points: para-social personalisation and familiarisation

Intently regarding depersonalised televisualised spectacles to sense suspicious motions and to detect disorderly rhythms is an arduous undertaking. The initial appeal of voyeuristic stimulation steadily dissipates as one is swiftly assimilated into labour process routines and corresponding feelings of disenchantment. While each shift in a CCTV monitoring room has the potential for visual unpredictability and visceral spontaneity in terms of viewing content, dedicated watching rituals typically involve scanning monitor screens and listening to radio messages for hours on end in the faint hope of spotting an abnormality – an expression of strangeness in the monolith of mundanity. Monotony and tedium are familiar companions in the daily grind of watching. Relentlessly scanning the silhouettes of anonymous things and musing on their likely bearings, inclines the camera operators to engage in actions that help them alleviate the de-personal aspects of the job and cope with the long durations of time they spend profiling motionalities in the search for unusual transits or risky indicators. This entails exerting resources that allow for meaning to be speculatively projected onto visual stimuli. It is particularly apparent from observing the camera operators in situ that hermeneutical narration is one such device. This interpretive storytelling expedient brings significance and definition to what are predominantly vistas of partialness or ambiguity. It is utilised purposefully and inventively for interfacing with transmuting visualisations (i.e. visualities stripped of context) and for breaching serial repetitiveness (i.e. visualities devoid of originality). Visibility making evinces core facets of the self, as a territory that has been inscribed with obdurate values and as a territory that is perpetually transforming in nature and scope. Paralleling the practices of mainstream television and cinematic audiences (Hill 2005), camera operators construe and ethnomethodologically arrange what they see via their own subjective inscriptions, as women, as young people, as white persons, as class referents, as parents, as citizens, as incapacitants, as believers, as consumers, etc. It is these contrasting social filters and systems of knowledge that both mediate *and* influence what is caught on camera and how it is subjectively profiled and processed. As there is no official criteria for objectively directing attention, or for determining dubiousness, cameras operators develop their own situated models, templates that reflect and extend their particular attitudinal orientations and biographical experiences. They imaginatively construct identities for the subjects they watch and furnish the unfolding action with a range of creative commentaries:

The time is around 11:30pm, and two camera operators are watching a woman who, it has been suggested, 'looks like ET dressed up'. The woman, no more than five feet in height and in her early fifties, appears to have had too much to drink and is currently walking along the street unaccompanied ... A short time later, one of the camera operators comes back into the room asking where and how 'ET' is.

What I do [when bored] is make up stories for people I watch on the cameras and call them names.

(Camera Operator 1)

Whilst looking at the pedestrian zone at the rear of a major shopping centre, Camera Operator 12 watches two boys around eight or nine years old for a number of minutes, one of whom is doing gymnastic cartwheels on the street. His mother appears to be in one of the public telephone boxes making a call: 'He's pretty good at the first two or three, although by about the seventh one in a row his shape is struggling a bit. It's more horizontal as opposed to vertical. Not sure if he'd win a gold medal for that one! Ha-ha!'

Camera Operator 12's attention is drawn to a young male of relatively short stature apparently arguing with a nightclub doorman. It would appear that he has been ejected from the club and wishes to re-enter. The young male squares up to the doorman, but decides to step back a few paces when a second doorman joins his colleague. Half jokingly, and orientated towards the screen, the camera operator advises: 'Just walk *away ... just get in a taxi, mate, and head home. You're never going to win this fight ... He'd never do that if he was sober.' The observed male walks towards the car park directly adjacent to the club and sits on the wall while making a call on his mobile phone. 'What he needs is for his girlfriend to come out and for them both just to leave and get a taxi home.'*

I did get some entertainment last night. I saw a group of seagulls in the middle of the road feeding on some leftover food. This taxi came along and slowed right down but the birds just weren't paying any attention, so he just speeded up and went right over one of them. It was really funny. Made my night!

(Camera Operator 5)

These individualised accounts of what is being viewed in the camera's field of vision exemplify how camera operators project speculative context onto what is teleoptically perused, imbuing with situational meaning and coherence compressed visual significations. They impose on what are witnessed as fractured events categorical diagnoses and prognoses: they dissect intriguing motions, displace them from what are unknown socio-spatial circumstances and attribute them with a surmised frame of reference. In other words, the supervisors of the street code what they perceive in a formulation that renders the strange, familiar and the familiar, strange. This practice assists the camera operators to *order* and *organise* what they see in accordance with intuitive understandings that arise from the watchers' historical experiences of simulacra and generalised social positioning. Storytelling typifies and reifies specific versions of reality and affords the camera operators, as a participatory, albeit absent, audience, a vicarious role in the action unfolding. It makes them privy to the 'rhythms of sociality' structuring the modern metropolis. It helps bring a contrived stability to what is perceptually experienced as a disjointed and multiplex social world. To this end, the practices availed actually create an intimate connection with what is being viewed and retrospectively prosumed. It immerses the camera operators in the *theatre of the street*. There is a further function to image narration. Depictions are often verbalised and shared among other camera operators in a process that helps consolidate the occupational culture – and forge a 'team' ethos and shared identity. Expressing anecdotes and anticipating trajectories induces banter, formulates solidarities and expedites shift durations. It solidifies the subjective and intersubjective experience of watching and gives it a nuanced purpose and perspective. It fetishises historic occurrences and vignettes. It passes the time. It can even intensify worker productivity as it ensures that the watchers are actively invested in viewing practices and are attentive in monitoring streetscapes for items of interest. Thus, a fusion of the para-social camera medium and work tactics integrates the camera operators into social rhythms of the municipality and systemic rhythms of the monitoring facility (Lockwood 1964). Such points are concretised and qualified in the following excerpts:

116   *Engaging the means of watching*

I just treat the screens in here like I'm watching television. Helps you cope with what you see. It's funny 'cos a lot of the people we watch are like characters from TV, so it does become a bit like that. And gradually you begin to learn who they are and which places they hang out.

(Camera Operator 5)

Camera Operator 6's attention is drawn to two cyclists hurtling along. Suddenly, as the two turn left, one of the cyclists decides it a good idea to cycle along the ledge of a forty foot high bridge! Despite being an extremely dangerous thing to do, the three of us sit amazed watching the male cycle across to the other end of the bridge, before jumping down and returning onto the road again ... 'It's better than SKY TV's extreme sports channels in here' (Camera Operator 11).

I used to watch a lot of telly but I don't bother watching 'real' TV any more as this is enough for me. The last thing I want to do when I finish a ten-hour shift in here is put on the TV – you see everything in here anyway.

(Camera Operator 9)

What we do in here is make up our own copies of things and show them to the team; we've got a whole portfolio of still mug shots on tape over there – we just do it so that the boys can learn the faces and for our amusement when it's boring.

(Camera Operator 24)

The time is 1:13pm. Camera Operator 11 is monitoring the red light area and notices a known prostitute: 'Blimey, she's out on the go early!' A male jogger suddenly stops beside the woman, chats for a short time and then enters into a nearby flat with her. Both camera operators burst into laughter, one saying: 'That's pretty sly [pretending to be the jogger speaking to his wife], "I'm just out for a run love, won't be long", and the boy's off with some prostitute. I tell you what, when my husband goes out for runs he better not be coming down here!' General laughter erupts before Camera Operator 9 makes the observation that the female camera operators, 'shouldn't just jump to conclusions' and that 'perhaps the fellow lives there and she was just letting him in.'

All the stations are like mini town centres – [in reference to the people] they seem to be like ants, dashing off on their various journeys. It's just like a computer game in here; you know, with this many cameras and all this computer equipment, that's the way I look at it.

(Camera Operator 19)

The practices encapsulated above closely parallel the classificatory and hermeneutical designations media audiences creatively construct for the 'characters' whose confidences they indirectly contact, particularly viewers of soap opera and reality TV broadcasts (Denzin 1995; Biressi and Nunn 2005; Andrejevic 2004, 2012). It is not altogether unsurprising that camera operators typically position anonymous CCTV subjects, and the divergent roles that they execute, within wider popular cultural frameworks, attributing characterisations to anonymous bodies in a bid to label what they see and to establish meaningful and enduring connections. It is understandable that in the greyness of visualised street routines and conducts, a genus of 'colourful' personas materialise, a set of urban celebrities whose disadvantaged position, unorthodox habits, behavioural eccentricities and regular brushes with the criminal justice system make them prominent virtualised targets for supervisory oversight. Of course, I am referring to members of the urban underclass, beggars, drug addicts and dealers, vagrants, prolific shoplifters, pimps and prostitutes, street theatre protagonists whose actions principally dictate the cameras that are wielded and where they are pointed. For the camera operators, these individuals are not victims of structural oppression, nor are they disempowered points of visibility. They are, in contrast, the *Stars of CCTV*. Their combatant presence made the circuitry possible, and it now makes the practice of watching stimulating and the stuff of titillation. Indeed, without their polluted appearance in sacrosanct cathedrals of consumption, the work of watching would be as good as obsolete. It certainly would not be as interesting and pleasure-inducing. These figures bring amusement and enchantment to what is a relatively depersonalised pursuit, and they present camera operators with an interminable challenge – to capture and log their details and whereabouts on a daily basis in a virtual archive. They focus the gaze, they entertain, they elicit speculation, and they symbolise recalcitrance:

> *Talking about a known individual, Camera Operator 28 tells me: 'At the start we didn't know what his real name was so we called him "Disco Dan" and it has just stuck and now the whole team [all the operators] know him as that ... as he used to always hang about outside the underage discos looking to pick up young girls.'*

He's ['Neil'] a right bugger him. He doesn't really shoplift, but his favourite trick is to block-up parking machines with something and then go back later and collect the trapped money with a coat hanger. Took us a while to catch him doing it, but he was stupid enough to target parking machines in the same street! He's got lots of tricks to make easy money, but as soon as he is picked up, he puts on this act of appearing illiterate, pretending he has learning difficulties and any other disorder that excuses his behaviour. But he's as sharp as they come when it comes to scams.
(Camera Operator 12)

> *The camera operators frequently partake in cat and mouse games with those whom they monitor, one habitual shoplifter and drug addict, 'Billy',*

118   *Engaging the means of watching*

garnering cult status among the monitoring staff for his underhand tactics: 'He's some boy' (Camera Operator 7); 'He just disappears into thin air' (Camera Operator 11); 'an absolute and utter pain in the arse' (Camera Operator 9). Billy is known for exploiting CCTV 'blind spots' when stealing and hiding items, and when making his escape. Moreover, it is not uncommon for him to literally 'hide' behind patrolling guards within the local shopping mall (where he is serving a life ban) so he can slip into shops and malls undetected. Billy's expert resistive skills enable him to steal and escape with vast supplies of merchandise. He even chooses an optimum moment to launch his attack, around closing time when the shops are quiet and staff are either tidying or cashing up; and are thus oblivious to his presence.

It is in this context that 'celebnotoriety' surfaces. Celebnotoriety is an analytic that refers to a process of 'negative celebritisation', whereby certain individuals involuntarily procure, based on their appearance or comportment, a pathological variance of what Robert van Krieken (2012, 10) terms 'attention capital', becoming the sources of intrigue for the supervisory monitors. Conceptualised in this light, CCTV monitoring is akin to soap opera watching, with the urban thoroughfares constituting the spatial set, the urban poor 'performing' as the principal cast (other publics playing minor cameo parts), the high-powered camera facilities establishing a means for para-social relations to intitate, and the audience comprising camera operators and the alternate supervisory threads – or order keepers – in the wider web of visibility. An outcome of this distinctly dramaturgical order of interactionism is the formulation of obsessive (almost fanatical) televiewing on the part of the audience, a spectatorship that searches tirelessly for these miscreants, that encounters their visualised and virtualised forms on a daily basis and that has intimate knowledge of their personal circumstances. Indeed, the constant economy of attention that these 'street performers' unintentionally court fosters in the watching community a certain familiarity; dare we say fondness. The camera operators are obliged to share insights (recording attributes in the SIB and transmitting verbal descriptions across the communications network) and to speculate on the predicament of the characters observed in what often amounts to a customary form of 'celebrity making'. A social upshot is that it becomes almost impossible for the Stars of CCTV to venture anywhere in the city nucleus without attracting almost paparazzi-style engagement:

> The time is now 11:21am and Camera Operator 12 is focusing on a known person as he makes his way along Central Square and then onto Fiddlers Lane. She asks Camera Operator 11 to: 'Check out the state of "Derek"! He's clean, and he's got matching shoes on; can you believe it? And he's had a haircut. He must have been in care somewhere.' Camera Operator 11 retorts: 'I can't believe that's him. That's the first time I've seen him looking like that. Mind you, I haven't seen him in a while. Just wait a few days though, bet you he will be up to his old tricks again. One missing shoe and a bottle of voddie!'

Camera Operator 10 has identified two prolific shoplifters, a male and female in their early twenties, scruffily dressed and pushing a young child in a pram. I am told that these two are the district's worst family of shoplifters: 'There's a whole family of them and they're all into crime. These two are the worst for shoplifting, they often hide stolen stuff in the buggy.' The camera operator immediately warns all ShopSafe radio users that the two are crossing Richmond Street and are currently heading in the direction of a music premises and the local shopping centre. She gives a detailed description of the two, stating that they have 'got the pram out today'. A minute or so after she has relayed the message, a security guard is heard stating that the two are presently crossing his shop entrance. This passing and sharing of information by CCTV camera operators and security guards from multiple retail stores, regarding the whereabouts and attire of the two, continues for some time. It becomes almost comical as the family make their way up and down Richmond Street, on either side of the road, their every move attracting incessant audio commentary and visual tracking.

A resonance of such overexposure is that the CCTV camera operators, much like Stasi agent Gerd Wiesler in the film *The Lives of Others* (2007), can develop ambivalent, even intimate, affinities with those whom they monitor. Notwithstanding the fact that they are formally employed to manage these 'individuals' dispassionately via the disciplinary medium of the camera, to identify them and to track their motions, recurrently encountering their magnified visualisations on screen can prompt unanticipated responses and anomalous states:

A call over the ShopSafe radio system that a known shoplifter is moving in the direction of Princess Street, has Camera Operator 10 quickly detecting and zooming in on the aforementioned individual. The male looks up at the camera as he walks towards the pedestrian crossing before sharply looking down as if to avoid the camera's glassy stare. The camera operator proclaims, 'Hello Mark', to the screen as if the man can hear her. 'What have you been stealing today then, Sunshine? ... He used to be quite cute, but he's got all thin and gaunt-looking now 'cos of all the drugs.'

It's a weird feeling [passing 'known' individuals when shopping]. To think we know so much about them, but they don't even know who we are; it's strange. I mean some of them we have a right laugh with when we're behind the cameras, you almost feel like smiling at them when you pass them on the street!

(Camera Operator 6)

Camera Operator 2 has located and is following a known prostitute/drug addict who is accompanied by a male: 'Yeah that's Suzanne. She used to be a very pretty girl, but she ballooned right up when she was on the drugs and drink.'

> I've managed to get a guy prosecuted who lives near me; he frequently speaks to me when I bump into him in my local shop, having no idea who I am, or that I've had him lifted!
>
> (Camera Operator 4)

> *I am told about the recent death of a known prostitute from a drugs overdose. Camera Operator 7 proceeds to tell me the circumstances surrounding her death and the type of person that she was, as all the camera operators 'knew' her well: 'She was pretty well known round the town. A nice girl ... just fell into the wrong crowd which is a typical story really ... I mean, I know it sounds strange, but you form a kind of relationship with some of the people you watch, some of them are alright. And it's sad to think that you won't see them going about anymore, but that's life isn't it?'*

The qualities that create a popular 'rogue' celebrity character differ depending on a camera operator's social background and attitude, and the spatial and institutional context, but common characteristics include a CCTV star who: is a screen regular (i.e. in public space a lot); has defining features (e.g. distinguishable attributes or an eccentric personality); acts up in front of the cameras (i.e. by smiling or gesticulating at them); has a noteworthy reputation or 'interesting' personal life (i.e. a prolific history of offending or a person involved in complex romantic liaisons); amuses the operators via staged behaviours or evasion tactics. The camera operators' access to institutionally-held databases and formalised (police-security) networks of data exchange means that they can supplement their visual conjectures with biographical knowledge concerning the celebrity's background and law-breaking trajectory. It is not uncommon for camera operators to know intimate details about those whom they monitor: their full name, address and date of birth; their friendships and familial nexus; their criminal records; their love interests; their health statuses and drug addictions. Some take 'star gazing' to relatively extreme levels:

> Yeah I've learnt most of their [the Stars of CCTV] dates of birth off by heart [by habitually checking their 'wanted' status on the PNC]. Pretty sad, isn't it?! It's funny, I know more about the criminals than I do about some of my family.
>
> (Camera Operator 13)

> Even though they've taken away the logbook [which included the pictures and names of a number of individuals], I still remember the faces of lots of them, and you just begin to memorise the dodgers and their hang out spots from spending weeks and weeks looking at certain [train] lines.
>
> (Camera Operator 33)

The personalisation and familiarisation of those watched can impact on decision-making protocols, influencing the course of justice actualised. This

Construing circuitries 121

can entail camera operators electing to turn a 'blind eye' to public order offences. Or, conversely, it can involve camera operators going to great supervisory lengths in an attempt to have a loathed character brought to justice and taken out of circulation – or at least brought to the attention of the police and broader security network. The camera operators' capacities to exercise discretion in the assessment of risk and in determining police involvement are patently revealed in the following excerpts:

> A doorman at Jonah's bar alerts the two camera operators to a male 'begging aggressively' and being a 'general irritant' outside their premises. He asks for a police unit to move him on. A description of the man is given and Camera Operator 12 quickly spots him: 'Oh that's Johnny, he's not a problem. We often watch him rake through the bins and try and sell stuff to taxi drivers and other punters.' The same camera operator watches the man approach numerous people apparently asking for money, before moving on without fuss when they either ignore him or decline his request: 'I'm not calling the dispatcher, as he's not causing anyone any harm. I feel kinda sorry for him.'

> Camera Operator 3 is watching a group of around six or seven teenagers drinking what appears to be alcohol on the top deck of the shopping mall. She watches them for a few moments and I ask her whether CCTV report such activities: 'Nah, 'cos for one thing the police don't have the resources to lift them or get rid of their alcohol, and they're not exactly causing any trouble or bother to anyone standing in the bandstand. They're always up there, that is their hangout spot. I mean, if they're not causing anybody any trouble, it would be a shame to spoil their fun ... The shopping centre is always harping on to us about it, saying that the kids are a real problem and frequently misbehave and take part in petty crime against their customers and staff, but the police want them to produce stats before they take any action as they haven't received any complaints from any members of the public. Yeah, we've had a few arguments in our time with the guards and management in the mall about the kids on the roof. We just ignore them now.'

> The time is 20:30pm and Camera Operator 8 is on general scanning duty when she spots someone getting out of a car: 'I'm sure that's Scott.' She asks Camera Operator 17 to check the PNC to see whether there is an arrest warrant out for the male before stating: 'I really hope he is wanted for something ... I really hate him, he's a nasty piece of work.' Camera Operator 17 says jokingly that she thinks Camera Operator 8 has a personal vendetta against the man: 'She's always after this guy every time he steps foot in town, she's absolutely possessed.' Camera Operator 8 responds, 'Nah, it's just he's better off locked up – he's really into his drugs and is incredibly aggressive ... It's where a scumbag like him belongs.'

122 *Engaging the means of watching*

While the targeting of individuals for scrutiny is largely determined by subjective standards, CCTV monitoring is not all about the exercise of curiosity and supervisory control. The virtual intimacy that camera operators experience via street magnification, and their personalisation of telemediated spectacles, when juxtaposed with their positioning as embodied subjects who bear divergent social filters and values as males and females, and who possess contrasting and unique belief systems and biographies, inclines some to adopt compassion as a default ethos. In contrast to Norris and Armstrong (1999), who found the 'protectional gaze' – i.e. concern for a watched person's welfare or safety – a rarity, this research established it as a much more prevalent practice. Camera operators perceive themselves as custodians of the vulnerable and guardians of the peace. This elemental perception orientates at what and at whom the cameras get pointed. It is undoubtedly the case that supervision is 'Janus faced', that is, influenced by desires to constrain and by duties of care, a proclamation that is evidently illustrated in the following field citations:

Camera Operator 11 flicks through the cameras and notices three very young children, around four to seven years old, playing games in a doorway. The time is 9:42pm. She zooms the camera in on the youngsters and continues to monitor them for several minutes. A teenage girl, a male in his twenties and an older woman appear on camera, and the three children leave the steps with the adult trio. The older woman (who is previously 'known' to the operators) is identified by the camea operator as being the children's mother and she continues to watch them as they make their way along the street.

The time is 04:30am and Camera Operator 1 is flicking through the cameras on general scanning duties when her attention is drawn to a single, elderly person walking west along Curtain Street. She zooms the camera in on the individual, clearly recognising the woman. She informs me: 'Dora is a "known" old dear who is currently registered as a missing person and whose safety has been a source of concern for the police over the past few days.' She alerts the police dispatcher and a unit is deployed to return the woman to the safety of her care home.

The time is 11:20pm and I notice Camera Operator 8 watching an elderly woman on her own, struggling with a bag of shopping as she moves along the sidewalk. I comment on the fact that it is quite late for a pensioner to be walking in the city on a Friday night: 'She has probably been at the Bingo or visiting a friend. She's very smartly dressed. I just feel I've got to follow them [i.e. the elderly] to make sure that they are alright.'

A doorman asks CCTV to keep an eye on a male who is 'far too drunk for his own good'. The male is monitored closely along Hope Lane, regularly colliding with people as he stumbles around. The camera operator is afraid that the young man, despite being in no way aggressive, might bump into the 'wrong person' and be subjected to an assault. He is watched for the next five minutes until the camera operator's attention is diverted: 'Maybe sometimes I'm too motherly for this job, but I can't help thinking that that could be my son out there' (Camera Operator 18).

Gender is undoubtedly a mediating factor influencing the initiation of such virtual safeguarding, with each of the above examples being instigated by female camera operators, the majority of whom were mothers. It is regrettable that, at the time, more analytical attention was not given to the gendering of the gaze, and how biographical factors shaped who was made legible and how they were duly deciphered. This lack of focus on the camera projected gaze as a *pluralised* phenomenon, contingent on the observer's social positioning and habitus, is an important limitation of this study and an important topic for future research. It is imperative that empirical inquiries ascertain whether significant variances exist between male and female, young and old, white and non-white camera operators in terms of their viewing habits, and how any divergences might alter the nature and quality of the service provided.

Camera operators do not merely use the cameras for monological projections of care and control. They do not only construct external spaces from internal logics and moral frameworks. On the contrary, these technicians of the teleoptic gaze are exceedingly responsive to their surroundings and susceptible to subjectivated osmosis from watching people in a sustained and systematised fashion as they conduct daily activities. They are exposed to an exceptional diverse range of motions, objects and practices and derive extraordinary insight regarding social grammars. Over time they become expert risk assessors and behavioural specialists. They are socialised and transfigured by what they see. Their identities come to be melded via their subjection to telemediated vistas. The following miscellaneous extracts are typical examples of the 'learned knowledge' accreted from witnessing mediated events from behind a screen.

> *I notice Camera Operator 1 focusing the camera on a woman's pink shoes as she crosses Richmond Street: 'Oh I like them, they must be very fashionable, I've seen lots of girls wearing them.' A short time later, she zooms the camera onto another woman's bag as she chats to a friend on Powder Lane and tells me that, 'I've got that bag. Cost £10 in New Look.'*

> When I go out [at night in town] I never go to the three main taxi ranks, as they're always slower moving than the Manchester Street one.
> (Camera Operator 6)

> *We get on to talking about whether camera operators can intuitively predict if there is going to be trouble on certain nights in town: 'Yeah I think you can. You just sense an atmosphere [in town] even from within here. A lot of it has to do with the weather. If it's raining, it means that*

124   *Engaging the means of watching*

people are more likely to want to get home quicker at the end of the night, so you don't get as many queues and people hanging around outside [food] takeaways when the clubs shut. Usually it means there's less trouble [i.e. violence and disorder]. In contrast, it all seems to kick off on a night that has a full moon up. We call it the "full moon fever" affect.' (Camera Operator 3).

Because the scummers are all creatures of habit, they always go to the same places and areas like the telephone boxes or to the chemist to get their Methadone. There are certain places where they just seem to congregate. You just develop an awareness of people.

(Camera Operator 10)

Camera Operator 18 is asked by door staff to monitor two men apparently squaring up. Although the potential for violence would appear great to the untrained eye, the camera operator refrains from alerting the police dispatch centre, instead monitoring the behavioural dynamics of the situation closely herself: 'A lot of these types of incidents don't actually come to anything', she informs me ... She continues to observe the incident attentively for around five minutes until the man is eventually pulled away by his friends ... Clearly this is an example of how the camera operator's behavioural intuition led to a correct diagnosis of the situation and saved putting excess pressure on finite police resources.

As Camera Operator 11 is pregnant, she has been recently zooming in and making verbal statements about each pram she comes across: 'Not sure I like that one, looks a bit like a shopping trolley.'

Collectively, these kinds of example illuminate how mediated streetscapes act as stimuli and function to perpetually train the camera operators into watching repertoires that inform and govern their understandings of social relations, states and events. They illustrate how complex syntaxes materialise – or 'working rules' (Norris and Armstrong 1999) – that come to frame the normative ecologies of street-based conduct. But they also reveal how watching the street through a medium of simulation operates to discipline the perceptions and perspectives of the watchers. Exposure to distanced, yet visually intimate spectacles, can touch the soul. It can program and re-program the values and belief systems of the camera operators and impact on how they conceptualise and participate in the social world around them. It can educate and incite, instruct and arouse.

Chapter 4 synopsis

A tendency exists within surveillance studies to simplistically equate the practice of watching with power asymmetries and with the operationalisation of disciplinary interventions. The ethnographic examples provided above reveal the pluralistic nature of the gaze emitted, and show how its nuanced projection is underpinned by a desideratum to personalise and familiarise what is screened – to make sense of anonymous bodies and events via the application of socially constructed impositions. Indeed, this chapter has shown how the CCTV circuitry functions as a medium for para-social interactivity, distanced, yet intimate, interplays between performers and their audiences. In response to the depersonalised and repetitive dimensions of their labour, CCTV camera operators engage in hermeneutics of the self. They project speculative fantasies ('fantasyscaping') on viewed simulacra and formulate meaningful identities for those theatricalisms deemed exceptional, salient and/or memorable. In the largely prosaic domain of CCTV monitoring, esoteric, miscellaneous or atypical performers bring colour and depth to the greyness and flatness of mundane telemediations, and they provide for the camera operators a multitude of visceral sensations. Telling and sharing stories about noteworthy characters or remarkable episodes enables camera operators to de-anonymise their daily work and eradicate the impersonalism and repetitiveness of visual sequencing loops. This practice augments the occupational culture and elicits a discursive context for exchanging amusing or disturbing anecdotes. But it also permeates processes of identity formulation and re-formulation. It trains camera operators to 'see' things in particular luminosities and in specific contextualised frames of reference. Supervisory circulations, from this reading, resemble relational texts, conjoining the real with the imagined, the scared with the profane, the playful with the poetical, the lived with the duplicate, and the motional with the inertial. They produce distinctive scripts which are then implicated in the ordering of territories of space, and territories of self.

Overture to Chapter 5

Having excavated the para-social interactivity occurring between the camera operators and the objects of their attention, Chapter 5, 'Enduring circuitries: supervisory subjection', considers resonances attendant on visibility making, especially how confronting visualisations comes to shape in profound ways the camera operators' subjective understandings of reality. There is a risk contingent on getting too immersed, too intimately involved, in rhythms and scapes of the televisualised street. Being vicariously exposed to the disorderly and disturbing patterns of urban living, the brutality, the poverty, the fragility and the suffering, can easily precipitate disenchantment and trepidation. A compelled gaze can draw an unsettling reflection, and this magnified portrayal can occasion a sense of insecurity and feelings of generalised despair. Thus Chapter 5 contemplates how visceral subjection to telemediated spectacles can agitate the self and refashion ways of gauging social life.

5 Enduring circuitries
Supervisory subjection

> The jury at the Old Bailey saw Mr Osman being punched, stamped on and stabbed 20 times on a Saturday night in January last year. Brian Finucane QC, prosecuting, said: 'I warn you, you are going to see [CCTV] footage of this young boy being murdered.' The court watched in silence as youths carrying wooden bats, bottles, hammers and knives assaulted Mr Osman. He was left rolling about in the road as his attackers ran off ... [1]

The epigraph above conveys the brutal dimensions of watching theatres of the street from behind a camera lens. It illustrates precisely what types of visualised spectacle CCTV camera operators must process as they habitually search for social disturbances. Monitoring duties expose them to a taxonomy of trauma items. They bear witness to prostitution, homelessness, drug addiction, alcoholism, shoplifting, heated disputes, assault, robbery, murder, suicide and terrorism, and must visually endure the effects of fires, road traffic accidents and environmentally produced catastrophes. For all its tedious, strenuous and distressing components, it would not be an exaggeration to claim that CCTV operation is emotionally intensive work. It involves fixing a gaze upon the unruly ends of social relations and the darker sides of human nature. Despite its prominence and salience in this occupational field, researchers of CCTV – and surveillance scholars more generally – have hitherto paid insufficient attention to the socio-psychological turbulences associated with supervisory operativity, particularly the affective tonalities arising from intermittent sensorial subjection to mediated reflections depicting tribulation and desperation. Indeed, the 'work of watching' – of enduring circuitries of supervision as a background and passive visual profiler – has been inadequately foregrounded in analyses. Instead, there remains a bias toward the dispassionate observer who wields and accrues disciplinary power from an impersonal stare and asymmetrical gaze (Foucault 1977). It is the related notions of unidirectionalism and instrumentalism that I wish to problematise in this chapter, by explicating the visceral dimensions of camera work – of encountering the reflected spectacle as a spectator experience. Particular attention is given to the *retrojective* and prism-like properties of CCTV circuitries, their capacity as mediums to reflect the vital and the brutal proportions of urbanism, as a milieu of socio-economic advantage and disadvantage. They display imagery that affect the camera operators' territories of self and senses of stability. Indeed, teleoptic and telemediated contact with situations of uncertainty, disorder and harm has profound subjective resonances. It impacts on how camera operators perceive themselves and how they conceptualise the ethics and morality of the world around them. It prompts them to cast a cynical gaze upon the theatre of the street (with its contrasting riskscapes) which, of course, duly beams back a reifying reflection. In the face of adverse sentiments, and in order to execute their various social roles as embodied subjects, camera operators experience internal and external pressures to engage in self work, in fortifying territories of the self from outside disturbances that threaten its very structural constitution and solidity. In other words, we probe the subjectivating features of supervision and visibility – not from the viewpoint of the watched but instead from the experiential depths of the watcher.

To date, insufficient empirical consideration has been given to the following substantive questions: how do screened images impact on the watchers' sense of self-identity and what corollary behaviours might they motivate? What is the emotional significance of being positioned as an impotent presence in telemediated action? How might territories of the self defend against external incursion via coping interventions? This chapter will address these issues by exploring critically how camera operators relationally interface with telemediated imagery and how they decode the semiotics of disorderly rhythms. It shows how the intimate scenes of mediated unruliness and wretchedness are not denied or restrained by the onlookers. In contrast, they intuitively inform camera operator reasoning and they reveal the inherent precariousness of the social order. Such sequences operate to structure the perceptual attitudes and subjective identities of those whom they contact. The chapter unveils an important paradox. Installed as measures to securitise spatialised territories of the social, it evinces how CCTV circuitries in fact insecuritise spatialised territories of the self. As such, we challenge conventional preoccupations with the power being projected from within, rather than from without, the 'black box'.

Affective labour: managing emotionality and caring for the self

Sociologists typically perceive affective sensations and emotional states as having *social* origins, as being socially located, and important drivers of social relations and social change (Franks and McCarthy 1989; Barbalet 2002; Turner and Stets 2005; Tenhouten 2007). Such experiences, it is argued, emerge as a result of micro-level conditioning and macro-level civilising processes and play an influential role in determining the relational structure and intersubjectivity of the interaction order (Goffman 1967; Bendelow and Williams 1998). Sociological interest in emotionality has spread to encompass the systematic study of organisations and technologies, and the role of these actants in structuring emotional experiences and placing performative demands upon users (Hochschild 1983; Fineman 2003; Bolton 2005). As Fineman (1993, 1) writes:

> Emotions are within the texture of organising. They are intrinsic to social order and disorder, working structures, conflict, influence, conformity, posturing, gender, sexuality and politics. They are products of socialisation and manipulation. They work mistily within the human psyche, as well as obviously in the daily ephemera of organisational life.

One strand of the literature focuses on how emotionality is increasingly a site of marketisation, and how emotional intelligence and staged affectivity are courted by neoliberalised corporations (the call centre being the classic exemplar), and utilised as marketable resources by a range of neoliberalised workers (Hardt and Negri 2000, 108). In a now classic treatise of this issue, Arlie R. Hochschild (1983) proposes the term 'emotional labour' as a means to conceptualise the ways in which employers commercialise feeling and exploit the emotional resources of employees, e.g. by demanding that the latter 'deep' and 'surface' act as a way of sustaining internal coherency and externalising socially appropriate performative scripts. The rationality for this activity is the economic primacy placed by the service sector on customer relations management, on ensuring that mutually profitable interactions occur between employees and patrons. From this perspective, 'labour' refers to productivity in self-management and self-presentation. It involves workers either suppressing or arousing a variety of felt and unfelt emotional states in accordance with a corporate program of stipulated 'feeling rules'. It entails the public display of organisationally endorsed emotions and the manipulation of sentiment such that traumatic or awkward incidents can be internally processed and externally managed. Studies of the Disneyland 'smile factories' reveal the degree of corporate training, monitoring and expectations staff endure in order to maintain and sustain their contractual employment (van Maanen 1991). Occupations encompassing the most demanding forms of emotion labour have, for Hochschild, three shared features:

> First, they require face-to-face or voice-to-voice contact with the public. Second, they require the worker to produce an emotional state in another person – gratitude or fear for example. Third, they allow the employer, through training and supervision, to exercise a degree of control over the emotional activities of employees.
>
> (Hochschild 1983, 147)

While this analysis is valuable in showing how employers and employees each marketise emotionality for performative ends, and to service the interests of global capital, the precedence placed on service sector workers, who generally experience direct contact with consumers, and the primacy given to the economic and instrumentalised impetuses structuring this relation, has drawn criticism. Lloyd Harris (2002), for example, argues that the emotional labour concept needs adaptation so that the relatively neglected practice of emotional suppression by, for example, legal professionals can be better represented. In addition, Sharon Bolton (2005) asserts that the 'emotional labour' concept has become overused and infused with divergent meanings. She contends that it presupposes the structural power of organisations to dominate territories of the self and it naively assumes that workers are 'emotional dopes' and 'systemic puppets', rather than theatrically skilled social actors capable of subverting organisationally structured etiquettes of emotionality. She claims that the concept presently ignores the differing types of emotional labour performed by workers in different vocations and it fails to account for:

> ... the public and private faces of emotion management: emotional labour appropriated by organisations for commercial gain, emotion in labour performed by professionals as a means of carrying out difficult tasks and emotion work used in interaction with colleagues or the extra emotion work which may be offered as a 'gift' to customers, clients or colleagues.
> (Bolton 2005, 63)

Bolton proposes an analytical overhaul of the term into four overlapping categories: *prescriptive*, i.e. emotion management according to organisational and professional rules of conduct; *pecuniary*, i.e. emotion management for commercial ends; *presentational*, i.e. emotion management according to general social feeling rules; and *philanthropic*, i.e. emotion manipulation for altruistic gift giving. This approach epitomises a more ethnomethodologically informed theorisation of emotion management as a technique of *self work*. This involves repertoires of self manipulation less to present appropriate dramaturgical performances to a watching client base, than to manage precipitated feelings from rupturing or paralysing its territories. It is a response by self-technicians to the pressures, fluctuations and uncertainties contingent on the proliferation of immaterial labour (Hardt and Negri 2000). That is to say, 'self work' contrasts with the emotional labour trope by its referring to the key emotional measures – ethnomethodological and hermeneutical – exploited by actors to ensure that their inner feelings are in sync with self desiderata for security, coherency and stability. Although self work is patently shaped by the structural contexts in which workers are socially embedded, it is less an activity dictated by commercial imperatives than an ethical procedure to restore order and balance to the self during processes of social flux and situational awkwardness. It is, in other words, part of a subject's responsibility to *care for the self*, preserve its intelligibility in the face of social transformations and conditions of variability. Caring for the self, as Foucault (2001, 11) notes, involves a sequence of actions – or practices – that are 'exercised by the self on the self' and 'by which one takes responsibility for oneself and by which one changes, purifies, transforms, and transfigures oneself'.

I would like to suggest in the following sections that CCTV camera operators, as self and spatial technicians, engage in interconnected processes of emotion management and self work. Emotion management refers to system-imposed requirements for camera operators to control their emotionality (through suppression) for instrumental-rational ends. Self work refers to self-imposed requirements to manipulate emotionality (through suppression and expression) for subjective and value-rational ends. Via the medium of the camera circuitry and in order to perform their role proficiently, these supervisory workers are externally and internally compelled to detect disturbing outlooks while remaining impassively composed. This is so that incidences of disorder are competently captured on camera as conclusive evidence and that instructive briefs can be effectually conveyed to proximate figures of authority on the ground. Delivering capable services to the employer and fulfilling duties to the self demands that a range of coping strategies are creatively and systematically drawn upon to help process what is witnessed and to prevent stressors from interfering with recesses of interiority. Thus, what follows in the chapter indicates how the CCTV circuitry black box is infused in discomforting sentiment. It excavates the degree to which camera operators partake in emotion managing protocols (for professional imperatives) and in self work rituals (for subjective imperatives), and it elucidates the rationalities for such action. It reveals the work of watching to be an activity that is as much about the management of external space as the management of internal space – so that consistent orders can be perceived and maintained in both perceptual lifeworlds. Camera operators require to be sensitised to the self and desensitised to the fields of vision that capture and visualise streetlife in its various manifestations.

Spectacle disenchantment: the work of watching

Gauging disorderly rhythms

> Some of the things we see and have to deal with are horrendous. Really quite traumatic. I've seen guys committing suicide right in front of my eyes, and people being stabbed and beaten unconscious. It's just one of those jobs where you're always looking at the nastier sides of life. You just never know quite what you are going to face next.
>
> (Camera Operator 2)

As is evident from the respondent's harrowing narration, the camera operators' role as symbolic custodians of the social order involves them routinely interfacing with telemediated riskscapes and scenes of disruption. This is the currency on which their trade was founded, and continues to depend. They are, of course, contracted not to detect harmonic aesthetics but to sense disorderly imminence and unruly incidents. It is in the very fine print of what they do and who they are. As such, via the visual simulacra that the camera circuitry exposes and presents, these social order supervisors are brought into indirect contact with the anarchic consequences of socio-structural inequities (i.e. the poverty, the squalor, the violence, the suffering and the excess), and with the harrowing eventualities instigated by random forces of nature. As impotent bystanders they find themselves either implicated in explosive scenes of conflict or privy to profound moments of despair:

> Everything you can imagine I've seen, from traffic accidents to murder. I don't think anything prepares you for seeing someone die in front of your very eyes, you've just gotta find your own way of dealing with it.
>
> (Camera Operator 7)

> *Two males begin throwing wild punches at one another, resulting in one of them being knocked backwards onto the road, before being struck by a passing car. Camera Operator 1, who has been filming the incident while waiting for the police to arrive, shouts out in shock, 'Oh my God.' The car stops and a number of individuals from the group run to the male who is now slumped over the pavement ... Camera Operator 1 turns to Camera Operator 16 and proclaims, 'It's gonna be one of those nights.'*

> Helping in suicide inquiries is a fundamental part of our job. What usually happens is that we'll receive an emergency call from the police, a train company or a member of the public that there has been a potential suicide at either a station or along a route and we will immediately contact the relevant people, the police, ambulance service, train operating companies and the coroner, and then update the system that the train has either been delayed or cancelled. If the fatality has occurred within the vicinity of the station, we will immediately pull the station up on the main monitor and review the footage to try and piece together exactly what happened, you know, whether there are any suspicious circumstances, like if the casualty was running away from individuals, whether he or she was pushed, fell over or tripped, or intentionally jumped. We will try and ascertain as quickly as possible with the use of the cameras whether there were any suspicious circumstances behind the death so that we can inform the transport police and they then know to set up a murder inquiry, or the like.
>
> (Camera Operator 33)

> *The 100mph winds of the previous week had caused severe damage to much of the city's infrastructure and the camera operator plays me recorded footage of a station roof collapsing on top of a member of the public: 'The wind just took the roof slates right off on top of them. It's a miracle that no-one was killed' (Camera Operator 19).*

> One of our boys [a security colleague] got a knife pulled on him last week – guy was just absolutely crazy; coppers ended up having to spray him with pepper in the end; was mental. But we got it all on camera for evidence.
>
> (Camera Operator 23)

These excerpts convey the seriousness and severity of what is encountered on the monitor screens. They indicate the trying and stressful nature of observing in fine detail the barbarous and tragic properties of social reality via the medium of the teleoptic circuitry. They evoke the dangerousness contingent on economies that celebrate and valorise excess, and on lifestyles that embody market-driven instrumentalism and intemperate consumption. But more than this, these illustrations demonstrate the capacity of camera circuitries to become technologies of the self: to discipline and shape the viewpoints of their overseers.

The disturbance reifying gaze

Camera operators are recurrently exposed to transgressive actions and uncivilised behaviours, the outcome of which is the gradual sedimentation of a perception that civil ideals of social harmony, passivity and cohesiveness are misguided in an uncivilised and unequal society that is imbued with social problems. What the camera operators visually encounter generates a very different impression of social life, as a structure entrenched in misery, viciousness and marginality. Repeatedly searching for parlous motions and at-risk social bodies means that camera operators are, by virtue of a process of gaze reification, frequently subjected to textual violence. Despite being tele-mediated as visualised stimuli, prolonged graphic exposure to these trauma-infused realities, that is, situations symbolising or depicting the distress of a living being, inculcates in camera operators an acute, albeit distorted, awareness of the precarious scaffolding on which the social order rests. They come to inherit a 'damaged consciousness', and exhibit a set of experientially derived attitudes that materialise from chronic subjection to outlooks of disorder. This mentality envisions the external world through a lens of distrust, cynicism, fearfulness and despair. It perceives social relations as being inherently merciless, untrustworthy and volatile. Camera operators, as a consequence of embodying a work-induced habitus of trepidation, correlate their internal value systems and external outlooks with the labour that they practice:

> I'm just more conscious of people now when I'm out and about on the streets. I don't know, just more wary, more alert. I know what people are like now and what they're capable of. I have just become much more suspicious since I started working here and am not as relaxed being out and about as I used to be.
>
> (Camera Operator 14)

> I mean, you never really switch off from this job when you're outside in your own time. You're always sizing people up and keeping your eyes open … but at the same time, there are plenty of days when I just can't be bothered as it's so boring in here.
>
> (Camera Operator 7)

> Yes, you see it all in here. It's not a job for the faint hearted. It takes you up close to human behaviour and you learn a lot about how dark and nasty people can be. I'm far less trusting than I used to be since working in here. I've seen people steal from the really vulnerable and it makes you see what kind of world we live in.
>
> (Camera Operator 10)

> At any one time we're usually three or four camera staff down due to sick leave, ranging from stress-related conditions like depression to more serious stuff like heart attacks and strokes. Problem is, having people off puts more pressure on those operators having to cover, as they're frequently a man down.
>
> (CCTV Manager 2)

As is patently evident in the above quotations, the images from the cameras have impacted on the camera operators' perceptions of trust, altering their characterisation of social relations. They have affected their judgement on how safe/unsafe public space has become – and what strategies they need adopt in order to steer the self successfully through the parlousness of the urban underworld. Witnessing people doing repugnant things becomes the dominant frame of reference for typifying the state of humanity. It gets generalised to the particular, while the particular is applied unreflexively to the general. Indeed, the vistas telemediated via the camera circuitry give camera operators the impression that social life itself is inherently risky and dangerous. The ontological insecurity produced as a product of watching, of peering onto urban degradation, has been so transformative of disposition that there are now certain spaces and situations in which camera operators will no longer engage:

> I worry that my family might fall victim to crime, as I am more aware of the extent of crime and its effects now. I also worry if my husband is on a night out, as I know how easily trouble can break out.
>
> (Camera Operator 3)

> The job has definitely effected my social life. Observing the city centre in all its bingeing glory every weekend has put me off socialising there.
>
> (Camera Operator 4)

> Nowadays I don't go out at night in case I bump into the wrong person in a bar or taxi queue, 'cos I've seen what happens to some unlucky people. You can get a beating from just being in the wrong place at the wrong time.
>
> (Camera Operator 5)

Camera operators are professionally contracted to detect disturbances, and they become convinced that these realities are the norm. That what they ingest through the cameras is representative of social life itself. They become, in other words, imprisoned by the spectacle – it is this vehicle that aligns the coordinates of their moral compass, their sense of (dis)trust of/in the discursive Other. This is, of course, because camera operators are embodied subjects and not impassive plug-ins. Their subjectivities are dialectically structured via their voluntary viewing habits and via their involuntary subjection to the disruptive activities of others. They do not direct the gaze as much as guide it toward externally occurring events:

> This is just such a negative job; I mean you never pick up good things on the cameras. It's always fights, drugs, prostitution or shoplifting, it can really get you down sometimes. Okay that wasn't a bad fight, but it's still a fight and it really becomes like, 'is this all that happens out there?'
> (Camera Operator 3)

Telemediated alienation

For Karl Marx (2007 [1844], 72), industrialised work under capitalism necessitates an exploitation of body-mind energies, as each gets expended in the production of surplus value capital:

> [T]he fact that labor is external to the worker, i.e., it does not belong to his essential being; that in his work, therefore, he does not affirm himself but denies himself, does not feel content but unhappy, does not develop freely his physical and mental energy but mortifies his body and ruins his mind. The worker therefore only feels himself outside his work, and in his work feels outside himself. He is at home when he is not working, and when he is working he is not at home. His labor is therefore not voluntary, but coerced; it's forced labor. It is therefore not the satisfaction of a need; it is merely a means to satisfy needs external to it.

The type of labour Marx describes entails workers being enrolled in projects of manufacturing where they exercise little control over the conditions, machineries and products of production. The way in which a service or good is fabricated (the order of its making), and its inflated market value (its fetishisation), are processes determined by external forces, conditions above and beyond the subservient worker. Labourers thereby are dispossessed (or estranged) from what it is they are producing, as they are not the owners of the good, they do not determine its pathway to the market, nor are they adequately remunerated for their embodied exertions. So how do these classical sociological insights help us better comprehend the work of watching? How might they be applied to camera operativity?

It makes sense for us to consider what it is precisely that camera operators are in the business of making. What exactly are they constrained to fabricate?

Camera operators are social order keepers. They work to guarantee the inviolability of civil rhythms and to preserve harmonic patterns of sociality – but they must do this indirectly and from long distance. This is the crux of their work, but it is also the origin of their felt discontentment. Camera operators scan the monitor screens for disorders breaching desired social flows and protocols, and they capture these in fine-grained detail. Yet, the social order does not belong to them, nor does the machinery used for its preservation; the technologies of vision/visibility. As such, and when combined with the other structural oppressions they endure (e.g. the long hours, the low pay, the scarce autonomy, the uncomfortable ergonomics, etc.), camera operators very easily become alienated from and disenchanted with the means and ends of their labour. This estrangement stems from the simple fact that they have no unique ownership rights nor direct control over the principal product that they are obliged to manufacture. Social order is not a property that they, or anyone for that matter, can exclusively 'possess'. In contrast, it is a fluid, contingent and susceptible entity, co-produced as a consequence of multiplex chains of interactivity. Its integrity is entirely dependent on the quintessence of such intricate interplays. The social order, in other words, is determined by the behavioural compulsions of external others, those over whom the camera operators have no coercive or physical authority. It is the actions of these remote bodies that either conserve or contravene the social order, not the actions of those positioned within order-manufacturing observatories. This truth necessarily makes the work of watching a fraught pursuit. Camera operators, for instance, are often the first order custodians 'present' (in a vicarious sense) at an incident. They can visualise its constituents in vivid detail but have commonly to endure the delay preceding an embodied, order reassembling, response. This can mean passively witnessing and filming any number of terrifying acts without capacity to influence their outcome; without means to intervene in their dynamics. This separation from the visualised action ensures the camera operators experience profound feelings of powerlessness, contrition and dejection:

> You feel helpless and guilty when someone gets a kicking and you can't get a unit there quickly enough. I remember once watching helplessly as this guy was kicking his girlfriend in the head full force before leaving her lying in the middle of the road.
> (Camera Operator 14)

> You know, it's not nice watching a guy getting his head stamped on while you're waiting for the unit to arrive. You can't do anything and it can be pretty frustrating and distressing at times. At least when you're reviewing tapes you kinda know what to expect, you've got pre-warning; but when you're watching the incident unfolding in real time, it's a different story. I mean, I've sat here before and watched a guy jumping [i.e. committing suicide] in front of my very eyes on the camera. That was pretty hard to

take. It's really difficult because you know you can't do anything, but yet you have to watch. It's a horrible feeling.

(Camera Operator 9)

It's really hard not being able to physically intervene, particularly if there is a significant delay in getting units to the scene of an incident. On one occasion, a shoplifter was being restrained for over two hours before the call was answered – I was very close to going to lend a hand during my lunch break. It's hard when you can't go and sort out what you're watching for yourself.

(Camera Operator 18)

Camera Operator 3 tells me how distressed and annoyed she gets, not only with painfully slow police response times to ongoing incidents, but also with how long it frequently takes the dispatch centre to answer calls: 'It's regularly five minutes or more before a unit will arrive to a Grade 1 call in the city centre, by which time the individuals responsible have long gone and we may have a serious casualty or incident on our hands. Sometimes it's just so frustrating we can't do more.'

You just feel sometimes that you want to help out but all you can do is sit back and watch until the police arrive. It can seem like such a long time, especially if someone is getting jumped on or is threatening suicide. You just feel powerless and a bit guilty that you can't do more.

(Camera Operator 7)

These narratives seem a quantum leap away from Foucauldian inspired characterisations of the power attendant on the dispassionate and objectivating panoptic stare. They illustrate the trauma associated with producing fields of visibility with technologies of vision – with tools that function only *to magnify* and *to exaggerate* the affects of marginality, victimisation and immiseration rather than eliminate their root cause.

Despite the obvious challenges associated with perusing disturbing actions without recourse to alter their outcomes, the camera operators receive scant emotional support from their employers. In fact, and apropos the points outlined in Chapter 3, the wider organisational system in which CCTV operativity is nested debunks and downplays the significance of emotionality, demanding that staff instead be almost robot-like in their viewing practices and viscerally indifferent to that which they indirectly contact. Directives are explicitly and implicitly stated that prohibit and/or deny the manisfestation of pathological sensations for concern that they will negatively disrupt viewing procedures. Where camera operators do exhibit signs of distress, these are presented as 'personal' failings in terms of their not being able to erect boundaries between self and screen:

There is quite a high number of staff who take leave at some point in their time here for stress-related medical conditions. But if they can't manage to handle their emotions, then they shouldn't be doing this job.

(CCTV Manager 2)

We have had to sit here and watch incidents where individuals could and have been killed, and yet there's no counselling or support offered to us. I know a lot of people have been off with stress-related conditions and I don't blame them.

(Camera Operator 1)

The emotive dimensions of the sequences viewed, juxtaposed with the lack of recognition that the circuitry proprietor is prepared to ascribe to occupationally derived stress and alienation, compels the camera operators to engage in their own techniques of screen neutralisation; their own distinctive styles of processing. This involves the suppression of feelings in line with organisational stipulations, but also the application of coping strategies that help them re-establish a sense of ontological security both in terms of the work that they do and in the order of social existence itself. It becomes apparent that these coping practices are a by-product of risk work, and are familiar in policing cultures and in health delivery contexts (Reiner 1978; Holdaway 1983; Chan 1997; Waddington 1999; Healy and McKay 2000). They are exercised in a bid to protect and insulate the self from its overexposure to strains of distress, and to forge durable and enduring folk solidarities. In the case of teleoptic obligations, external and internal disturbances are managed through the use of three interconnected forms of work: *emotion work*, *self work* and *camera work*.

Techniques of neutralisation: managing external and internal disturbances

Safeguarding subjectivity

In order for the CCTV apparatus to function at full capacity, verbal broadcasts and visual monitoring duties need be executed in a professional and composed manner. This necessitates that for the shift duration, camera operators effectively subdue any debilitative thoughts and feelings curtailing teleoptic productivity or compromising systemic objectives. Emotions, when they are officially acknowledged by system orchestrators, are perceived as impediments to the circuitry's economy and efficiency, as a source of vulnerability to be suppressed and repudiated. Camera operators, in a sense, trade as a marketable resource their ability to manage emotionality. By the same token, the supervisory organisation purchases impassive observers. As a result of this implicit exchange, sentiment manipulation becomes the sole responsibility of the individual camera operator; it forms part of the labour contract

138 *Engaging the means of watching*

that each party upholds and perpetuates. This kind of deliberate emotion work, expended and honoured predominantly for system ends, is personified in the following narratives:

> The key thing about doing this job is trying to stay calm, even if you don't maybe always feel it. You've just got to stay in control, as people out there rely on it, the people we watch and the people we work with.
> (Camera Operator 17)

> The staff are trained in using the radios professionally and are expected to not shout down them or get too excited when they're passing messages on.
> (CCTV Manager 2)

> The first time I saw something violent happen I was in shock, though now it's just second nature, and I don't even think about it. It's a part of the job that you just have to get used to. You just do your best to capture events comprehensively so that the evidence is clear. I mean, that's our job, to not get emotionally involved.
> (Camera Operator 2)

> At the time [of witnessing something serious], I normally have something of an adrenaline rush, and just do everything I can to get the incident dealt with in the most professional and speedy way possible. I rarely seem to consider the nature of the incident until afterwards. I just go into auto pilot, really, and follow the script.
> (Camera Operator 1)

However, enduring the trials and tribulations of on-screen activity and conducting such exertion over a prolonged period of time can desensitise the viscera of camera operators, and can estrange them from their previously held moralities and thresholds of tolerance. It can reach a point where even the most graphic violence becomes either routinised or celebrated:

> When I started the job, things used to get to me a bit. But over time, you just get used to it and nothing seems to shock me anymore.
> (Camera Operator 8)

> Saw a brilliant fight the other night, 'bout ten guys knocking lumps into each other. Got it all on tape if you fancy a look?
> (Camera Operator 22)

> The first thing I do when I come into work is check the incident sheet from the night before to see if there are any good fights to watch. I didn't

used to appreciate all the violence but it's actually quite amusing now. You just get used to it and it becomes a source of entertainment.

(Camera Operator 28)

Emotion work is not the only type of interiority training in which the camera operators must partake. Camera operators also exercise individualised self work programs that are orientated around private coping; that involve the management of screen and self via a process of preconscious and conscious disassociation. Whereas emotion work is a practice that predominantly benefits the wider organisation, camera operators engage in self work preceding, during and following shifts as a means of self-safeguarding, of assuring stability in territories of the self. Various methods are employed in an attempt to separate work and personal identities and to re-establish a sense of certainty and unity in what appears an uncertain and fragmented external world. They are exerted to resist self-shaping by simulacra bearing technologies of vision; technologies that act on the self in both instructive and destructive manners. These ethnomethodologies of coping transpire in multiplex ways. They can involve psychological detachment from the action taking place on screen, erasure of incidents from memory, utilising comedy and black humour as a cathartic means of processing traumatic memories and deriving self-worth from the part they play in consolidating supervisory circulations.

Distancing and depersonalisation

Whereas Chapter 4 illustrated how camera operators partake in processes of personalisation and familiarisation as a means to titillate and to organise, here we find them actively engaged in processes of depersonalisation and defamiliarisation as a means to cope. The dual enchantment and disenchantment the camera operators experience as they conduct their work evinces the equivocal nature of supervision: its capacity to thrill, to inform, to stultify and to shock. Mirroring the experiences of popular culture audiences that have an ambiguous relationship with what is broadcast on the televisual screen, as well as with the actual material screen itself, perceiving it as an obstruction to total escapism and a comforting safety mechanism (Hill 1997; Gauntlett and Hill 1999), camera operators also endure screen ambivalence. They forget its materiality when pursuing desires for stimulation and recall its materiality when confronting extremities. The following narrations elucidate the symbolic techniques camera operators utilise in order to disassociate subjectivity from on-screen action:

> Some of the incidents we watch are violent, which can be hard to take if you don't distance yourself from what's going on. I consciously maintain a level of distance from the persons involved, and luckily I have never

seen anything bad happen to anyone I personally know, which makes it a bit easier to sustain. It doesn't affect me at all, I mean, you see much worse stuff on the news and TV everyday and it kinda dulls you to the stuff we watch.

(Camera Operator 3)

What you have to do is just forget about what you've seen and put it out of your mind, really.

(Camera Operator 17)

I forget incidents as soon as they are over, they are dealt with, gone, forgotten about and you move on. It would be unfair of me to take all this stuff home to the wife and family. Once an incident is finished, it's finished.

(Camera Operator 9)

I have a technique to switch myself off from what is happening on the screens, otherwise I'd get ill. I pretend it's a film I'm watching, that it isn't real. Sure you maybe identify with some of the people, but you don't actually know them which helps. The camera, you know, makes it all seem slightly less personal.

(Camera Operator 6)

I never come home and sit and think, 'Oh my God that guy I saw getting beaten up has got a fractured cheek.' It's their life, it's not mine.

(Camera Operator 3)

Despite attempts to disconnect what is viewed on screen from what is registered in the memory and inscribed on the self, to systematically and methodically erase incidents from the mind, the camera operators would often verbalise accounts of previous traumatic occurrences that they had filmed. This would involve them demonstrating on camera where such episodes took place and describing in minute detail exactly what transpired. Some would also describe the after-effects of such exposure, especially its propensity to scar the self: to leave it with an impression of trepidation. Both points appear in the following excerpts:

Yeah I remember that I was on duty one night and it was around 10pm when I was doing a station patrol with the cameras and [showing me on camera the exact station and location] there were these two lads leathering the hell out of this poor sod who was sitting on the bench. Really vicious attack, it really shook me up for a while. He must have been punched upwards of ten times. So I immediately jumped on the public

Enduring circuitries 141

> address system and told them that they were being watched on CCTV and that British Transport Police were on their way.
>
> (Camera Operator 21)

> I remember when I was working on a big murder investigation ... Spent several weeks helping the CID [Criminal Investigation Department] piece together CCTV footage ... I couldn't sleep for weeks after that, kept on having nightmares and just seeing the victim's face in my mind over and over ... It was fucking horrible.
>
> (Camera Operator 2)

These narratives capture the longevity of shock and the corollary difficulties of deleting harrowing memories from the affective archive. Despite attempts to rationalise what is seen, and dislodge it from the mind, imagery has a habit of being embedded in the subconscious as a permanent marker and feature of self-identify.

Laughing it off: disassociating through humour

It would seem that the effectiveness of the 'memory erosion' strategy is, for some, difficult to achieve, especially in the long term. The application of humour was another self work technique that the camera operators exploited to render their labour subjectively meaningful:

> I think we all tend to use a fair bit of humour in here, which outside the room may be seen as insensitive and quite possibly offensive. I think being able to laugh about many of the things we see is a healthy way of dealing with them.
>
> (Camera Operator 4)

> *Camera Operator 16 makes a comment about the arrested male's length of hair: 'Gee that's some hairstyle!' and the conversation quickly turns (as it so often does) to comedy, and this time, to Camera Operator 16's lack of hair. Camera Operator 6 asks: 'Are you jealous like?!' to which Camera Operator 1 responds: 'Better watch what you say, I heard that Camera Operator 16 used to be a dish in his day ... that was 50 years ago like! [general laughter].' Camera Operator 16 tells Camera Operator 1 to 'piss off' and that 'at least I used to be a dish which is more than can be said for you' ... From this exchange, I find out that Camera Operators 6 and 16 have previously had a slanging match that was accidentally broadcast over the radio meaning that the whole force apparently heard their insults. This kind of horseplay is a frequent feature in the room, so too the operators incessantly being derisive toward one another.*

142 *Engaging the means of watching*

Such amusement also involved ridiculing and creating humorous biographies for the people watched:

> *Camera Operator 1 is focusing the camera on five males, all dressed in Hawaiian shirts and evidently under the influence of alcohol. She has a laugh to herself, and comments jokingly: 'Oh my God, there should be a law against wearing that sort of thing.'*

> That cop was running like he had a rocket up his arse! Never seen him move like that before, must have been finishing time or something.
>
> (Camera Operator 16)

These comical interludes helped the camera operators cast light on what was often experienced as gloomy and confronting labour. They functioned to bring ephemeral relief and recompense to the work of being exposed to unbridled simulacra, and they provided temporary escape from feelings of alienation and captivity generated by an exploitative and confined workspace.

Other comedy moments emerged either through camera operator interaction and general horseplay in the monitoring facility or via the more 'unusual' situations they encountered on screen:

> Camera operator 1: At the end of the day, if men are stupid enough to go with the prostitutes, then it's their own fault. They're just too quick to think with their anatomy as opposed to with their heads [laughter between the camera operators].

> Camera operator 16: Yeah well you lot [females] are too quick to think with our credit cards than with your own! [more laughter]

> *A call abruptly comes over the radio from a nightclub doorman informing CCTV that there are 'a couple of naked guys' walking along Chancelry Lane. There is sudden pandemonium as Camera Operator 1, who is heating up her supper in the microwave, races back to her terminal to focus on the two naturists: 'Oh my god, they've got their tadgers out and everything!' Camera Operator 16, also laughing as he watches the men on his monitor screen, comments: 'Must be pretty cold out there!' Camera Operator 1 responds, 'That's enough to put me off my corn beef hash, that is!' before turning to me and proclaiming, 'I told you we are subjected to some traumatic sights in here!'*

The format and content of the comedy was not merely light hearted in character. Camera operators also took solace in applying much darker modes of humour for carthatic and restorative ends. While appearing callous to the outsider who is unaware of the intense affective atmospheres in which CCTV observatories are steeped, such humour is core business in the occupational cultures of those working in vocational fields that are structured around the management of disease, dying, death and deviance. (McNamara et al. 1995; Rose et al. 1997; Anshel 2000; Hopkinson et al 2005). It operates as a separation mechanism for releasing incapacitating levels of feeling and for temporarily escaping the thresholds of trauma and impotence that characterise the work of watching social rhythms via a telescreen (Cohen and Taylor 1992). For camera operators, such tactics are likely employed to externalise and share distressing events, and to decouple self from society. As such, the use of dark comedy means that the lightning strike of discomposure can be safely conducted and deflected away from the sensitivities of the self. The following excerpts are typical examples of this procedure being operationalised:

> The police should get lasers put on the fronts of the cameras or machine guns, so we can shoot them all [the Stars of CCTV] when they step out of line.
> (Camera Operator 1)

> *The camera operators are scanning an area for a woman who has threatened suicide. Two paramedics have arrived on the scene and make their way onto the bridge where she was claiming to be, peering over the side to the road far below. On seeing this, Camera Operator 7 crassly states: 'Just look for the black hole in the road.'*

At times, the appropriation of humour was utilised for purposes of symbolic ordering and self-projection. In an environment where camera operators experience profound feelings of powerlessness and are alienated from their labour activities, the lateral bullying of colleagues becomes a way of re-establishing a social order in which they can exercise some influence. It can be imposed to exert hierarchical forms of control in a setting that is all too often permeated in entropy. The practice also functions to bind together certain individuals into mutual communities and to further isolate others. Its existence reflects the repetitive yet fraught nature of working in such locales, and the ease with which emotional drives can breach rationalised protocols that are designed to regulate and direct conduct in the occupational context. It becomes an outlet for camera operators to project their own ontological insecurities onto lateral others:

> *Camera Operators 2 and 7 are discussing Camera Operator 1, calling her a series of disparaging names. I had recently worked alongside the said individual on a nightshift prompting Camera Operator 2 to comment:* 'Oh I bet that was fun, she'll have kept you right did she?!' *'Right pain in the backside that one, she is always nipping my head about something. Got a mouth on her like nobody's business, so what was she saying?' (Camera*

144   *Engaging the means of watching*

Operator 7). Feeling incredibly awkward and not wishing to get drawn into discussing individual operators, I smile and reply jokingly, 'No, she was just keeping Camera Operator 16 from zooming in on all the ladies!' 'Yeah, but be honest, she's a real bitch isn't she, don't tell me you like her? Bet she says stuff about us?' (Camera Operator 2). Again, I have to think quickly on my feet and, using humour as a way of quelling the situation, reply, 'She's harmless and at least she doesn't try singing along to the radio like you two do!'

Camera Operator 14: I wonder if 'Shorty' will be on time tonight. He's been all high and mighty the past few months as he has been acting Team Leader.

Camera Operator 9: No, what you mean is he's been a TIT [laughter]. TIT stands for Team Leader in Training but it also refers to the little shit as he is a tit!

Camera Operator 14: He's the only guy in the world I don't have to jump up to head-butt!

Once Camera Operator 13 and her boyfriend leave the room, the discussion amongst the remaining camera operators turns to an evaluation of the former's 'new man': 'He seems quite nice, pretty quiet though' (Camera Operator 3). 'That's how she likes them, so they can do as they're told!' (Camera Operator 14). 'Where do you reckon she found him then? eBay?!' (Camera Operator 2) [general laughter].

Internalising the good citizen discourse

A final self work ritual practiced by the camera operators was assimilation of the governmental discourse that valorises responsible citizenship. These workers would perpetually justify their exposure to suffering apropos a self-narrative that their actions as 'safety guardians' and as 'street purgers' were making a positive and transformational difference to society; that their work was making an impact on street dynamics and was improving the image and security of the spaces under observation. They felt that their actions were apprehending the bad guys while protecting the good guys. Such a belief, verbalised in commemorations of influence and in celebrations of worth, is suitably encapsulated in the following accounts:

> It's nice safeguarding vulnerable persons, like lone females or drunk persons, at night, making sure they get home okay and keeping an eye on them. I like protecting the public.
>
> (Camera Operator 8)

It's not all doom and gloom in here. Getting the right result is always a good feeling, whether it's ensuring persons responsible for an assault on a Friday night are rounded-up and caught, or playing a part in reuniting a lost child with his parents on a busy Saturday afternoon. It's the feeling that you've made a difference which gives you the buzz.

(Camera Operator 4)

It's just such a good feeling when you get a result, and this is a very valuable job when you can contribute to stopping crime in the community where you live and raise your family.

(Camera Operator 3)

I like chases the most, when you're moving from camera to camera trying to second guess the boy's next movements.

(Camera Operator 5)

These articulations of job worth and self-worth are important explanations for why camera operators continue in their role as watchers. These workers are involved in producing knowledge about social life and sharing stories about what they have seen. They are implicated in the process of 'text making' as viewers and as authors, and thus their reflections on their scope of authority enables them to justify the ethics of what they do, and to rationalise their exposure to harms in guardianship terms. They believe that their expertise and proficiencies are needed and that their actions contribute to the betterment of humankind. And, of course, they can do all of this from the safety of the observatory and from a position of anonymity.

Reclaiming the screens: resisting domination and estrangement via camera work

I shall speak in these circumstances of the individual having a primary adjustment to the organisation ... I have constructed this clumsy term in order to get to a second one, namely secondary adjustments, defining these as any habitual arrangement by which a member of an organisation employs unauthorised means, or obtains unauthorised ends, or both, thus getting around the organisation's assumptions as to what he should do and get and hence what he should be.

(Goffman 1961, 171)

CCTV camera operators re-enchant themselves through regularised secondary adjustments, using the cameras informally as vicarious agents of both wonder and elusion. While camera circuitries are used as para-social mediums for virtualised interactivity, they are also recruited for their capacity to elicit aesthetical pleasures and structural solidity: a sense of order and peacefulness in what seems like a disorderly and turbulent social milieu. Camera work involves temporary escape pathways and 'ruptures' from the adrenalin-fuelled tension, explosive violence and suffering plaguing urbanism. Using the cameras artfully to locate harmonic patterns of the 'natural order', e.g. resting cameras on scenes depicting dew-covered cobwebs, cumulus cloudscapes, still rivers, autumnal trees, deserted beaches, dawn sunrises and other such orderly relaxation vistas, affords camera operators the opportunity to capture – albeit transiently – stillness and fixivity, and to re-establish a trust in the master patterns of the natural order. Such practices enable these visibility workers to regain and reclaim a temporary status of 'ontological security', an elemental, primal perceptual security (or trust in the stability of the cosmos) which seems so elusive in the frenetic chaos and unpredictability of social relations. Paradoxically, the vicariousness fuelling the camera operators' discontent with the social order also helps them locate a harmonious transcendentalism, an aesthetical appreciation for the natural order's structural reliability and predictability:

Camera Operator 12 is looking at the beach cameras, and zooms one out to sea: 'What a gorgeous sky. That is one of the small consolations of this job; you get to see all the sunrises over the sea. I do like watching the sun come up.'

You just kinda need a break now and again from all the fighting and watching of druggies, so it's nice just to have a few minutes by yourself looking at a field of cows outside the town. I think you need it just to remind you that it's not all doom and gloom out there!
(Camera Operator 10)

Camera Operator 15 tells me that, when bored, he 'frequently' checks the weather situation up and down the coast as one camera, positioned at the top of a high rise block of flats, facilitates such a distanced spectacle. In showing me his favourite outlook, he says: 'You get great views of the coastline from this camera and you can see for forty miles in either direction. It's a fantastic scene to look over.'

A spider has spun a silky web across one of the camera lenses. On finding this, Camera Operator 11 artfully magnifies the image so that her monitor screen shows a giant spider's web glistening in the morning dew: 'One pleasant thing about this job is finding little pieces of magic like this, especially when it is soaked through like this. I'm sure we could enter some of the pictures we come across in some wildlife competition, they give you a real close up appreciation of nature. That's the best and only good thing about being on early shift, I guess.'

Enduring circuitries 147

An appreciative aesthetical 'view' of nature, however, can easily encompass a voyeuristic tone, when the gaze falls on the visual pleasures offered by the objectified human body:

> *As Camera Operator 14 is turning the camera, he focuses on the public walkway and beach area and says:* 'Ah, this is great along here in the summer, lots of bikinis out!'
>
> He's a bit of a looker, isn't he?! I wouldn't say no.
> (Camera Operator 1)
>
> *Camera Operator 16 is watching a scantily dressed female making her way along the road. Referring to her cleavage, he states:* 'God look at the state of that. You could park a bike in there! In fact, forget a bike, more like a car or lorry. She must need scaffolding to keep them up!' *[Laughter in room].*
>
> *Camera Operator 22, meanwhile, is focusing the camera on a female standing in the doorway of a late night lap-dancing club. Watching the female for a few minutes as she makes a phone call, he turns to me and says,* 'Phwoar look at that, she has got legs to her bum that one! It's not good for me this job ... it'll give me a coronary!'

It is evident that, from the anonymity and sanctuary of the viewing room, amusement in terms of sourcing stimuli that would enrich the camera operators' disciplinary and scopophilic gaze, was a motive for manoeuvring cameras to visualise the graphic, the repugnant and the intimate:

> *Camera Operator 22 proudly informs me that he has made up a 'best of fights' tape:* 'Yeah these are some of my best captures. Pretty good stuff.'
>
> *Camera Operator 3 tells me a story about a male who was seen snapping a branch off a tree, before going round a corner beside a set of bank machines and abruptly defecating on the ground:* 'We initially thought he was planning to use the branch as a weapon so we kept our eye on him, but it turned out that he just wanted the leaves to wipe his arse on once he'd finished! It was disgusting.'
>
> *Camera Operator 2, having telephoned the food order into a local Chinese takeaway, turns to Camera Operator 3 and says:* 'Do you remember the boy in his car? Strangest thing I've ever seen.' *Camera Operator 2 then goes on to tell me about a car he spotted one morning around 3am which was parked in an empty car park:* 'There was a naked male sitting in the driver's seat; the thing that was strange was that he seemed to be smelling his own underwear. We kept watching him for a while and then he suddenly

148 *Engaging the means of watching*

> squatted over the passenger seat and did a shit on the seat, I kid you not. It was absolutely disgusting. He obviously gets off on getting naked and then defecating in his car in public places. You see some weird and wonderful things in here, I can tell you.'
>
> We saw them having sex just behind there. Yes, we see it all in here, it keeps us entertained!
>
> (Camera Operator 17)

> *A short time into the shift, Camera Operator 14 tells me that: 'We've got all sorts of games we play in here. Our current favourite is "identify the building roof". Basically, what we do is zoom the camera onto a landmark church or prominent building roof, and then you've got to guess which one it is.' The camera operator then tells me to look away and moves a camera to focus on a distinctive architectural feature, before asking me, 'What do you reckon this one is, then?'*

> What we sometimes do is find a funny incident on tape that one of us has captured and then have a game of 'What happened next', you know, like they do on *A Question of Sport*. So you play a bit of the clip to the others and they have to tell you what the boy does next. I'm brilliant at it – call it a CCTV operator's intuition.
>
> (Camera Operator 29)

These instances reveal the degree of creativity that is elicited by the camera operators to make their labour more subjectively meaningful. They show how camera operator derived tactics are artfully induced as a vehicle to struggle with and contest the forms of domination they routinely experience at the hands of the glassy monitor screens and the formal rules under which they must work (see Chapter 6). The technologies of vision and fields of visibility over which the camera operators have privileged rights of access are thereby directed to ends that provide the watchers with at least some degree of autonomy and satisfaction. They get used for informal activities which fracture and pass the time, and they get used to service the desires of those who often feel constrained by the desires of others on the street.

'Creative fracturing' is but another important feature of the camera operator lifeworld. It involves the use of cameras to achieve unconventional tasks. The following examples provide germane instances of this activity:

> *As Camera Operator 9 takes control of one of the newer cameras overlooking the retail park, I say to him that they should perhaps have been installed there much earlier when a now derelict nightclub was in operation. He agrees but adds, 'Ah, they still have their uses, especially when my wife is going to the cinema with the kids and is looking for a space in the car*

park. I can use this camera to direct her to an empty space. I can keep an eye on the car, too.'

What I usually do in the evenings when I'm on duty is to swing camera 8 round onto the car park so that I can watch my own car. I just leave it on it the whole time I'm working to make sure none of them little shits try and break in to it or vandalise it. Gives me a bit more peace of mind y'know.

(Camera Operator 32)

Camera Operator 6 is watching on his monitor screen live coverage of a soccer match. He has skillfully focused a camera on a large plasma screen showing the match inside a public house. He continues to watch, and commentate on, the game for the next twenty-five minutes until it reaches a conclusion.

It's like it [the CCTV circuitry] has given me this great opportunity of moving freely round the city, something I can't really do normally because of my bad legs.

(Camera Operator 20)

This section has outlined the multitude of ways camera operators both evade and re-appropriate the technologies of vision governing their work practices and social identities. A number of contrasting social meanings are attributed to these actions and these normalised activities function to supply the camera operators with some much needed restorative balance. They make the work of watching manageable and they render it a more rewarding pursuit. Self work and camera work helps the camera operators counter feelings of alienation and conduct the work of watching in a fashion that is subjectively tolerable. These practices deter visions from the street being traumatically transposed on the self, and they provide a sanctuary from harmful exposure to the disorderly rhythms that so often appear from the duty of riskscaping street vistas.

Chapter 5 synopsis

This chapter has sought to provide a nuanced reading of supervision, as a lived experience and as a vocational task. It has foregrounded the reflective aspects of onlooking, the fact that visibility rendering inevitably implies enduring visualisations as a passive spectator, the dimensions of which can be disjointed and unsettling. Indeed, far from being dispassionate teleopticians unaffected by labour processes, we have discerned how supervisors are easily assimilated into a subjective perturbative, a way of seeing and a way of being that encapsulates the perceived precariousness of urban space. Despite being introduced as a measure to purify and pacify municipal spatialities (re Chapters 2 and 3), CCTV circuitries make apparent to the camera operators just how disordered and anarchic socialities actually are. In the course of their duties, CCTV camera operators are intermittently subjected to visualisations of distress, about which they can do very little. They overlook the cruelties contingent on urban lifestyles, the addictions, the destitutions, the transgressions and the excesses. Selfhood must be continually defended from disturbance via interconnected exercises of emotional management and self work. Such methods have contrasting temporalities. The former (composure retaining) occurs simultaneous to events unfolding, the latter (trauma processing) transpiring post-event during tranquil moments. Each serves a vital purpose: employment continuance and self preservation. Adverse affective states are recurrently experienced by the camera operators as an outcome of their spatial and social positioning; as a feature of spectating on a scene over which they have no direct influence, and as a result of being expected to preserve a condition that they have no capacity to accomplish. Physical distance from, but vicarious situation within, the quasi-realities observed, when combined with the unattainableness of physical intervention, rouses feelings of frustration. Camera operators acutely recognise that they have no real influence over the action occurring on the screens and they, at times, despair at – or seek to deny – this fact. This realisation of role impotence is accentuated by an equally problematic actuality: that tribulation and chaos are endemic properties of the city and are attributes that transcend their correctional capabilities. The duty of the CCTV camera operator, therefore, is as much to risk-manage external behaviour as to self-manage internal dissonance, to defend selfhood from pathological incursions by the simulacrum. Overall, this chapter has shown the ways in which telemediated interfacing influences and incises subjectivity. In the process, it has ascertained an intriguing irony: that supposed technologies of security can spawn subjectivities of insecurity.

Overture to Chapter 6

The concluding chapter of the book, 'Sustaining circuitries: supervisory fluctuation', touches on the camera operators' multidimensional relations with power as a currency that has contrasting proportionalities when set against their professionally assigned, and personally ingrained, roles and responsibilities. It also brings together the book's key thematics.

Note

1 Cited in: news.bbc.co.uk/1/hi/england/london/6358975.stm (accessed 20 February 2014).

6 Sustaining circuitries
Supervisory fluctuation

> ... I don't know why they are not on but it's just like everything else; we get told: 'Right, we're getting this done and we're going to be doing this' and then nothing happens. It's like the ShopSafe thing. It's the one occasion where they actually said, 'What do you actually want?' And we actually said what we wanted, and they have come away with it half and half which is a waste of time. But see this unit here [the ShopSafe computer terminal], it's been sitting here for six months doing nothing. We said to them that the radios were crap, and that we need better ones, 'cos they keep breaking down. And this fancy new machine was supposed to tell us which unit was calling us rather than us having to ask them, you know, so we know which cameras to point where. But when the guy came up to sort it we asked him how long it would take and he said 'a couple of weeks', and that was six months ago. You know, it's the same with everything, we're just like 'Yeah, well when?' and they may say 'two weeks' and we'll say 'see you in two years time, then.' It just doesn't work out the way that it should work out.
>
> (Camera Operator 7)

The concluding chapter comes in two segments. In the context of issues raised in previous chapters and taking an alternative analytical perspective, section one returns to the theme of discretionary power as raised in Chapter 2 and as alluded to subsequently. By offering a more nuanced understanding of how power is actually operationalised and flows in a multiplicity of ways, this portion provides a further example of why *lived experience* is a valuable resource for analysis and why lifeworld studies provide such rich detail on social patterns and social messiness. Concentrating empirical attention on camera operators' ambiguous relationship with power, and adding some novel dimensions to this relation based on the experiential accounts proffered and practices observed, the first section critically reconfigures dominant conceptualisations of supervisors as 'empowered watchers'. Section two offers some brief concluding remarks in terms of how this book extends analytical horizons on supervisory practices as these relate to technologies of vision and fields of visibility. As indicated in Chapter 2, previous research on teleoptic workers has predominantly followed, either intentionally or inadvertently, a Foucauldian tradition emphasising the *power*[1] of the watchers over the

152 *Engaging the means of watching*

objects of their gaze.[2] Watchers of CCTV sequences, for instance, are considered 'empowered' by virtue of their access to asymmetrical vision and their capacity to influence the course of justice. Yet this depiction of camera operators privileges the power concomitant on the projected gaze and overemphasises the symbolism of *watching*: it fails to see watching as a form of work that demands attentiveness, rule following and emotional manipulation. While these individuals occupy observatories and perform a relatively important role as collectors and conduits of personal information, Chapters 3–5 have revealed that the lived experience of CCTV camera operators within supervisory circulations is characterised by far greater complexity. They are watchers, but also *workers*, subjected to the same systems of productivity measurement and regulation as any other neoliberal labourer. They are also susceptible to an emotive duress produced by the very technologies that earn them a wage. Disempowerment is further compounded by the camera operators' inheritance of a system over which they had no directive input (Chapter 3). For reasons previously outlined, camera operators posess a distinct *in*capacity to direct the social rhythms in the streets they oversee. However, as we have also seen, camera operators avail their agency to render the circuitry they operate into a parasocial medium of interactivity and marvel. In other words, camera operators discover methods of re-empowering and re-enchanting themselves through embodied practices and vicarious means. They get seduced by the spectacle as much as they get disillusioned from its unsettling reflection. The argument developed here is that power within and without these observatories is fluid and that camera operators experience both empowerment and disempowerment via their embodied intersections with the circuitry over which they preside.

In order to flesh out each of these contentions, what follows is brief coverage of the arguments situating the CCTV operator within a hermeneutics of power. While insightful and indubitably valid to a degree, a focus on only the 'official role' of CCTV staff as *watchers* and a simplistic understanding of enhanced vision as necessarily equating to power, i.e. neglecting the importance of how reflections need be processed, means that such claims have a tendency to fetishise the power that camera operators actually exercise and personally experience. This discussion contextualises the subsequent sections where we critically probe the extent to which camera operators themselves receive empowerment via their occupational positioning and subjection to visibility-visuality processes. This section incorporates a re-conceptualisation of camera operators that takes into consideration their alternative identities as workers and as citizens.

Empowered watchers: on capacities for influence

Vision and knowledge

Camera operators oversee intricate and sophisticated camera circuitries that compress space-time discontinuities. As such, they can access multiple realities simultaneously and accrete knowledge from the stimuli deciphered. As was mentioned in Chapter 2, a number of writers have equated the camera operators' anonymous gaze as generative of profound power asymmetries; the veil of the camera precluding the possibility of equivalent relations. Their capacity to scrutinise selected visualisations without offering explanation or justification has merited claims that they perform a privileged labelling role. Interaction reciprocity, it is contended, is eroded via telemediation and by virtue of the fact that camera operators have only an absent (and thus unaccountable) presence in the exchanges they initiate. Yet it is not only powers of vision that are thought to empower watchers, but also their abilities to source and profile the populations they inspect. Camera operators, as we saw, can often access official databases that contain sensitive biographical details on 'suspect' populations. Indeed, some of the camera operators observed had formal clearance to conduct their own PNC checks, to establish whether or not a warrant was served for a person's arrest. Regular involvement in intelligence-gathering operations being undertaken by serious crime units and being privy to their discursive exchanges is a further way in which camera operators acquire specialist authority. They are also given access to the informational interchanges occurring between grounded security personnel. Indeed, as we saw in Chapter 4, it was not uncommon for camera operators to use the radio system to ask whether an identity was known for a particular individual they were tracking. Thus, not only can camera operators profile people in great detail, and construct characterisations from what is seen, but they also learn a great deal about them. This knowledge, of course, is not generally reciprocal, with watched populations predominantly oblivious to the identities of their onlookers and not capable of contesting their degree of exposure.

Defining and editing realities: subjective power

While empirical research has focused attention on how camera operators draw upon subjective filters – biography and social identity – to construct ecologies of normality, Chapter 4 further demonstrated the role of these profilers in social constructions of reality. Far from being passive conduits of information, it illustrated how the watchers' personalisation of screenlife comes to affect the course of justice felt and experienced on the streets. When evaluating claims regarding their authoritative capabilities, the function of camera operators not only in orchestrating, but also in 'editing', reality should not be overlooked. The moment a criminal or anti-social incident occurs in view of a camera, it is the watchers who are entrusted, through their organisationally ascribed professional role as pictorial 'custodians', to employ a range of proficiencies to fuse together pieces of evidence in a sequential montage. This involves locating discrete pieces of footage and reassembling them so that they narrate a convincing story. Despite this practice being susceptible to corruption, legal prosecutors regularly use camera-captured sequences in the criminal courts as 'expert witness' accounts. As editing footage undoubtedly shapes the voting patterns of the viewing public in reality television programmes such as *Big Brother*, it perhaps would not be unreasonable to infer that a camera operator-construed depiction of external events influences the 'voting' protocols of judges and jurors in criminal trials (Edmond and San Roque 2013). Camera operators, therefore, not only possess the agency to construct suspicion and anticipate intent, but also have the ability to directly influence, through visual editing, the outcomes of criminal justice processes.

Expert risk assessors: conduits and gatekeepers

Camera operators, although not scholastically trained in the biomechanics of human comportment, assess visualised behaviours according to experientially assimilated risk metrics. They inform police and security staff about at-risk bodies and they alert those agents to ongoing incidents that require an embodied intervention by a street authority. This often involves CCTV staff contacting police control, alerting them to a disturbance they are watching that, it is felt, requires an urgent police presence.[3] Camera operators are in turn asked by police dispatchers to monitor confrontational relations and to alert them should there be any escalation in intensity. Not only do camera operators act as conduits, but they adopt a 'logistical' role in terms of directing those arriving on scene. Another facet of this duty occurs when police officers, after an incident, contact the camera operators to inquire about what was witnessed and recorded on camera. More often than not, it is the camera operators' verdict that determines subsequent action. Camera operators are also expected to act as police resource 'gatekeepers' to private security personnel. Should a security guard or door steward require a police unit to attend a fracas, the request must be made through CCTV channels. An oversupply in demand, a restricted number of police units and a convoluted communication protocol mean that, in practice, camera operators make their own discretionary decisions about whether a police response is appropriate:

> *Camera Operator 5 receives a muffled call from a bar doorman experiencing difficulties with a customer. The camera operator quickly selects the camera, before turning and focusing it on the entrance where a woman, accompanied by a male, is arguing heatedly with four door staff and seemingly refusing to leave the vicinity. The bar want a unit to move the woman on, but Camera Operator 5 ignores the request, telling them fallaciously that the units are, 'all tied up at the moment, but I'm monitoring your front door'. He does this for a minute or so before losing interest.*

The above examples illustrate how camera operators experience empowerment via their 'background' watching position, formulating their own decisions about whether or not a situation transgresses a perceived risk threshold. However, CCTV observatories are not merely a voyeuristic paradise; they are also workplace settings subject to rules, expectations and exploitative conditions.

Moreover, camera operators are not simply watchers; they are also workers and citizens who must manage a complex set of social roles and duties.

Disempowered workers: on experiences of impotence

> I've had to review footage recently of two poor souls committing suicide. I didn't want to, but it was my turn. It's really not a nice job, but the police need it done to check that there are no suspicious circumstances. You've just got to try and not let it get to you, though it's hard.
>
> (Camera Operator 20)

CCTV camera operators have, as this excerpt exemplifies, little agency to avert their gaze. They are paid to manufacture fields of visibility and to profile visualities, and by doing so, to ensure or *insure* the sanctitude of consumption rituals and patterns of orderliness. They must film and observe despite the severity or banality of the reflected spectacle. The job of watcher implies just that: compelled monitoring of the variable and the mundane, the shocking and the prosaic (apropos Chapters 4 and 5). Indeed, the general assumption in the literature that camera operators have complete discretion to observe who and what they choose is empirically and organisationnally misleading. Camera operators are often *told* who or what to watch, and are even challenged by superiors wishing to know why they were monitoring particular images (and not others). The following field extract was a fairly typical example:

> *Camera Operator 11 receives a radio call from a security guard alerting him to a 'dodgy' suspect. The operator follows the male in question for around five minutes. A short time later, Camera Operator 10 receives a call from the police controller asking why Camera Operator 11 is watching the man ... Camera Operator 11 is clearly angered by this call and asserts, 'There's too much accountability with this job.'*

It is not simply the setting, technology and organisational rules that constrain the agency of camera operators. Their lowly structural position in the wider surveillance assemblage also reinforces feelings of powerlessness. Camera operators are only one component in a much larger visibility reticulation. While being at the operational nucleus, and front line in terms of their exposure to suffering, such workers occupy the lowest position in a social control hierarchy. Indeed, officially and organisationally, CCTV staff have no authority over any of the other contributing cells. In contrast, they find themselves the subjects of external command, being regularly and brusquely instructed what to do and where to look:

> Police officer to the camera operators: Right, just to make you aware, from now on you're not to touch cameras four, fifteen, thirty-eight and fifty-one as they're set on numberplate duty, ok?

156   *Engaging the means of watching*

>   Doorman to the camera operators: CCTV, put your cameras on our front doors, we've got a male kicking off.

The arrangement of camera operators at the lowest rung of the policing command chain spawned feelings of frustration and resentment. The following three extracts provide germane context:

> *A police officer comes into the room looking for camera footage of an incident from the previous night. He describes where the incident was alleged to have taken place, and asks if there is a camera located anywhere close by. Camera Operator 7 tells the officer that the nearest one is 'some distance away' and therefore won't have picked up anything substantial enough to warrant checking the tape. The officer disregards his instruction and asks him to check it anyway.*

> *Two police officers enter the CCTV room and begin verbally instructing the camera operators where to focus the cameras. When the two constables leave, Camera Operator 1 blurts out, 'How dare they do that – I hate when the police interfere with our work. They think they can just come in here and take control of everything. They've got no right to do that.' Camera Operator 16 nods his head, stating: 'It used to be a lot worse. I remember times when they [i.e. the police] actually pushed you aside and took control of the cameras ... It's one of the reasons why I can't be doing with this job anymore.'*

> *Camera Operator 3 is trying to get a unit deployed to the town centre so that a wanted suspect, who had been involved in an earlier incident, can be arrested. Rather than take the camera operator's word that the female is wanted, the police despatcher instead puts out a call for the incident inquiry officer to confirm this detail. Hearing the despatcher effectively snub her own information, the camera operator angrily exclaims [though not over the radio], 'Do you not believe me, like?'*

Indeed, intense feelings of irritation associated with directional disempowerment are further incited when camera operators, in the hope of having a unit deployed, alert the police dispatcher to an incident, only to have their concerns either ignored or dismissed:

> *Camera Operator 8 contacts police despatch informing the despatcher that there are 'four guys squaring up and a unit down there sharpish should stop things escalating'. The camera operator is told to 'keep watching it' and to let them know if things progress. The camera operator slams down the radio in disgust: 'What a waste of time, what's the point? You can see how much they value my judgement!'*

As camera operators are ascribed the paradoxical role of police resource 'gatekeepers' without having any actual authority over the deployment of units, they are regularly pushed into a difficult role as intermediaries, with night-time economy doorstaff on the ground impatiently requesting updates on units which the police despatcher has either refused or simply does not have disposable. The following evidences an all too familiar scenario:

> *A call comes across the PubWatch radio from a doorman asking for a police unit to attend immediately, as they are currently restraining a violent customer. Camera Operator 13 takes the call, simultaneously pointing the nearest camera at the venue, while Camera Operator 2 monitors the establishment's entrance from another camera. A male is being held on the ground by two doormen, while another doorman stands in close attendance clutching a radio in some visible agitation. Camera Operator 13 contacts police despatch by telephone and describes the incident. The despatcher acknowledges the request and puts a call out for a unit to attend a 'Grade 1 call regarding a potential custody'. However, no units respond, and the despatcher has to make three further pleas before receiving an acknowledgement. By this time, the doorman has radioed CCTV a further two times asking for details on the requested unit. Despite not actually knowing whether or not a unit is en-route, Camera Operator 13 responds: 'I've alerted police despatch and there will be a unit on its way to you shortly' ... Commenting on the whole incident later, Camera Operator 2 tells me: 'I mean what they [i.e. police despatch] forget is that it's us who are accountable to and have to deal with all the boys [i.e. door staff] on the network. We're the ones who have to answer their questions about when or if the unit will be there. It's really annoying.'*

Although camera operators might be empowered via an ability to socially construct and define mediated realities, they are simultaneously disempowered via an inability to instruct and deploy systemic resources. Camera operators, like other workers, are also subject to the whims of the circuitry executive:

> *Camera Operator 6 informs me that the operators have a specific clause in their contract under the heading, 'Any Other Duties', meaning management has the power to introduce new equipment (i.e. more cameras and radios etc.) into the CCTV suite without having to increase the camera operators' salaries for any extra work that this incursion would involve: 'That basically means they can put in more cameras, but they don't have to give us extra pay to monitor them. It's not right.'*

> *Camera Operator 1 is told about the new signing-in sheets for staff and is clearly extremely angry about this development: 'There's no way I'm signing that sheet. We shouldn't be getting punished just 'cos of one person's actions ... it's not fair. I'm fed up of us being treated like children in here.'*

> *Due to police despatch being short staffed, Camera Operator 2 has been instructed to help traffic division conduct vehicle registration checks on the cars stopped at their checkpoint:* 'We shouldn't have to do vehicle checks as that's not our job. We were never trained to do half the things we actually do around here. We always have to do extra tasks 'cos they're short staffed.'

Not only do CCTV operators lack structural authority, but, as noted in Chapter 5, they have no control over the social action occurring on screen. Their gaze habitually finds individuals requiring care, compassion and physical safeguarding – that is, needing a proximate service that is beyond their means to deliver. Despite being introduced as social deities to protect the vulnerable via a system of vision, camera operators actually experience a structurally derived impotence. They are incapacitated from realising the very purpose of their vocation. The harmful will remain harmful, and the sufferers will abide as sufferers, notwithstanding first-rate or subpar camera work.

Camera operators are regularly subpoenaed to attend criminal courts to provide judge and jury with 'expert witness' accounts regarding captured footage.[4] Most of the camera operators researched dreaded going to court, finding such an event stressful and intimidating. This is because their identities are suddenly revealed and their positional anonymity is abruptly compromised. Some have to give evidence on serious crimes, others on the wrongdoing of those residing in nearby residential estates. For these reasons, several camera operators reported understandable feelings of trepidation that were contingent on this 'appearance':

> I had to describe the incident to the jury before formally identifying the accused in the dock. He was this big guy and he just sat there scowling at me. The guy ended up getting put away for a few months, and I always worry when I'm out and about that I'll bump into him, and he'll remember me.
>
> (Camera Operator 2)

> I had to go up there in a murder trial and give evidence against the boy who did it. Absolutely shit myself the whole day sitting outside the witness stand … When I did eventually get called, he just kept staring at me. Bloody daunting, I can tell you.
>
> (Camera Operator 14)

> I'm just scared that I'm going to be called to court some time to give evidence and someone's going to recognise me at a later stage. The whole point of being a CCTV operator is that our identities are anonymous and we are hidden from the public. If our faces become publicly known, then our personal safety could be jeopardised.
>
> (Camera Operator 17)

Going to court also involves the camera workers answering questions relating to the 'production' that they fabricated, often pitched by linguistically competent defence barristers. Questioning can range from the broad (i.e. what happened in the incident), to the more specific and difficult (i.e. why, in particular, the camera operator decided to film the accused and not another person in the vicinity). Despite recording the incident in often punctilious detail, the camera operator has, in all probability, not viewed the visual evidence for over a year. Defence teams, however, are quick to plug inevitable gaps found in the camera operators' recollections, leaving the latter to feel that their integrity is being directly challenged:

> It becomes quite hard to remember what exactly happened, especially when you are asked by a defence lawyer in court to recount it chronologically. It feels like they're attacking you and that you are the guilty party ... I hate going to court to give evidence.
> (Camera Operator 3)

> The thing is that we're doing a public service and they treat you like that [poorly]. You feel like you're the one on trial. It's a joke. We shouldn't have to go to court in the first place, I mean, surely the footage is enough and speaks for itself?
> (Camera Operator 14)

> There's far more pressure on us now to capture the whole event without missing anything. They [the defence] asked me questions about myself, the job, the actual incident and the production, trying to insinuate that I had made a mistake or that the production was in some way non-credible. Not pleasant.
> (Camera Operator 4)

The above sections have sought to problematise empirically the simplistic assumption that CCTV camera operators, by virtue of structural positioning within watch towers, have a cooperative relationship with power. They show the experience to be much more ambiguous, contingent on many external variables that are not directly manipulable by these workers. Camera operators experience power in various ways; they are agents *and* subjects of it. They are in the business of exploiting technologies of vision to render things visible but are simultaneously co-constructed and co-opted by the reflected visualities. It is therefore more productive to think of camera workers as conduits of power, as channels where power acts, sediments and flows.

Supervisory boxes of enlightenment

There has been a general, if unfortunate, reluctance among social inquirers to contact the daily operational realities of supervisory circuits and their wider circulations of supervision. As such, there has been a concomitant tendency to ascribe a formal rationality to these processes, to reify them as taken-for-granted procedures that automatically occur above and beyond the messiness of social mediation. That is to say, a focus on how fields of visibility act on exposed bodies has privileged the experiences of the watched over the experiences of the watchers. Surveillance research seems preoccupied with critically engaging 'systems of surveillance' vis-à-vis their technical structures, operating logics and end points (i.e. how they act on subjects), not via their means of exercise (i.e. how they are socially produced and experienced). Yet by abstracting a 'system' from its lived and sentient context and by exalting 'power' as the predominant unit of analysis, it is easy to: (a) perceive supervisory operativity as a mechanised propulsion; and (b) fetishise supervision as an action seemingly beyond social contact and interference. The complexities contingent on visibility making and visuality processing are consequently disregarded, an instrumentalism restricting nuanced understandings of supervisory phenomenologies. Specifically, the ambiguous nature of construing and enduring telemediated vistas as a vicarious witness – how, in other words, exposure to simulacra impacts upon and is managed by territories of the self. *Opening the Black Box* has revealed this relation to be fraught with complexity, reflecting the fact that the camera workers have an ambiguous relationship with the technologies of vision and fields of visibility for which they are ultimately responsible. They have no direct ownership over either entity and experience life behind the camera lens and telescreen as simultaneously enabling and constraining, enlightening and deadening, enthralling and shocking. It provides them with rights while it loads them with burdens. CCTV work both informs and distorts their view of the world, and it influences their vicarious and firsthand engagements with it. The conventional structural approach to the study of supervisory circuitries effectively bypasses and displaces the pivotal role performed by *supervisory* workers, construing them either as 'plug-ins' or as mechanised 'cogs' entrenched within a larger machinery of domination. It purges their lived experiences and relegates the transformativity of agency: their capacities to contort what is seen and to retrieve the means of vision for producing desirable visualisations. It makes invisible (or silences) the work expended in supervisory tasks, and it overlooks relational features of supervisory circulations – the para-social interactivity, the labour processes, the embodied experiences, the affective atmospherics, the symbolic meanings, the supervisory cultures and the frenetic interplays among spatially, temporally and culturally distributed actors and actants. It detunes such noise and expels it from analysis.

CCTV camera operators are an active audience for street theatrics. From this viewing position, the camera operators personalise what is being seen and construct biographies and narrations for those characters and situations deemed exceptional. Telling and swapping stories about noteworthy encounters enables camera operators to de-anonymise their daily labour and to eradicate apathies contingent on experiencing *overexposure* – i.e. on being subjected to relentless streams of disturbing and pedestrian textual imagery. What emerges through para-social encounters and visual processing is the creation of CCTV celebrities. These esoteric performers bring depth and colour (meaning) to the flatness and greyness (unintelligibility) of mundane tele-mediated rhythms. They provide a source of amusement. CCTV monitoring, from this point of view, becomes socially comparable to soap opera viewing – where para-social relationalities are formed between audience and performer, captivating scenes materialise, and reprobate or valorised protagonists emerge, figures involuntarily competing for economies of attention. And yet, camera workers are not always active in their casting as a supervisory audience. They experience profound passivity vis-á-vis their physical separation from behavioural sequences, be they orderly or otherwise, being perpetuated at the other end of the camera. They must endure the social scripts and actions of distanced Others in both their benign and malevolent manifestations. They are hostage to the glassy screen of the monitor and to the mediated spectacles it displays.

  This book has explored the experiences of CCTV camera operators as they inherited 'custom designed and built' CCTV circuitries and attended to tele-mediated social events. It has illustrated both the seductive and enchanting, and the traumatic and disenchanting nature of vicariously witnessing a sequence of visualised visibilities. It has also contemplated the various resonances associated with camera operators being organisationally constituted as symbolic custodians of a precarious social order. It has been argued that the distinctive positioning of camera operators as impotent overseers spawns affective atmospheres, especially feelings of excitement, impotence, merriment and distress. By focusing attention on the 'work of watching', we are able to discern that supervision is a far from straightforward mechanical or technical exercise performed by a collective of rule following, dispassionate and detached bureaucratic officials. On the contrary, camera operators are emotionally engaged in the labour that they practice and they routinely endure role ambivalences. At a professional level, camera operators are obliged to identify risky scenarios, to capture transgressive acts and to mitigate public disturbances via a set of communicative repertoires. At a personal level, they must manage an array of pathological sensations that correspond with the reflected vistas that they themselves harness technologies of vision to visualise. Camera operators, therefore, are locked into a recursive labour duality: social order manufacturing and management of the self. In supervisory circulations, fields of visibility and the reflected visualisations they retroject back can act as unintended traps: they can simultaneously entice and appal.

  The existing literature on surveillance operativity predominantly reaffirms the reasoning of Foucault that monitoring observatories are fields of power and that watchers are projectors of an inhumane, differential or disciplinary gaze. Yet this rationalist reading of power fails to account empirically for how the gaze projected gets reflected, and how it acts on its *caster*. While the techniques and rationalities for supervising society are well rehearsed, and so too the consequences for those experiencing excessive and disproportionate visibility, less is known about how supervisory workers experience screened visualities – how, in other words, these texts implicate their selfhood and demand careful management. CCTV camera operators are typically represented one-dimensionally as discretionary and discriminatory watchers, as bearers of power but not as receptacles of trauma. Yet these individuals are far from dispassionate and impassive in their role as custodians of the social and moral order. They are instead emotional and visceral beings with multiple identities and concerns; these circumstances filtering what they see and being transformed by what is seen. While current scholarship has focused attention on the subjectivities camera operators express at work, and the repercussions of such values on determining profiling protocol, future research must probe the reverberations of supervisory circulations – as technologies of domination (i.e. as self-disciplining mediums) – for the subjectivities that supervisors craft at home and need bear as they engage the lifecourse. *Opening the Black Box* has accentuated the struggle concomitant on the work of watching. It has demonstrated how the gaze borne from camera work is mediated by social factors that define its daily orientation and that construe its retrojected reflection. We have found that what gets seen and unseen is the complex consequence of multilayered and multicellular relationalities, of ongoing processes of interactivity that encapsulate life within a circulation of supervision. We have also discovered that a projected gaze embodies multiplicities of power – powers to magnify and identify objects, but also powers to subjectivate the territories of the self. We must perceive these as mutually constituting dualities – processes that operate at multiple levels of consciousness. The book has forged a pathway in its conceptualisation of supervisory work. But further fine grained research is required to open more black boxes to reveal their divergent and variant contents, particularly in an age when the making and profiling of visibility fields and their reflected visualisations is progressively the work of the computerised algorithmic code; a watching repertoire that is pre-programmable and subject to alternative practices of socio-material mediation. We should eagerly anticipate the results from this inquiry to establish whether or not automated softwares produce comparable assemblages of meaning and messiness, and whether or not they also complain of fatigue and seek shortcuts as a response to the trying and rewarding work of watching.

Notes

1 Classically one of the most contested concepts in the social sciences, 'power' or 'empowerment' in this chapter refers to all or any one of the following capabilities: the capacity of an actor *to know*; the capacity of an actor *to define a situation*; the capacity of an actor *to influence events or exert control*; and the transformational capacity of an actor to intervene in a given set of events *to achieve outcomes or to make a difference*.

2 This tradition dates back to Foucault's (1977) pioneering analysis of the Panopticon prison tower guards, which is still influencing, to some degree, works in the contemporary period, e.g. Fyfe and Bannister (1996); Norris and Armstrong (1999).
3 As previously stated, the camera operators have no directional power to demand attendance.
4 This is interesting for theoretical reasons, as it perhaps suggests that the objective power of the visual image is declining in a society characterised by infoglut.

References

Aas, K.F., H.O. Gundhus and H.M. Lomell. 2009. *Technologies of Insecurity: The Surveillance of Everyday Life*. Abingdon: Routledge-Cavendish.

Abi-Rached, J.M. and N. Rose. 2010. 'The Birth of the Neuromolecular Gaze'. *History of the Human Sciences* 23(1): 11–36.

Adey, P. 2009. 'Facing Airport Security: Affect, Biopolitics, and the Preemptive Securitisation of the Mobile Body'. *Environment and Planning D: Society and Space* 27(2): 274–95.

Amoore, L. 2007. 'Vigilant Visualities: The Watchful Politics of the War on Terror'. *Security Dialogue* 38(2): 215–32.

——2009. 'Lines of Sight: On the Visualization of Unknown Futures'. *Citizenship Studies* 13(1): 17–30.

Amoore, L. and M. de Goede. 2008. 'Transactions after 9/11: The Banale Face of the Preemptive Strike'. *Transactions of the Institute of British Geographers* 33(2): 173–85.

Andrejevic, M. 2004. *Reality TV: The Work of Being Watched*. Lanham, MD: Rowman & Littlefield Publishers.

——2012. 'The Work of Being Watched: Interactive Media and the Exploitation of Self-Disclosure'. *Critical Studies in Media Communication* 19(2): 230–48.

——2013. *Infoglut: How Too Much Information is Changing the Way We Think and Know*. Abingdon, Oxon: Routledge.

Andrejevic, M. and M. Burdon. 2014. 'Defining the Sensor Society'. *Television & New Media*, DOI: 10.1177/1527476414541552.

Anshel, M.H. 2000. 'A Conceptual Model and Implications for Coping with Stressful Events in Police Work'. *Criminal Justice and Behavior* 27(3): 375–400.

Armitage, R. 2002. *To CCTV or not to CCTV? A Review of Current Research into the Effectiveness of CCTV Systems in Reducing Crime*. London: Nacro.

Atkinson, P., A. Coffey, S. Delamont, J. Lofland and L. Lofland. 2001. *Handbook of Ethnography*. London: Sage Publications Ltd.

Atkinson, R. and G. Helms. 2007. *Securing an Urban Renaissance: Crime, Community and British Urban Policy*. Bristol: The Policy Press.

Ball, K., K.D. Haggerty and D. Lyon. 2012. *Routledge Handbook of Surveillance Studies*. Abingdon: Routledge.

Ball, K. and L. Snider. 2013a. 'Introduction: The Surveillance-industrial Complex: Towards a Political Economy of Surveillance?' In *The Surveillance-Industrial Complex: A Political Economy of Surveillance*, edited by K. Ball and L. Snider. Abingdon: Routledge.

References

——2013b. *The Surveillance-Industrial Complex: A Political Economy of Surveillance*. Abingdon: Routledge.
Ball, K.S. 2009. 'Exposure: Exploring the Subject of Surveillance Information'. *Information, Communication and Society* 12(5): 639–57.
Ball, K.S. and K.D. Haggerty. 2005. 'Editorial: Doing Surveillance Studies'. *Surveillance & Society* 3(2/3): 129–38.
Bannister, I., R. Fyfe, and A. Kearn. 1998. 'CCTV and the City'. In *Surveillance, Closed Circuit Television and Social Control*, edited by C. Norris, J. Moran and G. Armstrong. Aldershot: Ashgate.
Barbalet, J.M. 2002. *Emotions and Sociology*. Oxford: Blackwell Publishing.
Barnard-Wills, D. 2011. 'UK News Media Discourses of Surveillance'. *The Sociological Quarterly* 52(4): 548–67.
Baudrillard, J. 1994. *Simulacra and Simulation*. Translated by S.F. Glaser. Ann Arbor: The University of Michigan Press.
Bauman, Z. 1998. *Work, Consumerism and the New Poor*. Buckingham: Open University Press.
——2000. *Liquid Modernity*. Cambridge: Polity Press.
Becker, H.S. 1963. *Outsiders: Studies in the Sociology of Deviance*. New York: The Free Press.
Belina, B. and G. Helms. 2010. 'The Friendly Eye in the Sky: CCTV in Großbritannien'. In *Geographien eines europäischen Nachbarns*, edited by K. Zehner and G. Wood. Heidelberg: Spektrum Akademischer Verlag, pp. 167–75.
Bendelow, G. and S.J. Williams. 1998. *Emotions in Social Life: Critical Themes and Contemporary Issues*. London: Routledge.
Berger, P.L. and T. Luckmann. 1966. *The Social Construction of Reality: A Treatise in the Sociology of Knowledge*. London: Penguin Books.
Biressi, A. and H. Nunn. 2005. *Reality TV: Realism and Revelation*. London: Wallflower Press.
Bogard, W. 1996. *The Simulation of Surveillance: Hypercontrol in Telematic societies*. Cambridge: Cambridge University Press.
Bolton, S. 2005. *Emotion Management in the Workplace*. Basingstoke: Palgrave MacMillan.
Browne, S. 2012. 'Race and Surveillance'. In *Routledge Handbook of Surveillance Studies*, edited by K. Ball, K.D. Haggerty and D. Lyon. Abingdon: Routledge.
Calvert, C. 2000. *Voyeur Nation: Media, Privacy, and Peering in Modern Culture*. Boulder, CO: Westview Press.
Cartwright, L. 1995. *Screening the Body: Tracing Medicine's Visual Culture*. Minneapolis, MA: University of Minnesota Press.
Castells, M. 2010a. *The Power of Identity: Vol. 2, The Information Age: Economy, Society and Culture*. Three vols. Second edn. Chichester: John Wiley & Sons Ltd.
——2010b. *The Rise of the Network Society: Vol. 1*. Three vols. Second edn. Chichester: John Wiley & Sons Ltd.
Chan, J. 1997. *Changing Police Culture: Policing in a Multicultural Society*. Cambridge: Cambridge University Press.
Christie, N. 1986. 'The Ideal Victim'. In *From Crime Policy to Victim Policy: Reorienting the Justice System*, edited by E.A. Fattah. Basingstoke: Macmillan.
——2000. *Crime Control as Industry: Towards Gulags, Western Style*. Third edn. Abingdon: Routledge.

References

Clavell, G.G. 2013. 'CCTV in Barcelona: The Political Economy of Surveillance in the (Wannabe) Global City'. In *The Surveillance-Industrial Complex: A Political Economy of Surveillance*, edited by K. Ball and L. Snider. Abingdon: Routledge.

Coaffee, J., D. Murakami Wood and P. Rogers. 2009. *The Everyday Resilience of the City: How Cities Respond to Terrorism and Disaster*. Edited by S. Croft, New Security Challenges. Basingstoke: Palgrave Macmillan.

Cohen, S. 1985. *Visions of Social Control: Crime, Punishment and Classification*. Cambridge: Polity Press.

——2002. *Folk Devils and Moral Panics: The Creation of the Mods and Rockers*. 3rd edn. Abingdon: Routledge.

Cohen, S. and L. Taylor. 1992. *Escape Attempts: The Theory and Practice of Resistance to Everyday Life*. London: Routledge.

Coleman, R. 2004a. 'Reclaiming the Streets: Closed Circuit Television, Neoliberalism and the Mystification of Social Divisions in Liverpool, UK'. *Surveillance & Society* 2(2/3): 293–309.

——2004b. *Reclaiming the Streets: Surveillance, Social Control and the City*. Cullompton: Willan Publishing.

Coleman, R. and M. McCahill. 2011. *Surveillance and Crime: Key Approaches to Criminology*. London: Sage Publications Ltd.

Coleman, R. and J. Sim. 2000. '"You'll Never Walk Alone": CCTV Surveillance, Order and Neo-liberal Rule in Liverpool City Centre'. *The British Journal of Sociology* 51(4): 623–39.

Conrad, P. 1992. 'Medicalization and Social Control'. *Annual Review of Sociology* 18: 209–32.

Crofts, P., P. Hubbard and J. Prior. 2013. 'Policing, Planning and Sex: Governing Bodies, Spatially'. *Australian & New Zealand Journal of Criminology* 46(1): 51–69.

Davies, S. 1996. *Big Brother: Britain's Web of Surveillance and the New Technological Order*. London: Pan Books.

——1998. 'CCTV: A New Battleground for Privacy'. In *Surveillance, Closed Circuit Television and Social Control*, edited by C. Norris, J. Moran and G. Armstrong. Aldershot: Ashgate.

Davis, M. 2006. *City of Quartz: Excavating the Future in Los Angeles*. London: Verso.

Davis, M. and D.B. Monk. 2008. *Evil Paradises: Dreamworlds of Neoliberalism*. New York: The New Press.

de Certeau, M. 1984. *The Practice of Everyday Life*. Translated by S. Rendall. London: University of California Press.

Denzin, N.K. 1995. *The Cinematic Society: The Voyeur's Gaze*. London: Sage Publications Ltd.

Dillon, M. and L. Lobo-Guerrero. 2009. 'The Biopolitical Imaginary of Species-being'. *Theory, Culture & Society* 26(1): 1–23.

Ditton, J. 1998. 'Public Support for Town Centre CCTV Schemes: Myth or Reality?' In *Surveillance, Closed Circuit Television and Social Control*, edited by C. Norris, J. Moran and G. Armstrong. Aldershot: Ashgate.

Doyle, A., R. Lippert and D. Lyon. 2012. *Eyes Everywhere: The Global Growth of Camera Surveillance*. Abingdon: Routledge.

Dubbeld, L. 2003. 'Observing Bodies: Camera Surveillance and the Significance of the Body'. *Ethics and Information Technology* 5: 151–62.

Dupont, B. 2008. 'Hacking the Panopticon: Distributed Online Surveillance and Resistance'. In *Surveillance and Governance: Crime Control and Beyond*, edited by M. Deflem and J.T. Ulmer. Bingley: Emerald Group Publishing Ltd.

Edmond, G. and M. San Roque. 2013. 'Justicia's Gaze: Surveillance, Evidence and the Criminal Trial'. *Surveillance & Society* 11(3): 252–71.

Feeley, M. and J. Simon. 1992. 'The New Penology: Notes on the Emerging Strategy of Corrections and its Implications'. *Criminology* 30(4): 449–74.

——1994. 'Actuarial Justice: The Emerging New Criminal Law'. In *The Futures of Criminology*, edited by D. Nelken. London: Sage Publications Ltd.

Ferreday, D. 2011. 'Haunted Bodies: Visual Cultures of Anorexia and Size Zero'. *Borderlands ejournal* 10(2): 1–22.

Fineman, S. 1993. *Emotion in Organizations*. London: Sage Publications Ltd.

——2003. *Understanding Emotion at Work*. London: Sage Publications Ltd.

Finn, J. 2012. 'Seeing Surveillantly: Surveillance as Social Practice'. In *Eyes Everywhere: The Global Growth of Camera Surveillance*, edited by A. Doyle, R. Lippert and D. Lyon. Abingdon: Routledge.

Fisher, J.A. and T. Monahan. 2011. 'The "Biosecuritization" of Healthcare Delivery: Examples of Post-9/11 Technological Imperatives'. *Social Science & Medicine* 72(4): 545–52.

Fiske, J. 1998. 'Surveilling the City: Whiteness, the Black Man and Democratic Totalitarianism'. *Theory, Culture & Society* 15(2): 67–88.

Foucault, M. 1977. *Discipline and Punish: The Birth of the Prison*. London: Penguin.

——1988. 'Technologies of the Self'. In *Technologies of the Self: A Seminar with Michel Foucault*, edited by L.H. Martin, H. Gutman and P.H. Hutton. Amherst, MA: University of Massachusetts Press, pp. 16–49.

——1991. 'Governmentality'. In *The Foucault Effect: Studies in Governmentality*, edited by G. Burchell, C. Gordon and P. Miller. Hemel Hempstead: Harvester.

——2001. *The Hermeneutics of the Subject: Lectures at the Collège de France 1981–1982*. Translated by G. Burchell. Basingstoke: Palgrave Macmillan.

Franks, D.D. and E.D. McCarthy. 1989. *The Sociology of Emotions: Original Essays and Research Papers*. Greenwich, CT: JAI Press.

Fussey, P. 2007. 'An Interrupted Transmission? Processes of CCTV Implementation and the Impact of Human Agency'. *Surveillance & Society* 4(3): 229–56.

——2008. 'Beyond Liberty, Beyond Security: The Politics of Public Surveillance'. *British Politics* 3(1): 120–35.

Fyfe, N.R. and J. Bannister. 1996. 'City Watching: Closed Circuit Television Surveillance in Public Spaces'. *Area* 28(1): 37–46.

Gad, C. and L.K. Hansen. 2013. 'A Closed Circuit Technological Vision: On Minority Report, Event Detection and Enabling Technologies'. *Surveillance & Society* 11 (1/2): 148–62.

Gandy, Jr, O.H. 1993. *The Panoptic Sort: A Political Economy of Personal Information*. Boulder, CO: Westview.

——1996. 'Coming to Terms with the Panoptic Sort'. In *Computers, Surveillance and Privacy*, edited by D. Lyon and E. Zureik. Minneapolis: University of Minnesota Press.

——2006. 'Data Mining, Surveillance, and Discrimination in the Post-9/11 Environment'. In *The New Politics of Surveillance and Visibility*, edited by K.D. Haggerty and R.V. Ericson. Toronto: University of Toronto Press.

168 References

——2009. *Coming to Terms with Chance: Engaging Rational Discrimination and Cumulative Disadvantage*. Aldershot: Ashgate.
Garland, D. 1996. 'The Limits of the Sovereign State: Strategies of Crime Control in Contemporary Society'. *The British Journal of Criminology* 36(4): 445–71.
——2000. 'The Culture of High Crime Societies'. *The British Journal of Criminology* 40(3): 347–75.
——2001. *The Culture of Control: Crime and Social Order in Contemporary Society*. Oxford: Oxford University Press.
Gauntlett, D. and A. Hill. 1999. *TV Living: Television, Culture and Everyday Life*. London: Routledge.
Geertz, C. 1973. *The Interpretation of Cultures*. New York: Basic Books.
Germain, S., L. Dumoulin and A.-C. Douillet. 2013. 'A Prosperous "Business": The Success of CCTV through the Eyes of International Literature'. *Surveillance & Society* 11(1/2): 134–47.
Gerrard, G., G. Parkins, I. Cunningham, W. Jones, S. Hill and S. Douglas. 2007. *National CCTV Strategy*. London: Home Office.
Giddens, A. 1990. *The Consequences of Modernity*. Stanford, CA: Stanford University Press.
Gill, M. and A. Spriggs. 2005. *Assessing the Impact of CCTV*. Home Office Research Study 292. London: Home Office.
Gilliom, J. 2001. *Overseers of the Poor: Surveillance, Resistance, and the Limits of Privacy*. Chicago, IL: University of Chicago Press.
Gilliom, J. and T. Monahan. 2013. *SuperVision: An Introduction to the Surveillance Society*. Chicago, IL: The University of Chicago Press.
Goffman, E. 1959. *The Presentation of Self in Everyday Life*. London: Penguin Books.
——1961. *Asylums: Essays on the Social Situation of Mental Patients and Other Inmates*. New York: Doubleday.
——1967. *Interaction Ritual: Essays in Face-to-Face Behaviour*. Chicago, IL: Aldine Publishing Company.
Goold, B.J. 2004. *CCTV and Policing*. Oxford: Oxford University Press.
——2007. 'Privacy, Identity, Security'. In *Security and Human Rights*, edited by B.J. Goold and L. Lazarus. Oxford: Hart.
Goold, B.J., I. Loader and A. Thumala. 2013. 'The Banality of Security: The Curious Case of Surveillance Cameras'. *The British Journal of Criminology* 53(6): 977–96.
Goold, B.J. and D. Neyland. 2009. *New Directions in Surveillance and Privacy*. Cullompton: Willan Publishing.
Graham, S. 1998. 'Towards the Fifth Utility? On the Extension and Normalisation of Public CCTV'. In *Surveillance, Closed Circuit Television and Social Control*, edited by C. Norris, J. Moran and G. Armstrong. Aldershot: Ashgate, pp. 89–112.
——2001. 'CCTV: The Stealthy Emergence of a Fifth Utility?' *Planning Theory and Practice* 3(2): 237–41.
——2006. 'Surveillance, Urbanization and the US "Revolution in Military Affairs"'. In *Theorizing Surveillance: The Panopticon and Beyond*, edited by D. Lyon. Cullompton: Willan Publishing.
Graham, S. and S. Marvin. 1996. *Telecommunications and the City: Electronic Spaces, Urban Places*. London: Routledge.
Greer, C. 2009. *Crime and Media: A Reader, Routledge Student Readers*. London: Routledge.

Grey, M. 2003. 'Urban Surveillance and Panopticism: Will We Recognize the Facial Recognition Society?' *Surveillance & Society* 1(3): 314–30.
Groombridge, N. 2008. 'Stars of CCTV? How the Home Office Wasted Millions – a Radical "Treasury/Audit Commission" View'. *Surveillance & Society* 5(1): 73–80.
Haggerty, K.D. and R.V. Ericson. 2000. 'The Surveillant Assemblage'. *British Journal of Sociology* 51(4): 605–22.
——2006. 'The New Politics of Surveillance and Visibility'. In *The New Politics of Surveillance and Visibility*, edited by K.D. Haggerty and R.V. Ericson. Toronto: University of Toronto Press.
Hall, S., C. Critcher, T. Jefferson, J.N. Clarke and B. Roberts. 1978. *Policing the Crisis: Mugging, the State and Law and Order, Critical Social Studies*. London: Palgrave Macmillan.
Hall, S. and S. Winlow. 2006. *Violent Night: Urban Leisure and Contemporary Culture*. Oxford: Berg Publishers.
Hardt, M. and A. Negri. 2000. *Empire*. Cambridge, MA: Harvard University Press.
Harraway, D.J. 2003. *The Companion Species Manifesto: Dogs, People, and Significant Otherness*. Chicago, IL: Prickly Paradigm Press.
Harris, L.C. 2002. 'The Emotional Labour of Barristers: An Exploration of Emotional Labour By Status Professionals'. *Journal of Management Studies* 39(4): 553–84.
Harvey, D. 2005. *A Brief History of Neo-liberalism*. Oxford: Oxford University Press.
Healy, C.M. and M.F. McKay. 2000. 'Nursing Stress: The Effects of Coping Strategies and Job Satisfaction in a Sample of Australian Nurses'. *Journal of Advanced Nursing* 31(3): 681–88.
Hier, S.P. 2003. 'Probing the Surveillant Assemblage: On the Dialectics of Surveillance Practices as Processes of Social Control'. *Surveillance & Society* 1(3): 399–411.
Hier, S.P. and J. Greenberg. 2007. *The Surveillance Studies Reader*. Buckingham: Open University Press.
——2009. 'Response: David Murakami Wood's "Situating Surveillance Studies"'. *Surveillance & Society* 7(1): 71–75.
Hill, A. 1997. *Shocking Entertainment: Viewer Responses to Violent Movies*. Luton: University of Luton Press.
——2005. *Reality TV: Audiences and Popular Factual Television*. London: Routledge.
Hochschild, A. 1983. *The Managed Heart: Commercialization of Human Feeling*. Berkeley, CA: University of California Press.
Holdaway, S. 1983. *Inside the British Police: A Force at Work*. Oxford: Blackwell Publishing.
Holm, N. 2009. 'Conspiracy Theorizing Surveillance: Considering Modalities of Paranoia and Conspiracy in Surveillance Studies'. *Surveillance & Society* 7(1): 36–48.
Home Office. 1994. *Closed Circuit Television: Looking Out for You*. London: HMSO.
Hopkinson, J., C. Hallett and K. Luker. 2005. 'Everyday Death: How Do Nurses Cope with Caring for Dying People in Hospital?' *International Journal of Nursing Studies* 42(2): 125–33.
Horton, D. and R.R. Wohl. 1956. 'Mass Communication and Para-social Interaction: Observations on Intimacy at a Distance'. *Psychiatry* 19(3): 215–29.
House of Lords. 2009. *Surveillance: Citizens and the State*. London: The Stationery Office.
Hubbard, P. 2004. 'Cleansing the Metropolis: Sex Work and the Politics of Zero Tolerance'. *Urban Studies* 41(9): 1687–702.

Innes, M. 2004. 'Signal Crimes and Signal Disorders: Notes on Deviance as Communicative Action'. *British Journal of Sociology* 55(3): 335–55.
Jewkes, Y. 2004a. *Media and Crime*. London: Sage Publications Ltd.
——2004b. 'High-tech Solutions to Low-tech Crimes? Crime and Terror in the Surveillance Assemblage'. *Criminal Justice Matters* 58(1): 6–7.
Jones, A. 2006. *Self/Image: Technology, Representation and the Contemporary Subject*. London: Routledge.
Kalberg, S. 1980. 'Max Weber's Types of Rationality: Cornerstones for the Analysis of Rationalization Processes in History'. *The American Journal of Sociology* 85(5): 1145–79.
Konings, M. 2014. 'State of Speculation'. *South Atlantic Quarterly*.
Koskela, H. 2004. 'Webcams, TV Shows and Mobile Phones: Empowering Exhibitionism'. *Surveillance & Society* 2(2/3): 199–215.
——2006. '"The Other Side of Surveillance": Webcams, Power and Agency'. In *Theorizing Surveillance: The Panopticon and Beyond*, edited by D. Lyon. Cullompton: Willan Publishing.
Kroener, I. 2013. '"Caught on Camera": The Media Representation of Video Surveillance in Relation to the 2005 London Underground Bombings'. *Surveillance & Society* 11(1/2): 121–33.
Kruger, E. 2013. 'Image and Exposure: Envisioning Genetics as a Forensic-surveillance Matrix'. *Surveillance & Society* 11(3): 237–51.
Latour, B. 1994. 'On Technical Mediation – Philosophy, Sociology, Genealogy'. *Common Knowledge* 3(2): 29–64.
Levin, T.Y. 2002. 'Rhetoric of the Temporal Index: Surveillant Narration and the Cinema of "Real Time"'. In *CTRL [SPACE]: Rhetorics of Surveillance from Bentham to Big Brother*, edited by T.Y. Levin, U. Frohne and P. Weibel. Cambridge, MA: MIT Press, pp. 578–93.
Lianos, M. 2013. *Dangerous Others, Insecure Societies: Fear and Social Division*. Aldershot: Ashgate.
Lippert, R. and B. Wilkinson. 2012. 'Deploying Camera Surveillance Images: The Case of Crime Stoppers'. In *Eyes Everywhere: The Global Growth of Camera Surveillance*, edited by A. Doyle, R. Lippert and D. Lyon. Abingdon: Routledge.
Lockwood, D. 1964. 'Social Integration and System Integration'. In *Explorations in Social Change*, edited by Z. Zollschan and W. Hirsch. London: Routledge and Kegan Paul.
Lomell, H.M. 2004. 'Targeting the Unwanted: Video Surveillance and Categorical Exclusion in Oslo, Norway'. *Surveillance & Society* 2(2/3): 346–60.
Los, M. 2006. 'Looking into the Future: Surveillance, Globalisation and the Totalitarian Potential'. In *Theorizing Surveillance: The Panopticon and Beyond*, edited by D. Lyon. Cullompton: Willan Publishing.
Lyon, D. 1994. *The Electronic Eye: The Rise of Surveillance Society*. Minneapolis: University of Minnesota Press.
——2001. *Surveillance Society: Monitoring Everyday Life*. Buckingham: Open University Press.
——2003a. 'Surveillance as Social Sorting: Computer Codes and Mobile Bodies'. In *Surveillance as Social Sorting: Privacy, Risk and Digital Discrimination*, edited by D. Lyon. London: Routledge, pp. 1–30.
——2003b. *Surveillance as Social Sorting: Privacy, Risk and Digital Discrimination*. London: Routledge.

——2006. *Theorizing Surveillance: The Panopticon and Beyond*. Cullompton: Willan Publishing.
——2007. *Surveillance Studies: An Overview*. Cambridge: Polity Press.
——2008. 'Surveillance Society'. In *Festival del Diritto*. 28 September 2008, Piacenza, Italia, www.festivaldeloliritto.it/2008/pdf/interventi/david_lyonpdf, accessed 10 January 2014.
——2009. *Identifying Citizens: ID Cards as Surveillance*. Cambridge: Polity Press.
Lyon, D., A. Doyle and R. Lippert. 2012. 'Introduction'. In *Eyes Everywhere: The Global Growth of Camera Surveillance*, edited by A. Doyle, R. Lippert and D. Lyon. Abingdon: Routledge, pp. 1–19.
Marks, P. 2013. 'Monitoring the Unvisible: Seeing and Unseeing in China Miéville's The City & The City'. *Surveillance & Society* 11(3): 222–36.
Martin, A.K., R. van Brakel and D. Bernhard. 2009. 'Understanding Resistance to Digital Surveillance: Towards a Multi-disciplinary, Multi-actor Framework'. *Surveillance & Society* 6(3): 213–32.
Marx, K. 2007 [1844]. *Economic and Philosophic Manuscripts of 1844*. Translated by M. Milligan. Mineola, NY: Dover Publications.
Mathiesen, T. 1997. 'The Viewer Society: Michel Foucault's "Panopticon" Revisited'. *Theoretical Criminology* 1(2): 215–34.
——2013. *Towards a Surveillant Society: The Rise of Surveillance Systems in Europe*. Hook: Waterside Press.
May, T. 1997. *Social Research: Issues, Methods and Process*. Buckingham: Open University Press.
McCahill, M. 2002. *The Surveillance Web: The Rise of Visual Surveillance in an English City*. Cullompton: Willan Publishing.
McCulloch, J. and V. Sentas. 2006. 'The Killing of Jean Charles de Menezes: Hyper-Militarism in the Neoliberal Economic Free-Fire Zone'. *Social Justice* 33(4): 92–106.
McGrath, J. 2004. *Loving Big Brother: Performance, Privacy and Surveillance Space*. Abingdon: Routledge.
McNamara, B., C. Waddell and M. Colvin. 1995. 'Threats to the Good Death: The Cultural Context of Stress and Coping Among Hospice Nurses'. *Sociology of Health & Illness* 17(2): 222–44.
Miller, P. and N. Rose. 1990. 'Governing Economic Life'. *Economy and Society* 19(1): 1–31.
Monahan, T. 2010. *Surveillance in the Time of Insecurity*. New Brunswick, NJ: Rutgers University Press.
——2011. 'The Future of Security? Surveillance Operations at Homeland Security Fusion Centers'. *Social Justice* 37(2/3): 84–98.
Monahan, T. and P.M. Regan. 2012. 'Zones of Opacity: Data Fusion in Post 9/11 Security Organizations'. *Canadian Journal of Law and Society* 27(3): 301–17.
Murakami Wood, D. 2012. 'Globalization and Surveillance'. In *Routledge Handbook of Surveillance Studies*, edited by K. Ball, K.D. Haggerty and D. Lyon. Abingdon: Routledge.
Newborough Police Force. 1996. *Force Medical Advisor's Report*. Newborough: Newborough Police Force.
——1997. *CCTV Monitoring Suite – Staffing*. Newborough: Newborough Police Force.
——1998. *Newborough CCTV Unit Newsletter*. Newborough: Newborough Police Force.

References

——2005. *Newborough City Public Space CCTV System 1996–2005 Overview*. Newborough: Newborough Police Force.
——2008. *CCTV Business Case Report*. Newborough: Newborough Police Force.
Newburn, T. 2001. 'The Commodification of Policing: Security Networks in the Late Modern City'. *Urban Studies* 38(5/6): 829–48.
Newburn, T. and S. Hayman. 2001. *Policing, Surveillance and Social Control: CCTV and Police Monitoring of Suspects*. Cullompton: Willan Publishing.
Neyland, D. 2004. 'Closed Circuits of Interaction?' *Information, Communication and Society* 7(2): 252–71.
——2006. *Privacy, Surveillance and Public Trust*. Basingstoke: Palgrave Macmillan.
Norris, C. 2003. 'From Personal to Digital: CCTV, the Panopticon and the Technological Mediation of Suspicion and Social Control'. In *Surveillance as Social Sorting: Privacy, Risk and Digital Discrimination*, edited by D. Lyon. London: Routledge.
——2012a. 'The Success of Failure: Accounting for the Global Growth of CCTV'. In *Routledge Handbook of Surveillance Studies*, edited by K. Ball, K.D. Haggerty and D. Lyon. Abingdon: Routledge.
——2012b. 'There's No Success Like Failure and Failure's No Success at All: Some Critical Reflections on the Global Growth of CCTV Surveillance'. In *Eyes Everywhere: The Global Growth of Camera Surveillance*, edited by A. Doyle, R. Lippert and D. Lyon. Abingdon: Routledge, pp. 23–45.
Norris, C. and G. Armstrong. 1998. 'Power and Vision'. In *Surveillance, Closed Circuit Television and Social Control*, edited by C. Norris, J. Moran and G. Armstrong. Aldershot: Ashgate.
——1999. *The Maximum Surveillance Society: The Rise of CCTV*. Oxford: Berg.
Norris, C. and M. McCahill. 2006. 'CCTV: Beyond Penal Modernism?' *The British Journal of Criminology* 46(1): 97–118.
Norris, C., M. McCahill and D. Murakami Wood. 2004. 'The Growth of CCTV: A Global Perspective on the International Diffusion of Video Surveillance in Publicly Accessible Space'. *Surveillance & Society* 2(2/3): 110–35.
O'Driscoll, C. 2008. 'Fear and Trust: The Shooting of Jean Charles de Menezes and the War on Terror'. *Millennium – Journal of International Studies* 36(2): 339–60.
Orwell, G. 1949. *Nineteen Eighty-Four*. London: Secker and Warburg.
Parker, J. 2000. *Total Surveillance: Investigating the Big Brother World of E-spies, Eavesdroppers and CCTV*. London: Piatkus.
Pugliese, J. 2006. 'Asymmetries of Terror: Visual Regimes of Racial Profiling and the Shooting of Jean Charles de Menezes in the Context of the War in Iraq'. *Borderlands ejournal* 5(1).
Reeve, A. 1998. 'The Panopticonisation of Shopping: CCTV and Leisure Consumption'. In *Surveillance, Closed Circuit Television and Social Control*, edited by C. Norris, J. Moran and G. Armstrong. Aldershot: Ashgate, pp. 69–88.
Reiner, R. 1978. *The Blue-coated Worker: A Sociological Study of Police Unionism*. Cambridge: Cambridge University Press.
Rose, K.E., C. Webb and K. Waters. 1997. 'Coping Strategies Employed by Informal Carers of Terminally Ill Cancer Patients'. *Journal of Cancer Nursing* 1(3): 126–33.
Rose, N. 2000. 'Government and Control'. *British Journal of Criminology* 40(2): 321–39.
——2013. 'The Human Sciences in a Biological Age'. *Theory, Culture & Society* 30(1): 3–34.
Rosenberg, J.M. 1969. *The Death of Privacy*. New York: Random House.

References

Samatas, M. 2013. 'The SAIC–Siemens "Super-panopticon" in the Athens 2004 Olympics as a Case of "McVeillance": The Surveillance Industrial Complex's Unscrupulous Global Business'. In *The Surveillance-Industrial Complex: A Political Economy of Surveillance*, edited by K. Ball and L. Snider. Abingdon: Routledge.

Sarno, C., M. Hough and M. Bulos. 1999. *Developing a Picture of CCTV in Southwark Town Centres: Final Report*. London: Crime Policy Research Unit.

Simon, J. 2007. *Governing Through Crime: How the War on Crime Transformed American Democracy and Created a Culture of Fear*. Oxford: Oxford University Press.

Skinns, D. 1998. 'Crime Reduction, Diffusion and Displacement: Evaluating the Effectiveness of CCTV'. In *Surveillance, Closed Circuit Television and Social Control*, edited by C. Norris, J. Moran and G. Armstrong. Aldershot: Ashgate.

Smith, G.J.D. 2004. 'Behind the Screens: Examining Constructions of Deviance and Informal Practices Among CCTV Control Room Operators in the UK'. *Surveillance & Society* 2(2/3): 376–95.

——2012. 'Surveillance Workers'. In *Routledge Handbook of Surveillance Studies*, edited by K. Ball, K.D. Haggerty and D. Lyon. Abingdon: Routledge, pp. 107–15.

——2012a. 'What Goes Up, Must Come Down: On the Moribundity of Camera Networks in the UK'. In *Eyes Everywhere: The Global Growth of Camera Surveillance*, edited by A. Doyle, R. Lippert and D. Lyon. Abingdon: Routledge.

——2013. 'Surveillance Technology and Policing'. In *Encyclopedia of Criminology and Criminal Justice*, edited by G. Bruinsma and D. Weisburd. New York: Springer Science and Business Media, pp. 5094–104.

——2014a (forthcoming). 'Disembodied exhaust and embodied exhaustion: engaging the management of data-bodies in the informatic age'. *Body & Society*.

——2014b. 'Les répercussions sociales de l'e-living'. In *Le futur est-il e-media?* edited by P.-Y. Badillo and D. Roux. Paris: Economica, pp. 168–75.

Smith, G.J.D., M. San Roque, H. Westcott and P. Marks. 2013. 'Surveillance Texts and Textualism: Truthtelling and Trustmaking in an Uncertain World'. *Surveillance & Society* 11(3): 215–21.

Surveillance Studies Network. 2006. *A Report on the Surveillance Society*. London: Information Commissioner's Office.

Taylor, E. 2013. *Surveillance Schools: Security, Discipline and Control in Contemporary Education*. Basingstoke: Palgrave Macmillan.

Tenhouten, W.D. 2007. *Sociology of Emotions*. London: Routledge.

Thrift, N. 2005. *Knowing Capitalism*. London: Sage Publications Ltd.

Tilley, N. 1993. *Understanding Car Parks, Crime and CCTV: Evaluation Lessons from Safer Cities*. London: Crime Prevention Unit.

Turner, J.A. and J.E. Stets. 2005. *The Sociology of Emotions*. Cambridge: Cambridge University Press.

van Krieken, R. 2012. *Celebrity Society*. Abingdon: Routledge.

van Maanen, J. 1991. 'The Smile Factory: Work at Disneyland'. In *Reframing Organizational Culture*, edited by P. Frost, L. Moore, M. Luis, C. Lundberg and J. Martin. London: Sage Publications Ltd.

Wacquant, L. 2007. *Urban Outcasts: A Comparative Sociology of Advanced Marginality*. Cambridge: Polity Press.

——2009a. *Prisons of Poverty*. Expanded edition. Minneapolis: University of Minnesota Press.

——2009b. *Punishing the Poor: The Neoliberal Government of Social Insecurity*. Durham, NC: Duke University Press.

Waddington, P.A.J. 1999. 'Police (Canteen) Sub-culture: An Appreciation'. *The British Journal of Criminology* 39(2): 287–309.

Walby, K. 2005a. 'How Closed-Circuit Television Organizes the Social: An Institutional Ethnography'. *Canadian Journal of Sociology* 30(2): 189–215.

——2005b. 'Institutional Ethnography and Surveillance Studies: An Outline for Inquiry'. *Surveillance & Society* 3(2/3): 158–72.

——2006. 'Risky Spaces, Algorithims, and Signifiers: Disappearing Bodies and the Prevalence of Racialization in Urban Camera Surveillance Procedures'. *Topia: Canadian Journal of Cultural Studies* 16: 51–67.

Waldby, C. 2000. *The Visible Human Project: Informatic Bodies and Posthuman Medicine*. London: Routledge.

——2001. 'Digital Archives, Virtual Norms: The Visible Human Project as a Technology of Anatomical Inscription'. In *Digital Anatomy*, edited by C. Lammer. Vienna: Turia and Kant Verlag.

——2002. 'Stem Cells, Tissue Cultures and the Production of Biovalue'. *Health: An Interdisciplinary Journal for the Social Study of Health, Illness and Medicine* 6(3): 305–23.

Weber, M. 1978. *Economy and Society: An Outline of Interpretive Sociology*. Berkeley: University of California Press.

Webster, W. 2009. 'CCTV Policy in the UK: Reconsidering the Evidence Base'. *Surveillance & Society* 6(1): 10–22.

Wells, H.A., T. Allard and P. Wilson. 2006. *Crime and CCTV in Australia: Understanding the Relationship*. Gold Coast, Queensland: Centre for Applied Psychology and Criminology, Bond University.

Welsh, B.P. and D.C. Farrington. 2002. *Crime Prevention Effects of Closed Circuit Television: A Systematic Review*, Home Office Research Study 252. London: HMSO.

——2008. *Effects of Closed Circuit Television Surveillance on Crime*. Campbell Systematic Reviews.

Wise, J.M. 2013. 'Introduction: Ecstatic Assemblages of Visuality'. In *New Visualities, New Technologies: The New Ecstasy of Communication*, edited by J.M. Wise and H. Koskela. Aldershot: Ashgate.

Wright Mills, C. 1959. *The Sociological Imagination*. Oxford: Oxford University Press. Reprint, 2000.

Yar, M. 2003. 'Panoptic Power and the Pathologisation of Vision: Critical Reflections on the Foucauldian Thesis'. *Surveillance & Society* 1(3): 254–71.

Young, J. 1999. *The Exclusive Society: Social Exclusion, Crime and Difference in Late Modernity*. London: Sage Publications Ltd.

Yurick, S. 1985. *Behold Metatron: The Recording Angel, Foreign Agents Series*. New York: Semiotext(e).

Index

Aas, K.F., H.O. Gundhus and H.M. Lomell 25n3
Abi-Rached, J.M. and Rose, N. 17
Adey, P. 27
affective labour 127–30, 149–50
agency, space-time fusion of 81–82
airwave accessibility 96
Amoore, L. 20
Amoore, L. and de Goede, M. 20
Andrejevic, M. 19, 20, 28, 117
Anshel, M.H. 143
Armitage, R. 46, 57n27
ascendant publics, concerns of 39–40
asymmetrical (il)legibility 9–11
Atkinson, P., A. Coffey, S. Delamont, J. Lofland and L. Lofland 51
Atkinson, R. and Helms, G. 42
Automatic Number Plate Recognition (ANPR) 56n5

Ball, K. and Snider, L. 7, 25n3
Ball, K.S. 13–14
Ball, K.S. and Haggerty, K.D. 50
Ball, K.S., K.D. Haggerty and D. Lyon 25n3
Banksy (street artist) 31
Bannister, I., R. Fyfe, and A. Kearn 39, 40
Barbalet, J.M. 127
Barnard-Wills, D. 45
Baudrillard, Jean 19, 33
Bauman, Zygmunt 19, 39, 42
Becker, H.S. 40
Belina, B. and Helms, G. 30
belonging (and unbelonging) 31, 40
Bendelow, G. and Williams, S.J. 127
Berger, P.L. and Luckmann, T. 63
Big Brother (Channel 5 TV) 154
biomechanics 20–21, 154

biopolitical compulsions, bioeconomical imperatives and 28
Biressi, A. and Nunn, H. 117
Bogard, W. 11
Bolton, Sharon 128, 129
Brown, Gordon 36
Browne, S. 9
Bulger, James 40
Burdon, M. 28
bullying 143
business corporations, jurisdictional authority of 42

Calvert, C. 32
camera circuitries *see* circuitries
camera (in)effectiveness 45–48
camera networks: instigation of 63–77; socialities and 63–64, 149–50
camera operators 4; camera positioning and 89–91, 95–99; CCTV circuitry example, operator experiences within 70, 73–74, 75, 77, 78–82, 83, 85, 93–94, 96–98, 102–3; contractual indemnity for 86; court appearances as expert witnesses 158–59; creative commentaries by 114–15; desensitisation of 138–39; directional disempowerment for 156; discontents with working environment 93–95; duties of 76–77, 78, 80–81; emotional engagement of 127–30, 159–62; emotional support for, lack of 136–37; escape pathways for 146; guardianship and devotion duties 98–99; impotence, experiences of 150, 155–59; influence, capacities for 152–55; informal tasks of 81; institutionally-held databases, access to 120; interactions between watchers

176 Index

and watched 106–13; interpretation of circuitries, operator experiences and 108–13, 115–16, 117, 119–24; interpretive decision-making 80; 'learned knowledge' accrued by 123–24; logistical role of 154; non-professionalised communicative ambiguities for 97; operational negligence 87–88; operators' interrelationships with circuitries, experiences of 137–39, 139–41, 141–44, 144–45, 145–49; organisational constraints on 155; powerlessness of 135–37, 155; relational affinities with system 64; responsiveness to surroundings of 123; sharing depictions between 115–16; social order and work of 132; socialisation and transfiguration of 123–24; speculative content, projection of 113–14, 125; 'star gazing' by 120; structural authority of, lack of 158–59; structural positioning of 152–55, 159; subjective inscriptions, ethnomethodological arrangement of 114; subjectivities of 4; suicide inquiries, experiences of 131; sustainment of circuitries, operator experiences and 151–63; symbolic interactivity of 110–11; trauma and death in experiences of 126, 128–32, 139; trust, social relations and experiences of 132–34; unanticipated responses from 119–21; vicarious witnesses 160; visceral dimensions of camera work 126–27
camera unit ownership, distribution of 34–35
camera usage, operating procedures 48–49
camera work: resistance to domination by 145–49; visceral dimensions of 126–27
cameras and equipment, life of 92
capitalism, industrialised work under 134–35
Cartwright, L. 9, 16
Castells, Manuel 17
CCTV circuitry, example of social history in 'Newborough' 64–102; agency, space-time fusion of 81–82; airwave accessibility, struggles for 96–97; camera networks: instigation of 63–77; socialities and 63–64,

149–50; camera operators: camera positioning and 89–95, 95–99; contractual indemnity for 86; discontents with working environment 93–95; duties of 76, 78, 80–81; experiences of 70, 73–74, 75, 77, 78–82, 83, 85, 93–94, 96–98, 102–3; guardianship and devotion duties 98–99; informal tasks of 81; interpretive decision-making 80; non-professionalised communicative ambiguities for 97; operational negligence 87–88; relational affinities with system 64; cameras and equipment, life of 92; community safety partnerships (CSPs) 66; dependency fragilities 72–77; discrimination 82; expedience, socio-material sedimentation of 77–82; false allegations, disproval of 80; fragilities in structures and operations 83–104; functionalism 77–82; germination of CCTV network 65–66; impression management, precedence for 69–70; improvidence, socio-material sedimentation of 83–103; inflexibility, sedimentation of 64–77; instrumentalism 38, 82; interconnectedness 66, 102; intra-organisational tensions and interpersonal conflicts 87–88; material, fragilities of 89–95; membership of working group 67–72; monitoring rooms, ergonomic features of 93–94; multi-agency collaboration 66, 78–79; positioning, fragilities of 95–99; powers in formation of supervisory circuitries 64; proprietary fragilities 99–102; public-private quango, formation of 66; solidities in structures and operations 77–82; staffing, fragilities on 84–89; structures, making of 63; surveillance, Lyon's perspective on 8–9, 63, 65; working group activities 64–65, 74–75, 76, 77, 82, 83, 84, 88, 89–90, 92, 98–99, 100, 101; camera arrangement or positioning 89–91, 95–99; consultation process 75–76; defective planning and deficient acuity 82; details, systematised management of 70; external organisations, working with 72–73; formalised functionalism 77–82; ideological management

campaign 72; impression management, precedence for 69–70; internal memorandum at system launch 88–89; investment, problems of 100; lateral groups, dealing with prerogatives of 73–74; media, relationships with 74–75; ownership rights 100–101; persuasion, methods of 71; public opinion, engagement with 65, 68–69; 'publicity subgroup,' formation of 70–71; recession plagued political economic environment, supervisory circulations in 101; revenue dispersal 83; specialist incompetence 89–90; working group membership 67–72; exclusion from 68; legislative privileges 68–69; organisational structure of 67–68
CCTV (Closed-Circuit Television): arrival of 42–44, 44–45; civil milieu, deployment in 42; cultural acceptance of 33; dependence on 35–36; 'fifth utility' of modern urbanism 27, 30, 34–35; literature of operation of 161; physical and cultural depth 33–36; prominence of 30–33; research on 45–49; social identities and 32; *Stars of CCTV* 117, 118, 120, 143; strategic deployment of 30; struggles for, strategies and tactics 106–8; symbolic (im)materialisation of 31–33; synoptic platform 35, 45; technical sophistication and operational capabilities of 35; (un)visibility of 28–30, 36, 37–45; visibility and 35–36
CCTV Today 35
celebnotoriety 118
Chan, J. 137
Christie, Nils 39–40
circuitries 4–5; CCTV circuitries 23; closed circuitries, opening of 23; visuality circuitries 17–18; *see also* CCTV circuitry, example of social history in 'Newborough'; engagement with circuits; instigation of circuits; interpretation of circuits; operators' interrelationships with circuits; sustainment of circuits
Clavell, G.G. 7
close observation 5
closed circuitries, opening of 23
Coaffee, J., D. Murakami Wood and P. Rogers 42, 44
Cohen, S. 37, 39

Cohen, S. and Taylor, L. 34, 143
Coleman, R. 9, 30, 31, 37, 39, 40, 42–43, 55n3, 66
Coleman, R. and McCahill, M. 25n3
Coleman, R. and Sim, J. 44, 58n31
collaborative data sharing 109
collection means 54–55
comedy moments 141–44
communication protocols 154
communicative fluency 20–21
community safety partnerships (CSPs) 66
conduits 154
confrontational relations, monitoring of 154
conjecture, process of 20
Conrad, P. 9
contact points 105, 108–13, 113–24
Copeland, David 41, 57n28
correlation, process of 20
coverage and comportment 33–36
creative fracturing 148
Crimewatch UK (BBC TV) 40
Crofts, P., P. Hubbard and J. Prior 40

data capture 27
data provision 27
Davies, Simon 9, 41, 58n31
Davis, M. 40
Davis, M. and Monk, D.B. 38, 40
de Certeau, Michel 106, 107–8
decision-making protocols, impact of personalisation and familiarisation on 120
dedicated watching, interpretation of 5–11
Denzin, N.K. 117
dependency fragilities 72–77
depersonalisation 139–41
detectors 25n1, 28
Dillon, M. and Lobo-Guerrero, L. 9, 66
disassociation through humour 141–44
disciplinary power, accrual of 126
discretionary decision-making 154
discrimination 82
disempowerment 152, 155–59; directional disempowerment for camera operators 156
Disneyland 128
disorderly rhythms, measurement of 130–32
dissemination ends 54–55
distancing: interpretation of circuitries 111; operators' interrelationships with circuitries 139–41

Index

distressing proceedings, externalisation and sharing of 143
disturbance management 137–49
disturbance reifying gaze 132–34
Ditton, J. 46
Doyle, A., R. Lippert and D. Lyon 55n3, 58n31
Dubbeld, L. 48
Dupont, B. 15
Durkheim, Emile 57n29

economics 37–39, 40, 42, 43, 44, 45, 67, 101, 128
Edmond, G. and San Roque, M. 20, 21, 32, 58n31, 154
emotion work 129, 137, 138, 139
emotional intelligence 89, 128
emotional labour 128–29
emotionality, management of 127–30
empowerment 152–56, 162n1
engagement with circuits 24, 27–59; ascendant publics, concerns of 39–40; belonging (and unbelonging) 31, 40; biopolitical compulsions and bioeconomical imperatives 28; business corporations, jurisdictional authority of 42; camera (in)effectiveness 45–48; camera unit ownership, distribution of 34–35; camera usage, operating procedures 48–49; CCTV (Closed-Circuit Television): arrival of 42–44, 44–45; civil milieu, deployment in 42; cultural acceptance of 33; dependence on 35–36; 'fifth utility' of modern urbanism 27, 30, 34–35; physical and cultural depth 33–36; prominence of 30–33; research on 45–49; social identities and 32; strategic deployment of 30; symbolic (im)materialisation of 31–33; synoptic platform 35, 45; technical sophistication and operational capabilities of 35; (un)visibility of 22–30, 36, 37–45; visibility and 27, 28–30, 35–36; collection means 54–55; coverage and comportment 33–36; data capture 27; data provision 27; detectors 28; dissemination ends 54–55; economics 37–39, 40, 42, 43, 44, 45; gaze orientation 44, 105; insecurity, perceptions of 40–41; intersubjective experience, research and 53–54; longitudinal aggregation 28; media coverage, malicious exaggeration of 40; mobilitants (mobile bodies) 27, 30; motion-sensitivity 27; neoliberal crusades 37–45; neoliberal rationalities 30–32; neoliberal system 38–39; neoliberal technocracy 44; personal information 9–10, 28; poor, problematisation of 37–45; privileged, protection of 37–45; role transitions 53–54; sensing unvisibility 28–30; 'sensor society,' emergence of 28; sensorial output 27; signal events, effects of 36, 41–42; space, management of 39–41, 42, 44; street prohibitions of neoliberal cities, monitoring of 42–43; supervisory lifeworlds 49–55; Town Centre Management (TCM) quangos 42; ubiquity of sensors 27–28; underclass, emergence of 39–40; verisimilitude 17, 32–33; visibility making 27, 28–30; visualisation 28; watching, closed circuitries and chains of 50–53
expedience, socio-material sedimentation of 77–82

fallaciousness 20
false allegations, disproval of 80
Feeley, M. and Simon, J. 43, 57n23, 66
Ferreday, D. 9
Fineman, S. 128
Finn, J. 32, 35, 45
Finucane Qc., Brian 126
Fisher, J.A. and Monahan, T. 9
Fiske, J. 20, 48
Foucault, Michel 4, 10, 22, 26n7, 126, 129, 161, 162n2
fragilities in structures and operations 83–102
Franks, D.D. and McCarthy, E.D. 127
functionalism 77–82
Fussey, Pete 43, 49, 55n3, 64
Fyfe, N.R. and Bannister, J. 36, 163n2

Gad, C. and Hansen, L.K. 22
Gandy Jr., O.H. 9, 10
Garland, D. 31, 40, 66
gatekeepers 154–55, 157
Gauntlett, D. and Hill, A. 139
gaze orientation: disturbance reifying gaze 132–34; engagement with circuitries 44; interpretation of circuitries 105–6

Index 179

gaze projection 16; interpretation of circuitries 105–6; reception and, social construal in 19–21
Geertz, Clifford 55
gender, mediating factor of 68, 123
geo-spatial awareness 20–21
Germain, S., L. Dumoulin and A.-C. Douillet 48, 55n3
Gerrard, G., G. Parkins, I. Cunningham, W. Jones, S. Hill and S. Douglas 38, 56n5, 56n12
Giddens, Anthony 18
Gill, M. and Spriggs, A. 46–47
Gilliom, J. 15
Gilliom, J. and Monahan, T. 25n3
Goffman, Erving 69, 127, 145
good citizen discourse, internalisation of 144
Goold, B.J. 16, 31, 55n3, 58n31
Goold, B.J. and Neyland, D. 25n3
Goold, B.J., I. Loader and A. Thumala 30, 36, 37, 41, 45, 47, 55n3, 57n18, 57n20
Graham, S. and Marvin, S. 39
Graham, Stephen 11, 27, 30, 31, 35, 39
Greer, C. 37
Grey, M. 11
Groombridge, N. 47

Haggerty, K.D. and Ericson, R.V. 5, 6, 7, 8, 11, 20, 25n3
Hall, S. and Winlow, S. 38
Hall, S., C. Critcher, T. Jefferson, J.N. Clarke and B. Roberts 40
Hardt, M. and Negri, A. 128, 129
Harraway, Donna 56n7
Harris, Lloyd 129
Harvey, David 38
Healy, C.M. and McKay, M.F. 137
Hier, S.P. 11
Hier, S.P. and Greenberg, J. 7, 25n3
Hill, A. 114, 139
Hochschild, Arlie R. 128
Holdaway, S. 137
Holm, N. 15
Home Office 29, 46, 56n12
Hopkinson, J., C. Hallett and K. Luker 143
horizons, fusion of 15–23
Horton, D. and Wohl, R.R. 13, 25n5
Hubbard, P. 40
humour, disassociation through 141–44

impotence, camera operators' experiences of 150, 155–59
impression management, precedence for 69–70
improvidence, socio-material sedimentation of 83–102
inflexibility, sedimentation of 64–77
influence, camera operators' capacities for 152–55
infoglut 20, 163n4
Innes, M. 57n26
insecurity, perceptions of 40–41
instigation of circuits 24, 63–104
instrumentalism 38, 82; operators' interrelationships with circuits and 126, 132
interactivity 15, 21, 65, 84, 108, 110, 124, 135, 145; para-social interactivity 24; symbolic interactivity of camera operators 110–11
interconnectedness 66, 102
interpretation of circuitries 24, 105–25; camera operators: creative commentaries by 114–15; experiences of 106, 108–13, 114–24; institutionally-held databases, access to 120; interactions between watchers and watched 106–13; 'learned knowledge' accrued by 123–24; responsiveness to surroundings of 123; sharing depictions between 115–16; socialisation and transfiguration of 123–24; speculative content, projection of 113–14, 125; 'star gazing' by 120; subjective inscriptions, ethnomethodological arrangement of 114; symbolic interactivity of 110–11; unanticipated responses from 119–21; CCTV (Closed-Circuit Television): *Stars of CCTV* 117, 118, 120, 143; struggles for, strategies and tactics 106–8; celebnotoriety 118; collaborative data sharing 109; contact points 105, 108–13, 113–24; decision-making protocols, impact of personalisation and familiarisation on 120; distancing 111–12; gaze orientation 105; gaze projection 105–6; gender, mediating factor of 123; informal usages of circuits 110; interactivity 108, 109, 110, 124; 'Janus faced' nature of supervision 122; market, ethics of 107; media audiences constructions of

classificatory designations 116; neoliberal agenda, CCTV as material manifestations of 107–8; para-social facilitation 105; para-social personalisation and familiarisation 113–24; risk flow tracking 108; scanning rituals 106; social action, co-produced reciprocities of 108; spectacle enchantment 113–24; strategies, de Certeau's definition of 107; supervisory circuitries as para-social mediums 108–13; supervisory circulations, relational character of 111–12; text-mediated interactions 105; theatre of the street 113–15, 117; unidirectional observation, depersonalised nature of 106; unpredictability of viewing content 113; visibility, making of 106, 114; visibility dialectics 106; visuality processing 106; watching: monotony and boredom in 113–14; relationship between watcher and watched 12, 24, 48, 106–13; seduction of 113–24, 124–25; watchers and watched, interactions between 106–13
intersubjective experience, research and 53–54
intra-organisational tensions, interpersonal conflicts and 87–88

'Janus faced' nature of supervision 122
Jewkes, Y. 7, 37, 45, 57n30
Jones, A. 34

Kalberg, S. 14
knowledge, vision and 152–53
Konings, M. 20
Koskela, H. 10, 34
Kroener, I. 41
Kruger, E. 21

Latour, Bruno 18
Levin, T.Y. 32
Lianos, M. 38
Lippert, R. and Wilkinson, B. 58n31
lived experience, analytical value of 149–50, 151–52
Lives of Others (film by Florian Henckel von Donnersmark) 119
Lockwood, D. 115
Lomell, H.M. 39, 48
longitudinal aggregation 28
Lords, House of 34, 35, 56n12

Los, M. 11
Lyon, D., A. Doyle and R. Lippert 34
Lyon, David 5, 7, 8–9, 18, 25n3, 25n4, 63, 65

McCahill, M. 42, 44, 55n3, 58n31
McCulloch, J. and Sentas, V. 20
McGrath, J. 10, 34
McNamara, B., C. Waddell and M. Colvin 143
Major, John 29
market, ethics of 107
market capitalisation 128
Marks, Peter 29
Martin, A.K., R. van Brakel and D. Bernhard 15
Marx, Karl 134–35
material, fragilities of 89–95
Mathiesen, T. 11, 25n3, 45
May, T. 51, 53
media audiences, constructions of classificatory designations 116
media coverage, malicious exaggeration of 40
membership of working group in 'Newborough' 67–72
de Menezes, Jean Charles 20
Miller, P. and Rose, N. 18, 31
mobilitants (mobile bodies) 27, 30
Monahan, T. 9, 25n3
Monahan, T. and Regan, P.M. 9, 50
monitoring rooms, ergonomic features of 93–94
motion-sensitivity 27
multi-agency collaboration 66, 78–79
Murakami Wood, D. 11

National Security Agency (NSA), PRISM programme of 5–6
neoliberal agenda, CCTV as material manifestations of 107–8
neoliberal crusades 37–45
neoliberal rationalities 30–32
neoliberal system 38–39
neoliberal technocracy 44
neoliberalised work 128
neutralisation, techniques of 137–49
Newborough Regional Council Public Protection Committee (PPC) *see* CCTV circuitry, example of social history in 'Newborough'
Newburn, T. 41
Newburn, T. and Hayman, S. 58n31
Neyland, D. 25n3, 58n31

Nineteen Eighty-Four (Orwell, G.) 6
normality, taxonomies of 21–22
Norris, C. 19, 40, 41, 43, 48, 55n3, 56n12, 57n27
Norris, C. and Armstrong, G. 9, 15, 19, 122, 124, 163n2; engagement with circuits 29, 30, 33, 36, 39, 41, 42, 44, 48, 49, 55n3, 56n12, 57n18, 57n22, 58n31, 58n32
Norris, C. and McCahill, M. 19, 29, 58n31
Norris, C., M. McCahill and D. Murakami Wood 55n3, 56n12

O'Driscoll, C. 20
operativity problem 9–11, 12
operators' interrelationships with circuitries: affective labour 127–30, 149–50; bullying 143; camera operators: desensitisation of 138–39; emotional engagement of 127–30, 159–62; emotional support for, lack of 136–37; escape pathways for 146; experiences of 130–32, 132–34, 135–37, 138–39, 139–44, 144–45, 146–49; powerlessness of 135–36, 143, 155; social order and work of 132; suicide inquiries, experiences of 131; trauma and death in experiences of 126, 128–32, 139; trust, social relations and experiences of 132–34; camera work: resistance to domination by 145–49; visceral dimensions of 126–27; capitalism, industrialised work under 134–35; comedy moments 141–44; creative fracturing 148; depersonalisation 139–41; disassociating through humour 141–44; disciplinary power, accrual of 126; Disneyland 128; disorderly rhythms, measurement of 130–32; distancing 139–41; distressing proceedings, externalisation and sharing of 143; disturbance reifying gaze 132–34; disturbances, management of 137–49; domination via camera work, resistance to 145–49; emotion work 129, 137, 138, 139; emotional intelligence 89, 128; emotional labour, concept of 128–29; emotionality, management of 127–30; good citizen discourse, internalisation of 144; humour, disassociating through 141–44; instrumentalism 126, 132; market capitalisation 128; neoliberalised work 128; neutralisation, techniques of 137–49; pecuniary emotion management 129; philanthropic emotion management 129; powerlessness 143; prescriptive emotion management 129; presentational emotion management 129; screens, reclamation of 145–49; self, practices of caring for 127–30; self-identity, impact of screened images on 127; self work and self-technicians 127, 129–30, 137, 139, 141, 144, 149–50; selfhood, defence of 150; sentiment manipulation 137–38; social origins of affective sensations 127–30; socio-psychological turbulence, supervisory operativity and 126; spectacle disenchantment 130–37; street reality, disconnection with cognitive reality 140; subjectivity, safeguarding of 137–39; supervisory operativity, socio-psychological turbulence associated with 126; telemediated alienation 134–37; telemediation 112–13, 122–23, 125, 130–37, 160–61; trauma items, taxonomy of 126; unidirectionalism 126; visceral dimensions of camera work 126–27; watching: brutal dimensions of 126; work of 130–37
Orwell, George 6

para-social facilitation 105
para-social interactivity 21, 109, 124, 160
para-social personalisation and familiarisation 113–24
Parker, J. 9
pecuniary emotion management 129
personal information 9–10, 28
personal memoirs 19
philanthropic emotion management 129
poor, problematisation of 37–45
positioning, fragilities of 95–99
power: disciplinary power, accrual of 126; empowerment 151–56, 162n1; formation of supervisory circuits and 64; sight, powers of 3–4; subjective power 153; surveillance, power conveyances in 11; technologies of 4; unidirectional power, surveillance and 9–10
powerlessness 58n30, 135–36, 143, 155

prescriptive emotion management 129
presentational emotion management 129
privileged, protection of 37–45
productivity, measurement of 152
proprietary fragilities 99–102
public-private quango, formation of 66
Pugliese, J. 20

realities, definition and editing of 153
Reeve, A. 39, 42
Reiner, R. 137
risk assessment, expertise in 154–55
risk flow tracking 108
riskscapes 4–5, 22, 127, 130
role transitions 53–54
Rose, K.E., C. Webb and K. Waters 143
Rose, Nikolas 17, 57n24
Rosenberg, J.M. 9

Samatas, M. 7
Sarno, C., M. Hough and M. Bulos 46
scanning rituals 106
screens, reclamation of 145–49
self: practices of caring for 127–30; territories of 4, 24, 107, 125, 127
self-identity, impact of screened images on 127
self work and self-technicians 127, 129–30, 137, 139, 141, 144, 149–50
selfhood, defence of 150
sensing unvisibility 28–30
'sensor society,' emergence of 28
sensorial output 27
sentiment manipulation 137–38
sight, powers of 3–4
signal events, effects of 36, 41–42
Simon, J. 40
Skinns, D. 31, 46
Smith, G.J.D. 6, 15, 16, 18, 19, 28, 31, 32, 34, 45, 48, 55n4, 101
Smith, G.J.D., M. San Roque, H. Westcott and P. Marks 7, 10, 11, 19
social action, co-produced reciprocities of 108
social order, camera operators as symbolic custodians of 161
social origins of affective sensations 127–30
social relations 18–19
socio-psychological turbulence, supervisory operativity and 126
solidities in structures and operations 77–82

space, management of 39–41, 42, 44
spectacle disenchantment 130–37
spectacle enchantment 113–24
spectacle reflection 16–17
staffing, fragilities on 84–89
strategies, de Certeau's definition of 107
Straw, Jack 37, 38
street prohibitions of neoliberal cities, monitoring of 42–43
street reality, disconnection with cognitive reality 140
street theatrics 113–15, 117, 160
subjective power 153–54
subjectivity, safeguarding of 137–39
supervision: 'Janus faced' nature of 122; supervisory circuits as para-social mediums 108–13; watching 12–13, 13–14, 14–15
supervisory circulations: envisioning of 12–15; relational character of 111–12; relational features of 160
supervisory coordinates, engagement with 13–15
supervisory enlightenment 159–62
supervisory lifeworlds 49–55
supervisory operativity 160–63; socio-psychological turbulence associated with 126
supervisory structures and rhythms 15, 21–23
surveillance 5–11; ambiguities of 6–8; equivocal notion of 7; flattening of 12–15; hyper-rationality and 10; Lyon's perspective on 8–9, 63, 65; power conveyances in 11; social meanings attendant on 7; struggles for 6–8; studies on, foci and characterisations of 7–8, 8–9; unidirectional power and 10; watching 5–11
Surveillance & Society 8
Surveillance Studies Network (SSN) 5, 25n3, 35
sustainment of circuits 24–25, 151–63; camera operators: court appearances as expert witnesses 158–59; directional disempowerment for 156; emotional engagement of 127–30, 159–62; experiences of 151–52, 154–59; logistical role of 154; organisational constraints on 155; structural authority of, lack of 158–59; structural positioning of 152–55, 159; vicarious witnesses 160; CCTV,

literature of operation of 161; communication protocols 154; conduits 154; confrontational relations, monitoring of 154; discretionary decision-making 154; empowerment 152–56, 162n1; gatekeepers 154–55, 157; impotence, camera operators' experiences of 150, 155–59; influence, camera operators' capacities for 152–55; knowledge, vision and 152–53; lived experience, analytical value of 149–50, 151–52; productivity, measurement of 152; realities, definition and editing of 153; risk assessment, expertise in 154–55; social order, camera operators as symbolic custodians of 161; street theatrics 113–15, 117, 160; structural approach to study of supervisory circuitries 160; subjective power 153–54; supervisory circulations, relational features of 160; supervisory enlightenment 159–62; supervisory operativity 126, 160–63; telemediation 160; visibilities, making of 151–52; vision and knowledge 152–53; visualities, processing of 151–52, 160; watching: disempowerment of watchers 152, 155–59; empowerment of watchers 152–56; symbolism of 152; work of 159–62

Taylor, E. 25n3, 34, 58n31
telemediated alienation 134–37
telemediated renditions of social life 18
telemediated riskscapes 4–5, 130
telemediated territories of attention 21
telemediation: operators' interrelationships with circuitries 112–13, 122–23, 125, 130–37; sustainment of circuitries 160–61; watching and 17–19
teleoptics 17–19
Tenhouten, W.D. 127
text-mediated interactions 105
textualism 7
Thatcher, Margaret 43
theatre of the street 113–15, 127, 160
Thrift, N. 39
Tilley, N. 46
Town Centre Management (TCM) quangos 42
trauma items, taxonomy of 126
Turner, J.A. and Stets, J.E. 127

underclass, emergence of 39–40
unidirectionalism 126; unidirectional observation, depersonalised nature of 106
unpredictability of viewing content 113
utility of observational interventions 6

van Krieken, Robert 118
van Maanen, J. 128
verisimilitude 17, 32–33
virtualisation 10
visibility 3, 15–23
visibility dialectics 107
visibility making 9–10; engagement with circuitries 27, 28–30; interpretation of circuitries 106, 114; sustainment of circuitries 151–52, 160; watching and 21–23
visibility-visuality alternations 15–23
vision and knowledge 152–53
vision manufacturing, visibility and 16
vista rendering, visuality and 16–17
visualisation 9–10, 19, 26n7, 29
visuality 3, 15, 16–17
visuality processing: interpretation of circuitries 106; sustainment of circuitries 151–52, 160; watching and 21–23

Waddington, P.A.J. 137
Walby, Kevin 15, 19, 40, 48, 50, 58n31, 105
Waldby, C. 17, 28
Wacquant, Loic 40, 57n23, 57n24
watching: asymmetrical (il)legibility 9–11; brutal dimensions of 126; closed circuitries, opening of 23; dedicated watching, interpretation of 5–11; disempowerment of watchers 152, 155–59; empowerment of watchers 152–60; engagement with circuitries 24, 27–59; gaze projection 16; gaze projection and reception, social construal in 19–21; horizons, fusion of 15–23; instigation of circuitries 24, 63–104; interpretation of circuitries 24, 105–25; monotony and boredom in 113–14; operativity problem 9–11, 12; operators, subjectivities of 4; operators' interrelationships with circuitries 24, 126–50; relationship between watcher and watched 12, 24, 48, 106–13; seduction of 113–24, 124–25; spectacle reflection 16–17;

supervision 12–13, 13–14, 14–15; supervisory circulations, envisioning of 12–15; supervisory coordinates, engagement with 13–15; supervisory structures and rhythms 15, 21–23; sustainment of circuitries 24–25, 151–63; symbolism of 152; telemediation 17–19; teleoptics 17–19; utility of observational interventions 6; visibility making 21–23; visibility-visuality alternations 15–23; vision manufacturing, visibility and 16; vista rendering, visuality and 16–17; visuality processing 21–23; watchers and watched, interactions between 106–13; watching rituals 6, 23–24; work of 3–5, 130–37, 159–62
Weber, Max 14, 51
Webster, W. 34, 47, 55n3, 101
Wells, H.A., T. Allard and P. Wilson 47
Welsh, B.P. and Farrington, D.C. 46, 57n21
Wise, J.M. 34
working group activities 64–65, 74–75, 76, 77, 82, 83, 84, 88, 89–90, 92, 98–99, 100, 101; camera arrangement or positioning 89–91, 95–99; consultation process 75–76; defective planning and deficient acuity 82; details, systematised management of 70; external organisations, working with 72–73; formalised functionalism 77–82; ideological management campaign 72; impression management, precedence for 69–70; internal memorandum at system launch 88–89; investment, problems of 100; lateral groups, dealing with prerogatives of 73–74; media, relationships with 74–75; ownership rights 100–101; persuasion, methods of 71; public opinion, engagement with 65, 68–69; 'publicity subgroup,' formation of 70–71; recession plagued political economic environment, supervisory circulations in 101; revenue dispersal 83; specialist incompetence 90
working group membership 67–72; exclusion from 68; legislative privileges 68–69; organisational structure of 67–68
Wright Mills, C. 29

Yar, M. 14
Young, J. 40
Yurick, S. 28